"...there can never be too many books on prison life. This is an area that is still a great mystery to much of the public and needs to be communicated from a variety of perspectives. And each person who has spent time in prison has a unique story to tell."

—Marc Mauer, Assistant Director of The Sentencing Project

Prison Ragout

Prison Ragout

◆

Musings While Incarcerated

"Pop"

iUniverse, Inc.
New York Lincoln Shanghai

Prison Ragout
Musings While Incarcerated

iUniverse, Inc.

For information address:
iUniverse, Inc.
2021 Pine Lake Road, Suite 100
Lincoln, NE 68512
www.iuniverse.com

ISBN: 0-595-33634-5

Printed in the United States of America

No amount of appreciation is sufficient to be expressed to my wife, children, extended family and many friends who gave me the morale support and encouragement to survive this ordeal.

All names of people (except those of public figures) and places have been changed to protect the innocent and the guilty.

I wish to thank all of those who read the manuscript and offered constructive criticism—most of which I incorporated. The final result, good or bad, is mine. I wish to acknowledge my youngest son for the original artwork that evolved into the book cover.

Contents

Adams County Detention Center

Sentencing + 6 days

Dearest Wife,

10:30AM. I finally have paper and pen so I can write even if I don't have stamps. What Odyssey have I forced upon us? This is a strange and foreign world. I'm scared and cautious. The COs seem more hostile than the inmates. So far I'm OK.

My introduction to tier life was scary. The tiers are isolated from each other by locked doors. My tier has seven cells and a common area. In the common area are two hexagonal tables with attached wooden benches around the periphery. There are also three chairs. I was put in the tier during a lock-down—the other inmates were locked in their cells. I had to stay in the common area until after the lock-down. I selected a chair to sit on and wait. An inmate had apparently forgotten his ID on the chair. I placed it on a table. When the lock-down was over, a young muscular black with a scar across his cheek erupted from his cell and proclaimed that the chair was his. Naively—wondering why I should surrender the chair to him—I asked, "Why?"

"Pops, my ID was there. You messed mit my muther-fuckin' ID. Get the fuck up." Having been educated about the reservation system, I decided not to force the issue and "got the fuck up." I also concluded he would've pulverized me before the COs got there—if they made the effort. Inasmuch as the same inmate has sat in the chair during the six days since, the chair is essentially his private property. If he is called away by the COs and has to take his ID, he asks a "home-boy" to save the chair for him. If he returns to his cell momentarily, he leaves the ID on the chair. The same routine is followed for the other two chairs. There was no way for anyone else ever to sit in a chair. I have as little to do with as possible with the three chair-sitters. They seem totally corrupted and irrational. Luckily I'm comfortable sitting at a table.

I'll probably be here another week at least before being sent to the Classification Center. They keep the transfer schedule a secret, presumably to prevent ambushes and escapes. I love you deeply and remember the great times we've had and the great times in the future still to be had.

2:15PM. Morning medication went OK. Had a TB test. Walked 22 laps in exercise period. Lunch was sloppy joes, potato salad (good), green beans, milk and juice. Got clean sheets and towels today. I've been hand-washing socks and underwear. I don't yet fully realize how my life has transmogrified. I have a cell to myself—a blessing—in the medical tier. The cell was designed to accommodate wheelchairs and is quite spacious. It is irregularly shaped and is furnished with a bed, a desk and a sink-commode. At the head of the bed is a window—a slit—perhaps five inches wide and five feet tall, through which one can view the razor wire fence. An electronically controlled sliding steel door to the common area has a small window to allow the COs to peer in during lock-down.

One of the other inmates is Jack Wiley, early 60s, white, short and rotund, with a gray crown of hair. He's in for growing and selling marijuana—for medicinal purposes, of course. He seems fragile and vulnerable, but "jail-wise." He engenders the obsequiousness of the three chair-sitters by buying things for them from the commissary. He makes many telephone calls to his attorney, to those involved in the marijuana business with him, and to his wife. Because he's a bit deaf he yells into the telephone and the whole tier is privy to the details of his case. He's skittish. A couple of days ago, I sat beside him while he was reading the paper. His deafness may have concealed my approach and I'm not sure he was aware of my presence. I cleared my throat with the intent of asking if I could barter for a pencil and paper. He almost jumped out of his skin and quickly moved to another table before I could speak. He saw me as a threat—a surprising concept. I expected to feel endangered, not to be perceived as a danger.

I saw a case counselor this morning. Not much new (except I got paper and pen!). I love you deeply and look forward to every contact with you.

9:00PM. Had a good visit with Walt, Brad and Elgin. The support of our church friends is a sharp contrast to the lack of support from the church. Dinner was a turkey casserole and green beans. There's a gospel concert on Friday. I'm on page 200 in "Primary Colors." Will call you tomorrow. I'll see you in my dreams tonight, love. I'm sure glad you're strong and are there for me

Sentencing + 7 days. 6:00AM First week done! Got your second letter this morning. They're going to become a habit. ☺ Cold is gone. Didn't sleep well last night.

By taking the trip to Pinesburg, you're not abandoning me! You need this trip. You're doing what is best for everyone. In Pinesburg, you have family. You can escape concerns and troubles for a bit. We need your strength and I, too, am optimistic. My new location will have +'s and-'s. We'll probably be able to have contact visits, but it will be further away. Fewer but better visits.

I hope you give the church thought. They, markedly because they're humanistic Unitarians, could've been more supportive, especially given all we have done for them, but they seem intent on increasing the shame and isolation. It would be easy to find hypocrisy and apostatize. They could still provide needed support for you, however. Whatever you think is best. Have you given further thought to have your mother come out and spend time with you?

3:00PM. Exercise was outside. Did 20 laps. I walked with Tom, another inmate on the tier. He's in his late 40s, white, quiet, slight built, with a string of DWIs, and in for two months. He was in a car wreck eight or so years ago and suffered brain damage. A bit slow. Tomorrow his youngest brother is getting married. Tom will be the only one absent from a large family. It'll be a bad day for him. I told him we'd play chess to keep his mind busy.

He has a college degree and until eight years ago, at the time of his car wreck, had a successful career managing hotel restaurant staff. He steadily moved upward in the quality of the hotels in which he worked. He came from a large loving family, had a fiancée, a sports car and was enjoying the "good life." Then came the tragic accident. He was a passenger in the car. Alcohol was not involved. He was in the ICU for six weeks and had brain damage. He had to relearn how to walk and talk. He lost much of his mental acuity. His fiancée, who couldn't cope with his diminution, left him. He could no longer handle responsibility so his career was gone. An older brother, in the landscaping business, gave Tom a menial labor job. The most destructive aspect of the tragedy, however, is that he was cognizant of his previous self and was aware of his new limitations. The degradation gnawed at Tom and he wanted his former life. He yearned for his sports car and, in order to afford more materialistic trappings, took a second job at night delivering pizza. He wanted his fiancée and her love back. Whiskey soothed the lost and pain. He worked all day; came home, had a few belts, ate a microwave dinner, and delivered pizza.

One night, at his first delivery, the customer smelled the alcohol and called the police, who waited for him at the second stop. His blood alcohol content measured .12%—enough for a DWI. However this was not the first such arrest. The judge sentenced him to two months.

Tom is proud that he never had an accident while driving drunk. He doesn't admit the possibility of causing another accident because of his drinking. He has tried AA, a requirement of probation from previous offenses, but it hasn't worked for him. The memories were too stark—the hurt too deep. He is worried about losing his driving license permanently and not being able to continue his land-scaping job. A further spiral downward in his deteriorating life. If I were omnipotent, I would make the memories go away, for then Tom could be happy.

After exercise, I weighed myself. Will see if I lose weight. As you know, I don't eat much bread. I need a way to distribute my allotment fairly among the other guys. I don't want to invite trouble by perceived favoritism.

9:00PM. Called Brad to tell him your travel plans. He had asked last night. He is genuinely concerned about you.

Tom and I play chess. He takes forever to make the simplest moves and then brags about how long it takes for me to beat him. Quirky. Cell inspection came an hour early and some cells were in turmoil. Mine was fine.

Damon is a tall thin black man. He has chopped hair. He's well educated and spoken. Caught in a car with crack. Says he has terminal cancer. He told the following joke last night, *"Why do Scots wear Kilts?"* Answer: *"Because sheep can hear a zipper from 500 feet away."* We had to explain it to Tom. I'm at page 270 in "Primary Colors." I solved the bread distribution problem. I simply made a list of the guys and cycle through it—duh!

Marshall, early 20s, black, small and effeminate, was a victim of insidious injustice today. It's his first time in the penal system as well. I'm still not sure of his offense. He has a wife and a daughter, whose first birthday is today. He talks about his daughter constantly.

He's being held for a trial tomorrow. He feels as if he got a raw deal in the preliminary hearing. Everyone I've met so far believes they got a raw deal, but Marshall's protestation of innocence has a flavor of verisimilitude. He's naïve enough to be incapable of a polished lie. Marshall is indigent and was appointed a public defender. When he discusses his case with the jailhouse lawyers—our fellow inmates—they ask if he had discussed these issues with his attorney. "No," he responds. He didn't realize the significance and his attorney didn't ask the right questions or something. He was urged to convey the "new" information to his attorney before his trial. So he wrote a letter to his attorney a couple of days ago, but he didn't have a stamp. Marshall asked a CO what to do. The CO said that for indigent offenders the county provides postage for legal mail and not to worry about it. So, Marshall mailed the letter sans stamp amidst high hopes, nourished by other inmates, that something good would happen. This morning the letter was returned for insufficient postage and now it's too late to convey the information to his attorney. He was counting on the letter to change his life. The lesson he learned is to distrust the system. He believes the CO purposely misled him. I counseled that he inform his attorney and suggest that his attorney ask for a continuance. Marshall wants to get out and sees a continuance only as further incarceration.

Today, I remembered our cruise. My cell is approximately the size of our living room on the ship but not as grandly furnished. My bed is on an interior wall, which I am told is warmer. I learned today that all future exercise periods will be inside the gym—getting too cold. I have the postcards you've sent on the wall. Love you. I can feel your warmth and closeness.

Sentencing + 8 days. 10:30AM. The menu is weekly so it is starting to repeat itself. No meals are a total disaster. Glad to hear that you're sending a stamped envelope. We'll see how sending in stuff from the outside works.

We frequently get apples and oranges with our meals, but they are the smallest things. The oranges are like limes, but I'm glad to have them and even eat the rinds. Had a good discussion with Damon this morning after I called you. He is quite intelligent and sensitive. Why the hell is he in here?

Jose, late 30s, Hispanic, seems to be a career jailbird, short and wiry, loud, and obnoxious. He got upset this morning. His commissary order for peanut butter was refused again and he didn't know why. He had $3.30 in his canteen account and the peanut butter was $3.25. We calmed him down by explaining that the tax made the total more than $3.30. The lack of any explanation from the canteen needlessly created tension, paranoia and suspicion. In ways, the control of information is the most abusive. Plays with your mind.

It turns out that Jack has been in the Classification Center a couple of times. Sounds grim. Two to a cell. Come out only for meals and exercise (two times a week). No library, but a book trolley comes around. He wasn't clear about the telephone situation. He was there once for two weeks and once for four weeks. He says the length of stay depends on the availability of a vacancy at your final destination.

Finished "Primary Colors" (thank goodness).

Everything seems routine now. It's amazing how full the day seems. Once I'm at my final destination, I wonder if I can get religious material from the denomination's outreach program, *The Church of the Larger Fellowship?*

I'm forming a theory about the incarcerated population. Since I've been here for eight days, which makes me an expert, right? ☺ Jail has to meet society's sense of minimum humane conditions. That standard includes 3 meals, warmth, safety, a modicum of medical care and a bed. That level of sustenance is more than many inmates have on the outside. I've heard stories of homeless people committing a crime at the start of cold weather so they can survive the winter using the state's hospitality. What kind of society forces its citizens to commit crime to live? All is not what it appears to be.

9:30PM. Went to the gospel concert tonight. Big disappointment. Overt Christian evangelizing offering eternal salvation and heaven. Singing was a white male quartet. I was hoping for a black gospel choir.

Medicine is delivered OK. As I was waiting in the holding area for a TB test (negative) I tried to strike up a conversation with the CO. I asked if he followed college basketball. He paused, glared at me, said, "No" and continued to stare at me. I looked at the far wall and said nothing more. Are COs able to cope only by viewing inmates as alien? What cosmic law would've been violated if he had replied in a human fashion? "Naw, I'm more of a football fan."

I read the Inmate Handbook. I borrowed a copy from Damon. (Why don't they give each inmate one? Information control!) It says specifically that stamps, envelopes and paper cannot be sent in because they're available through the canteen. I notice that they charge 35¢ for a 34¢ stamp. At the next opportunity, I will place a small order and include stamps. If I am moved before the order is filled and the money is lost, then it's lost. For the first time, I can say I'm hungry. A candy bar or something would go well. I am, however, getting enough to eat.

Have a safe flight home, my love. Hope the time with your mother was relaxing.

Sentencing + 9 days. Noon. Got a card from you and a letter from Troy. I tried calling Troy and got his answering machine. It is ironic that Troy, my youngest brother, is offering me encouragement and support. It should be the other way around.

I worry about pens again. Apparently they don't last long and the canteen hasn't filled an order for one in two weeks. When this one goes dry...? No exercise today. ⊛ All my dirty clothes were laundered. Damon has ordered and will give me a stamped envelope (Monday?) and I'll send these notes at that time. I'm on page 25 of "Mexico." I remember starting it before. I'll get further this time.

The menu doesn't repeat itself. I was wrong.

A month after I get to prison, I plan to stop the Prozac. Deal with the world on my own.

Look forward to seeing you tomorrow. College football today. Maybe chips, dip and Auslese. Should we build a fire in the fireplace? Light a candle? You can play computer bridge behind me and yell at your stupid partner for leading trumps! Let me reach.

Sentencing + 10 days. 9:00PM. Gosh, it was good seeing you and talking with you. You're the innocent victim of all of this. You're showing so much courage, strength and love. I need all of those for you and from you.

Watched football. I won "tomorrow's dinner cookie" in a bet on the Minnesota-Detroit game. With regard to "human interaction," I may have it easier than you. I can talk or not talk at my will. I can leave the common area and go to my cell if I wish. I can't always go to the common area (lock-down periods), but largely the degree of human interaction is my choice.

Tomorrow is David's birthday. Troy reminded me in his letter. I'm sure that David will write me a letter of support. We three brothers always stuck together.

Up to page 100 in "Mexico." The writing seems forced for Mitchner.

In my canteen order are three Baby Ruths, three peanut bags, three rolls of Life Savers, three bags of instant coffee, a legal pad, five stamped envelopes, a pen, a felt tip pen, and a pencil/eraser.

I hope they don't handcuff me behind my back for the whole trip to the Classification Center. Causes back spasms. I'll call in the morning. This epistle may get in the mail tomorrow! Tomorrow's newspaper will have the chess column. I can replay the games in my cell during lock-down.

Sentencing + 11 days. 9:00PM. No exercise today. Called David to wish him a happy birthday. Had a great dream about you. You were lying next to me in a blue silk slip. Realistic. Saw a doctor today. He seemed extraordinarily compassionate for a prison employee. Maybe because he was young.

Sentencing + 12 days. 2:00PM. Two letters this morning! Lovely letters. Pretty pictures. No stamped envelope yet. Not optimistic about ever receiving it.

Page 205 of "Mexico." Not as interesting as "Chesapeake." Did we read "Texas?" Seems as if I remember it.

Should be leaving here any day now. But I do have my canteen order in, if my stay is longer. On my wife-to-do list are 1) water plants, 2) write the mortgage company, and 3) start the writing campaign. How's that for a nag? ☺ Hope my pen lasts.

Sentencing + 13 days. 6:00AM. Going to the Classification Center. No time to call. All my love,…your husband.

Classification Center

Sentencing + 14 days. I suspect yesterday will be the worst day of the whole experience. The trip wasn't too bad. Our wrists and ankles were shackled, but the handcuffs were in front—no coffle. I missed the morning meds.

This is a maximum-security institution and is unbelievable. During the intake processing, they put you in a holding tank between trips to various stations. The holding tank has seating for perhaps twenty people. At times there are over 50 of us, so we had to sit on the floor. The floor is covered with trash. There is plenty of space for additional benches. There is an unshielded commode, which every-one managed to avoid using. The COs' attitude, I'm sure, is that the inmates cre-ate their own environment. At times, I was one of three or four white guys. I returned from the pharmacy carrying blister packs of pills. One conversation scared the hell out of me.

"Hey, Pops. What's the pills?" asked a black guy across the room. The whole damned room went silent. He had a scar running down a cheek from his eye to his chin.

"Ah, just my damned blood pressure medicine," I answered as I sat on the floor. I tried to be nonchalant.

"Make you high?"

"Hell, doesn't make me feel anyway."

"Yeah? How did you granpoppy feel when he had my granmaw as a slave? You know what I mean?" The room was silent. I tried to think of a suitable response. I didn't want to appear scared or arrogant. I decided not to point out that there was a problem of several generations. I suspect he would've considered that as beside the point.

Another black guy sitting beside me rescued me. "Let me see those," he said as he grabbed the pills. He looked at them for a moment, tossed them back into my lap and said, "These aren't fucking shit." He paused and then spoke to my antag-onist across the room, "I don't know about you, my man, but my granpoppy slave loved to sink his meat in the missus of the plantation." The whole room laughed. I smiled—mainly from relief. I never saw my savior again and wonder if he knew what he did. Did he sense the atmosphere and stepped in purposefully? I like to think so.

I was deloused. I also got my quota of state clothes. One has to sign the receipt BEFORE receiving the goods. One signs the blank form. They put in whatever number they wish. How does this engender trust in the system? *"Hey, I only got one pair of pants!" "You signed right here that you got two."* I was asked about the required size of pants. Knowing I could wear pants that are too large, but not if they were too small, I asked for and received pants that are several sizes too large.

I'm doing OK. I was all screwed up about being able to receive personal property. I probably caused you much useless activity. Sorry, I just didn't know. I hope you got my massive letter from the County today. A bit of good luck, getting the stamped envelope through. I don't know how the commissary works here, so I haven't ordered anything.

Best-case scenario: A few days here and then I will be transferred to the State Psychiatric Evaluation Center (PEC). They do an evaluation and determine that I'm neither a raving lunatic nor a threat to society. A motion for reconsideration is filed and I get out in a few months. Could happen.

I was given an Inmate Handbook (finally!). I found that I'm eligible for parole after serving half of the sentence.

There is no opportunity for physical exercise here. My medicine wasn't right this morning—no Dynacirc, no Prozac. I understand I'll never get any Dynacirc or Minoxidil because they're not in the Department of Prisons (DOP) pharmacology. They'll make substitutions. Procardia for the Dynacirc and something for the Minoxidil. I'm anxious about it. It took so long to find a combination to keep the blood pressure under control. I did see a doctor today. He'll schedule an appointment with a psychiatrist to get a prescription for Prozac. Supposed to happen today. We had an AIDS awareness program this morning. No library here. ☻ I'll be OK.

The doctor gave me a form that states, because of my medical condition, I am entitled to a lower bunk. He told me to keep the form and carry it with me. When I got to the tier where my cell is, I showed the form to the black CO in charge, who promptly took it from me, crumpled it while glaring at me, and threw it in the wastepaper basket. No explanation. I was too intimidated by his imperious attitude to make an issue of it. I did get the lower bunk because my cellmate likes the upper. Not sure about my next cell. The system doesn't work because the parts don't function together. My cellmate is an older black man.

I find I'm sleeping more, not out of necessity, but rather for escape. In sleep, I go to isolated sandy beaches with you. In sleep, I dine in fine restaurants with you. In sleep, I walk with you on shaded forest trails. In sleep, I'm with beautiful you.

8:00PM. I was moved to the medical tier. Don't know what a difference that will make, except that, so far, I have a cell to myself and, thus, have the lower bunk. The cell is a rectangle about ten feet by seven feet. A bunk bed is against the short outside wall. The swinging door, with a peep window, is controlled by key. There is a desk and a wall-mounted shelf accessible from the upper bunk. The commode-sink is identical to that at County. Someone left a copy of the paper so I have some reading material. I haven't showered in a couple of days. Only taking Vasotec, Minoxidil (both from the supply you furnished from home) and aspirin now. Hope the delivery is squared away. My mood is still strong and positive. I understand that you can send in stamps. We knew this would be the roughest part. Two days down!

Sentencing + 15 days. 7:30AM. I did get my medication last night. Slept well. Still have the cell to myself. Finished the crossword puzzle from the paper left here. Breakfast was just served. Two hard-boiled eggs, ½ pint of 1% milk, 1 cup of coffee (has a faint taste of kerosene), a bit of jelly, 4 slices of bread, and oatmeal. They forgot to give me a spoon!

Some of the COs and inmates treat me with a modicum of deference because of my age. They call me "Pops."

I read that PEC is not part of the DOP and has its own policies about parole.

1:30PM. Had more blood work done. Also, saw the psychiatrist. Prozac is not available so he substituted Zoloft. One of two good things will have to happen. I'll get out of here soon or I'll see you in eight days! I understand the visits are contact visits and you can stay from 9:00AM until 4:00PM. We'll run out of things to talk about. ☺ Lunch was again served without a spoon. What am I missing? Each hour passed is an hour closer to the end. I hope I can call tonight. Love,…your husband

4:00PM. Hooray, I got your Monday letter with the stamped envelope. I'll mail this during the TV period when I have access to the mailbox. To print e-mail, there are several ways. The simplest way is to "cut & paste." Cut from within the terminal program and paste into Notepad or Word and then print from that program.

The schedule here alternates. One day we're allowed out of our cell from 1:30PM—3:00PM and on the next day, from 6:30PM until 9:30PM. We can come out into the common area where there is a TV and card tables. Cartoons and trash-talk shows are the TV fare as determined by the assertiveness of the dumb.

Please keep sending me stamps and envelopes. They are allowed in. I have a few small envelopes. I'm OK with pens. Worried about paper. Go ahead and address the envelopes. Makes them less valuable to others. Other inmates don't think I'll go to the PEC with a sentence of only 2 ½ years. They think I'll go to a minimum-security prison.

This period is the hardest. My cellmate yesterday had been sentenced to 18 months and he asked for 2 years. If he had received 18 months, he would've served the whole sentence in the County Detention Center whereas he would serve a two-year in a minimum-security prison, which, he says, is much better than the County's jail.

Dinner just was served. I found out that spoons are delivered *en masse* to the CO on duty and you have to ask for one. How was I supposed to know? Information control! Dinner looks OK, but I'm not hungry. Swiss steak (?), green beans, bread and chocolate cake.

Had another TB test. The state didn't trust the one from the County. Even the system doesn't trust the system. Got a tetanus shot. The nose pad broke off my glasses. I can still wear them. Another inmate told me that showers would be available tomorrow. I sleep and dream a lot. I'm sure it's a reaction to sensory deprivation. This indolent life style is addictive. Three days here past. Love,…your husband.

Sentencing + 16 days. 7:00AM. Sorry I couldn't call you last night. Should be able to tonight. Besides stamps, can you send me the crossword puzzle and bridge column from the paper? They help pass the time.

My medicine was delivered last night. I asked the nurse what the pills were. I understand now and won't double dose. The Zoloft should start this morning. Mood and spirits are OK. The sunrise is beautiful from my cell (5th floor). I think I've done all the medical stuff (hmmm, no urine test yet). I expect written tests, but none yet. The culminating event is an interview with the case manager. A numerical score is calculated that dictates your assignment to minimum-, medium-, or maximum-security.

I'm still trying to understand the judge's remarks about alcohol. The only source of information about alcohol usage, to which he conceivably had access, was the interview I had with the pre-sentencing evaluator who asked if I ever worried about excessive use. I, remembering the extra glass of wine drank at a party, answered "yes." Can anyone who drinks alcohol, truthfully answer "no"? The thought does not verify the supposition.

Your letter yesterday was a pleasant surprise. I've received none that were forwarded from County. Since my canteen order wasn't delivered, I should have about $11.25 there as well. My dress suit that I wore in court is being mailed to you. Time is going relatively quickly. I love you.

10:00AM. Got Zoloft this morning. I asked about commissary. It's closed this week. Next week, I can order on Tuesday and have delivery on the following Monday. Luckily, I have no emergencies. Today is dead. No tests. I traded a small bag of chips for an orange. Proud of me? I figure the more vitamin C I get, the better. Asked about personal laundry. There is none. One exchanges trousers, shirts and bedding. You're expected to hand wash your own shorts and socks in the tiny sink.

5:00PM. I showered! Changed into clean clothes. Feeling better. During rec (in an hour or so), I'll try to call you and then force myself to watch TV for variety. Cartoons will be on, but they offer relief from a cell wall filled with graffiti.

Looks cold outside. People are wearing coats. My cell is warm enough, but this place makes County look like a spa.

9:20PM. It was good talking to you. Telephone access is easier here, but the calls are limited to 10 minutes. Discontinuing my health insurance is OK. There's no way we could benefit from it. I was able to watch football for a short period and then the TV was switched to the black entertainment network.

I'm making a deck of cards. It will serve quite well for solitaire. Crossword puzzles and a deck of cards will entertain me for a long time.

Sentencing + 17 days. 7:30AM. Another pretty day. Been playing solitaire. Plan to wash clothes today. The only other thing on the calendar is a call to you. I looked on the fruit juice drink they give us—0% vitamin C. Hope church goes well for you.

Noon: Morning medication OK. I believe I'm OK for paper and pens until I can buy some. Read all the reading material three times or more. Wish I knew more about the news. I understand there is a Mid-East peace? How's the market been doing?

Did my laundry. One advantage to this cell is that, because of the heating vent location, things dry fast. It took forever to dry something in County. I understand that when I get to minimum security you can bring me lots of stuff. Get my own clothes. Other inmates are surprised when I mention that I expect to go to PEC. Apparently, that's where the criminally insane go. Am I crazy?

5:15PM. It was nice talking to you. Glad the Minister at least made a token effort. I do four things—sleep, write you, watch out the window, and play cards. I'm starting to talk to myself, but I'm aware I'm doing it, so it's OK, right? ☺ Hope you're paying the bills, watering the plants, and putting the garbage out. My dreams are nice and include you. I feel your warmth and cold toes!

Sentencing + 18 days. 6:30AM. I didn't sleep well last night. Maybe 18 hours a day is too much. ☺ I saw two pieces of heaven this morning. There were low clouds to the east, which made a fantastic sunrise. Spectacular colors. I imagined the two of us, warmly dressed, sitting on a beach with a blanket around our shoulders watching the rising sun. We have a thermos of cinnamon coffee and our cups are steaming as we huddle together. The second piece of heaven is, "I've got a pet!" Well, sort of. From my window this morning, for the second time, I saw a black cat. It cagily darts across a busy one-way, four-lane street to a paved-over lot. The lot is bare except for one bush growing against a building at its border. The cat crosses the lot and goes directly to that bush. Why? Does it have kittens there? Does it hunt for mice and birds there? I'll look for it again tomorrow.

Noon. Nothing has happened today. I was hoping for a flurry of activity to complete the classification process so I can get out of here. I haven't seen the cat since this morning. Food is worse here than the food in County, but I'll survive. My arm is tingling more. Lying down so much? No muscle relaxant? I picture my spinal cord slowly being severed!

2:30PM. Had early rec. Through a bizarre sequence of events I got a book! An inmate loaned me a book and then five minutes later the CO demanded the book! No explanation from her. I tried to explain that it wasn't mine—that I had borrowed it. The CO didn't care and didn't want to hear anything out of my mouth—she just wanted the book! I gave the book to her. It turns out that the book was the CO's and she had loaned it to the inmate who then loaned it to me. This irritated the CO. Because of a strange and strong sense of street ethics, the inmate felt obligated to get a book for me! The book that he borrowed (again!) from another inmate is "The Jeweled Spur" by Gilbert Morris. Looks like I won't be able to call you tonight. The rec schedule isn't periodic, as I had thought.

4:00PM. The book is terrible! Thinly disguised theistic proselytism. A minimum plot and all problems are solved by a belief in God. I'll probably read it out of boredom. I don't know when I'll be able to call.

5:00PM. Lots of mail came. I got a letter from Carl with 10 photos and a letter from Bud with a bunch of word puzzles. My sons, like my brothers, are having to patronize their role model. I also got a postcard from Alice, your sister, which the CO read while I waited for her to give it to me. Nothing from you, but that means more later.

I watched out the window and saw Zorro, the name I've given the cat, cross the street again. If Zorro can make it across the street as often as he does, then I can make it through this. I think, at the risk of being melodramatic, of Solzhenitsyn's gulag and Burt Lancaster in Alcatraz and draw resolve and strength.

I hope you've explained to our family and friends that I haven't answered their letters because of the lack of stamps. God, I hope they keep writing. Showered today and exchanged a pair of trousers for a clean pair.

9:30PM. Having a rec period and being able to use the phone was a surprise. I'm not sure if there is a schedule.

I wonder by what legal theory the prosecutor thinks he can keep the computer? I'm sure the judge will set him straight.

They brought four new guys to the tier tonight, but I still have the cell to myself—a blessing. No one has measured my blood pressure here, yet. Hope I can call you in two days.

Sentencing + 19 days. 8:00AM. Got a cellmate last night about midnight. Older quiet black man. He's small and has frost in his short hair. His face is wrinkled beyond his age. He won't be any trouble. I wonder if the system is compassionate enough to try to pair like individuals in a cell.

They had a shakedown. Two COs entered my cell as I was taken outside to the tier, handcuffed. They searched the cell and my personal items. They took two of my three pens. I'm sure the pens, being mightier than the sword, were viewed as a threat to the stability of Western civilization. I asked why they were taking the pens. They answered that it was the rules. Then the brute in charge warned me, "Don't you be developing an attitude. This is you first time and you be cool if you keep you mouth shut. Know what I mean?"

Cloudy morning. No sunrise. I haven't seen Zorro this morning, but having someone in the upper bunk limits my viewing time.

The Inmate Handbook says that one needs at least three years remaining on one's sentence to go to PEC. Why didn't Herb or the judge know that? My cellmate will probably be in medical most of the day.

9:30AM. My cellmate was moved out. I haven't seen Zorro today. Just had my medication and will get clean sheets and towels today. Such is my day that this is a big event! I'll work on Bud's puzzles and watch out the window for Zorro.

P.S. I've found a way to get exercise—squats. They cause the heart to pound.

Noon. I got my classification—medium-security. It will be reviewed after a year. Disappointing. Probably go to Rochelle or to Centerville. Worst case is 15 months. We can get through this! I'm a bit down. I got two letters from you today with crossword puzzles, photos and stamps! Thank you.

Sentencing + 20 days. What a beautiful picture of you. I taped it to my wall so I can see it as I lay on my side in bed. It has to serve as your avatar.

My cellmate returned. He's OK. His name is Ralph Smith.

Cloudy again this morning. No sunrise. ⊛ Slept well last night. I finished one crossword puzzle and played solitaire. I traded the book for another. It's the same genre but better written, so it may be tolerable

An evangelistic preacher, flabby jowls and a huge potbelly, came on the tier last night. The COs allow any inmate to leave their cell to hear the preaching. However if you wonder off to the TV or phone, they return you to your cell. If out, you have to hear the Lord's word. From a chair—being too heavy to stand—the preacher predicted quite confidently that the "rapture", the Second Coming, would be eight to twelve months after the "true" year 2000. He also described a politician (Bill Clinton thinly disguised) who was the anti-Christ. Many of the inmates give every indication of believing all that is said. The first week here is over! Got both fruit juice and apple juice with breakfast.

Later: Lunch was the best meal yet here—chopped beef, salad, peas and carrots, pasta, applesauce, a bit of jelly, and bread. I'm drowning in bread. They give three to five slices with each meal. I eat the wheat bread and give the white away.

The second book is as bad as the first. I'm skimming it and reading the parts that attract my attention. Need to wash socks today. Worked another crossword puzzle—keep them coming!

My biggest problem herein is information. How does the mundane—showers, laundry, mail—work? None of this explained officially and you have to learn from the other inmates. This reinforces the attitude that the system is not to be trusted, doesn't function, and you have to rely on your fellow inmates. Is that the message the system wishes to convey? The penal system would reduce recidivism if it inculcated the inmates with a trust of society—*"Do what's right and you'll get a square deal."*

Most of these guys have been here before, know what it's like, and yet do things that bring them back. Do they not have a chance or a choice?

I can mail these letters more frequently now that I have a supply of stamps.

Sentencing + 21 days. A clear sky this morning so the sunrise was non-spectacular. I didn't see Zorro. I had one coughing spell, but it didn't last long. I requested vitamins in my commissary order.

I'm enclosing a draft of a letter to the Commissioner requesting a classification reduction. Copies should go the local warden, the judge, and to Herb Diamond as our attorney. If you think it's a good idea, could you please send it ASAP? Feel free, of course, to edit it as you see fit. I called Bud and Carl last night. It's amazing to watch your kids grow. I love those young men, my sons, and am proud of them. Bud is redoing his front porch.

Many of the guys in here, including my cellmate, are technical parole violators. They get a hearing within a few weeks and in many cases (I suspect because of overcrowding) are released again on parole. I don't know my cellmate's original offense.

The populations (inmates and COs) here and in County are predominantly black. Most of the blacks are incarcerated because of drugs. Drug use, of course, is not confined to the black community, but it is certainly, because of socioeconomic reasons, more prevalent there. The problem isn't drug use but rather the conditions that promote the use of drugs as a mechanism to escape from reality. We need to make reality better.

An argument could be made that prohibition failed because too many whites were arrested for drinking, distilling and selling alcohol. If blacks had violated prohibition predominantly, would it have ever been repealed? The racial ratio in prison is startling.

Hope you had a good time at the opera tonight. The thought of being with you again makes all of this tolerable.

P.S. I just learned that pictures on the walls are prohibited.

Sentencing + 22 days. Just got the mail. Letter from you and one from Troy. I appreciate the six stamps and the poems. Troy had a brilliant idea and sent me a chess set made of paper and a few game scores. One of the crossword puzzles you sent has a chess column on the back! A Unitarian miracle! Life can give you wondrous moments if you're receptive. I can escape in solitaire, crossword puzzles and chess and let the troubles pass.

Since I've had time to add onto my commissary order, it currently has one package of envelopes, two writing tablets, two ball point pens, ten stamps, three disposable razors, one small can foot powder (these state shoes make my feet perspire and with the diminution of laundry facilities foot odor is a problem), one dandruff shampoo, a deck of playing cards, a bottle of vitamins, a box of laundry detergent, and, of course, the necessities—three Baby Ruths, a package of butterscotch, three rolls of Life Savers, two bags of popcorn, three packages of instant coffee and lastly, for my indigent cellmate, a package of cookies.

From my current supply, I will use one stamp to write Troy and one stamp to write Mary, leaving me two after this letter. I feel rich!

Something new for me. The blacks herein routinely call each other "nigger." The word is acceptable coming from a black, but I'm sure my usage would be anathema.

When I get to my final destination, after a couple of weeks of acclimation, I hope to stop the Zoloft.

Sentencing + 23 days. It was wonderful seeing and kissing you. You looked stunning. Thanks for the deck of cards. I worry that in three or four months, the support from friends may taper off. People get bored, get other interests, and the concern diminishes. If we recognize the possibility, then if it happens, it will be less disheartening.

I want to pursue retrieving the $11.25 from County from the aborted commissary order. They impose the time delay, are cognizant of when you are being transferred, and yet don't curtail the ordering process. I'm sure many of the inmates don't follow up and believe the system has screwed them again.

When I left the visiting area, there was a waiting line, so the earlier you arrive, the better. After our visit, I was sent to medical to receive my medication.

Sentencing + 24 days. I've been playing chess with Ralph, my cellmate. Although he hasn't beaten me, he is a good player and our games last over an hour. I've finished all of the crossword puzzles.

The inmates in here for drug offenses generally have no support from the outside. My hypothesis is that they have begged, borrowed, and stole from their family and friends to support their habit and thereby alienated the very people they need for support. Government *control* (avoiding the trigger word, "decriminalization") is the answer

Sentencing + 25 days. Another pretty sunrise. Zorro was AWOL again. Ralph tells me that you are informed by the COs on the morning of your transfer.

I have to find a way to clip my toenails. They had clippers on the County commissary list but not here. Perhaps at my final destination, I can get a pair.

Thanks for mailing the letter to the commissioner. I called Troy and asked for another paper chess set for Ralph. I'm surprised that some support organization doesn't distribute paper chess sets.

For the first time, I didn't eat any of the breakfast. They have started using a sugar substitute. I find it too bitter for the cereal. The scrambled eggs are from reconstituted eggs and are never good. I'll drink the milk and take my vitamin.

I lent my deck of cards to the inmate who had loaned me the book. I could hardly refuse. Following the example of another inmate, I gingerly chewed the blade out of a disposable razor. I tried to trim my beard but the blade must be quite dull.

I haven't seen Zorro recently, but I haven't seen a squashed black mass in the middle of the road either. I hope he/she is still OK.

Sentencing + 25 days. There's nothing except good news in our cell today. I got my commissary order filled so life improved significantly (I say, as I eat a

Baby Ruth). I have real laundry soap and real dandruff shampoo. I'm using "my" paper, "my" envelope and one of "my" stamps to write you.

Ralph is in here because he is a technical parole violator. He failed to provide a urine sample. He claims that he had trouble urinating in front of another person. Finally, he just quit reporting. He was on the street for two years, holding a job without any arrests, before they caught him. His case manager is recommending that he be released on parole again. That could happen in two days. It is good for him, but I have mixed feelings. He's probably as good a cellmate as one can expect.

I've submitted a sick-call request to have my blood pressure measured, "to check the efficacy of the current medication."

Later: The afternoon rec period is over. Many of the guys play pinochle and others watch TV cartoons. A couple of guys spend their time talking to the female COs, who seem to like the attention. I watch TV.

I'm up to fifty squats in my aerobics. I do them two or three times daily. They do get my heart pumping. For informational purposes only—you can send in money orders. I have $47, which is enough for now. I have a supply of paper, envelopes and stamps.

I got lots of mail—your letter about the church, opera, and the magazine articles (thank you), a card from Dianne, a card from Alice, a letter from Brad, and a letter with e-mail jokes from Dottie. I don't have Dianne's address. Could you send it?

I've eaten one of three Baby Ruths, one of two bags of popcorn, and one of approximately twenty-five butterscotch drops. Admirable restraint, agreed?

Sentencing + 26 days. I just wrote Dottie and hinted for crossword puzzles. I had a good night and morning medication. I will ask that an Inmate Handbook be sent to you. They can deduct the cost of mailing, etc., from my account. I'll ask a higher-ranking officer, who comes through from time to time on inspection. The laundry soap helps. I'm going to drink a cup of "real" coffee in a bit. I'm not sure how they prepare the prison coffee but is doesn't compare with "Taster's Choice"—available from the commissary.

There was another religious service last night in the common area. The evangelist gives Bibles away. Ralph is a Muslim as are many of the blacks herein. There are enough of them to have a scheduled religious service. Ominously the Muslim religion, herein, speaks of the evil of white Europeans.

An oddity—we haven't had any salt or pepper for the last week. Lots of sugar, jelly, and bread. It's not just my medical diet; Ralph isn't getting any either.

If I'm still here in three days, I'll submit another commissary request—aftershave lotion, cough drops, and, of course, more popcorn.

No mail today. That means twice as much tomorrow. After three weeks or so without, the shampoo was very refreshing in the shower today. Nothing has happened in response to my request to have my blood pressure measured. I sent my request of a copy of the Inmate Handbook directly to the warden. Might as well start at the top.

It's poignant that none of the considerable graffiti herein or in County is erotic, in contrast to the restrooms in service stations or college dormitories. Most of the graffiti is religiously oriented. I guess that inmates see "spreading the word" as salvation.

I made a cup of "real" coffee. Boy, it tasted good! I'll definitely order more. I had forgotten the dark roasted taste.

I view the delay in my assigning me to a prison as a positive sign. Others who came with me already know where they are going. Maybe the system is waiting for an opening at PEC or my case is receiving more scrutiny. Anyway I'm settled in here and am adjusted to the routine.

I'll call tonight and even if you're not there, you'll get the message that I'm still here.

Sentencing + 27 days. Breakfast was a disaster. All the milk served on the tier was sour. I had poured it on the grits before the discovery. Luckily, I hadn't used any in the coffee. The expiration date is in three days so it wasn't old, just mishandled. A fresh supply wasn't distributed. I ate the hard-boiled eggs and that will suffice.

Later: I got a real book, "The Last Sanctuary" by Craig Holden. Ralph borrowed it from a newly arrived inmate, but Ralph is reading the Bible.

My blood pressure was 150/90. Not perfect but better than I had expected. At the time of the measurement, I hadn't taken my morning medication yet.

We had a nice piece of ham for lunch, which surprises me because the Inmate Handbook clearly states that no pork products are served. The foot powder works. I'm sure Ralph is pleased.

The mail came. I got letters from Troy, David, Phyllis and Barbara. Phyllis sent a couple of large crossword puzzles. I got a notice that the order from Amazon.com was returned. Barbara sent a copy of one of her late husband's sermons. I found it interesting, intellectual, and thought provoking.

I ate a second Baby Ruth and started the next roll of Life Savers. I've been eating the butterscotch drops and sharing them with Ralph. Dinner—beef patty, mixed vegetables, mashed (creamed?) potatoes, bread, milk, apricots and apple juice—was good.

Ralph finally beat me at chess. He says now he can go home.

Sentencing + 28 days. I had real coffee this morning as I watched a so-so sunrise.

Ralph is at his parole hearing now to determine his fate. He has his hopes up. I hope it's warranted.

They measured my blood pressure this morning, 122/80! Today is shower day. I've done my laundry. I need to order more coffee, another bar of soap, and a supply of laundry soap. Ralph tells me that one can take commissary items when being transferred from here to prison—unlike from County to here.

Later: Ralph is getting out. They reinstated his parole. He's not sure when he leaves, today or tomorrow, but he's happy and I'm happy for him. I'll miss the chess games and will have to replace them with recorded game scores.

I still have no access to the current events—no newspapers, no TV news shows. World War III could've started as far as I know.

Later: Ralph is gone. I had a follow-up visit with the psychiatrist. She tells me that I probably won't go to PEC and I shouldn't want to go. The DOP policy is not to send anyone to PEC unless they have at least three years remaining. Most PEC programs have a two-year waiting list. She says that medium-security is not so bad.

Mail was just delivered. Three letters from you! I was just called for my shower.

Sentencing + 29 days. There was a beautiful moon last night, but clouds hid the sunrise. Last night, another inmate told me that this portion of the process is the worst. The second time through the system would be easier because you'd know what to expect.

I also learned a bit of inanity. The penal system defines a classification of crime—not an individual crime—as violent or non-violent. The state legislature just changed the designation of daytime burglary as a non-violent crime from its previous classification as violent. Is that all there is to reducing violent crime—just redefine it? Shouldn't the jury or judge evaluate each transgression to determine violent content? The system defines murder as a violent act, but is the 83-year old man who feeds his terminally ill wife an overdose of medication, sits down, holds her hand, and cries as she dies, committing a violent act? The penal system uses the word "violent" in a different way than is generally accepted. The implications mislead the public. Reports of rising or falling violent crime are based on the system's definition of the word. Reports of the numbers of violent inmates may include inmates who have never committed a violent (conventional usage) act, but their offense is labeled as violent. Injustice results because the inmate's job possibilities inside prison, his security classification, accumulation of good-time, and eligibility for parole are all affected by the *classification* of his crime as violent or non-violent—not by the particulars of his individual offense.

Cooler this morning. A bit chilly here in the cell. I've saved my last coffee packet for tomorrow. I'll eat the last bag of popcorn during the weekend. I've ordered five more. Not having a cellmate has its advantages, but I miss the conversation and the chess games. Ralph gave me his address, but I'm hesitant to write him. Prison friendships may not be as significant as they seem.

Inmates have told me that the warden is sensitive to requests from the outside. He wants to avoid negative publicity. If my request that a copy of the Inmate Handbook be sent to you isn't honored, perhaps you can call and request one.

Today is laundry day. I also have to organize my papers again, add the new addresses you sent to my address list and write my brother David. I wrote Alice yesterday. One can tell that she is your sister.

Tomorrow, I see you again.

Sentencing + 30 days. In a couple of hours you visit.

I had a good night. I had a dream that I was back in college—a big college—and I was having trouble finding my classes. I've had similar dreams a few times in the past. This is a common theme, I've heard. I wonder what anxiety it's indicative of?

The sunrise was pretty. The clouds were corrugated in a north-south direction so, as the sun rose, there were alternate bands of yellow and blue. Striking. Got letters from Walter and Troy yesterday. Walter sent me articles from "Science." Thoughtful of him.

I'm trying to finish "The Last Sanctuary." I'm not sure how long I'll be here and probably can't take it with me. It's a "cops and robbers" thriller. I'm on page 275 of 430.

At about 8:30 I plan to use my last packet of coffee so I can sip the coffee as I watch for you out the window.

Later: It was great seeing you! The event at the end was just the CO telling me to go to medical. I got my medication and had my blood pressure measured (130/94). More later.

Almost to the end of the book, page 380.

Sad about your conversation with the Minister. Even among Unitarians, compassion is in short supply. Our kith, kin and car club are more supportive than the Unitarian-Universalist Church. The Unitarian scalpel that removed dogma from the body religion also excised the heart.

The end of a visit means that I must wait for another and live in the memory of the last.

Sentencing + 31 days. One month gone by. The worst, I suspect, is behind us. I expect to be transferred this week. I finished the book—a good way to spend time. It shows the importance of a library at my final destination.

I wrote David and Nancy. It was hard writing Nancy because she's like a sister to me. I was the best man at their wedding.

There was a demonstration against the death penalty in the street outside the jail. I could see it from my cell.

I've lost nine pounds

Sentencing + 32 days. Commissary order came. I ordered a mechanical pencil and refills. I fear not having writing supplies after my experience at County. Got after-shave lotion (non-alcoholic, of course), cough drops, fifteen stamps and ten packets of coffee (one of which I immediately used). Also got snacks. I still have $43 in my account. Should be enough for awhile.

The psychiatrist ordered blood drawn—the third sample I've given.

Lunch was a hamburger patty, three pieces of wheat bread, rice, coleslaw and a fruit drink. Ate it all.

The mail arrived. Two letters from you, a letter from Carl, a letter from Phyllis and a letter from Dianne. The CO was impressed by the quantity of my mail. Dianne, the sister of yours that I knew the least, is the one writing the most. Carl sent me a bunch of crossword puzzles, word games and a chess column. Playing myself chess. I win! Helps maintain my sanity for a while.

Sentencing + 33 days. I saw a drug deal on the tier last night for the first time. One inmate traded cocaine for a bar of soap. Twice before, I was aware of marijuana being smoked. I can't imagine how the stuff gets in—venal COs? I had heard at County that drugs were prevalent here.

I feel safe and get along with the other inmates. I have not seen a fight although I heard of one. "Dude A" and "dude B"—young guys—fought over who was next in the food line. B is HIV+ (as are $1/3$ of the guys in here). "A" bit "B" and got "B"'s blood in his mouth. When "A" found out about "B"'s HIV status he became hysterical—crying, rocking back and forth, and incessantly wiping his mouth with his hand.

My cell is still the only one with one occupant.

Herb's call to the local psychologist has had an effect. I wonder if many attorneys make such telephone calls. I was summoned and interviewed by the psychologist as a candidate for group therapy. It was a good discussion and we talked about many things. The problem is that the group therapy would be here, where there is no physical activity and no library. I thanked them for the offer but declined it. The psychologist understood completely and my refusal won't be viewed negatively. No physical activity for months will ruin my health.

I hadn't realized how much I miss erudite conversation until I spoke with the psychologist. I just sort of let loose. It wasn't an emotional release. We spoke of racism, survival in jail, etc. He seemed willing to talk as long as I wanted. I appreciated it. It made me wish for the times, in front of the fireplace, when we sip wine, and talk.

I feel that either the appeal panel or parole board will drastically reduce my sentence. I can't see the benefit to anybody of my staying incarcerated, but the whole system is so askew that rationality has no weight. I'm trying to remain realistic, but one has to be receptive to miracles.

Sentencing + 34 days. I wrote Herb Diamond to thank him for his efforts as my attorney in exploring the group therapy program here and explained my refusal.

For 10¢, a cup of coffee is a bargain for the benefit it gives as a mood enhancement.

Sentencing + 35 days. Drat! I missed the telephone last night. I got in line at 8:45 and they cut off the telephones at 9:00. I didn't know that. How was I supposed to know that? I was next in line when it went dead. I'll try to call Phyllis this morning and have her relay a message to you. I'm still here.

No cellmate, yet. The predominant benefit in being alone in a cell is the privacy obtained, especially for defecation. There is no screen or door to separate the commode from the rest of the cell. There is a minimum amount of air circulation and the mephitic air hangs heavily.

Got my commissary order. I had a bit of a problem with another inmate, whom I barely know. He wanted to borrow a bag of popcorn until next week. I lent him one, but he wanted a bag every night. He said he'd order some to pay me back. In response to his second request, I deceitfully said I had no more. He could be shipped out or I could. Why is it so necessary to have the popcorn now? When I wanted something (stamp, pencil) I waited or bartered rather than borrowing. I believe it will be OK, but such things can lead to trouble. Hopefully I'll be shipped out soon.

I have to fight to stay positive today. The monotony wears on you. I must think positive! I got *two* apples for lunch. I *did* relay the message to you. I wish something would happen to change my environment. In the meantime, I have your letters, the telephone calls, cups of coffee, Baby Ruths, bags of popcorn, and sunrises. Much to be thankful for.

Seinfeld is watched on TV during the late rec session, but the noise level is so high that I miss most of the dialogue. A dude in the common area will yell to their "home-boy" still confined in a cell (only half of us are allowed out at a time). Two or three such conversations are concurrent. There seems to a cultural value placed on loudness that I don't appreciate. Because of the yelling, the TV volume is increased, which causes the yelling to get louder. The acoustics—mortar walls, plastered ceilings, small spaces and concrete floors—amplifies the cacophony. Calls for muting would be invidious, so the chaos is accepted.

I've saved the large manila envelopes I've gotten in the mail. They make an adequate filing system.

I'm told by other inmates that, because of the length of time I've been here, I will be given a job, such as helping deliver the meals, distributing the clean linen, or mopping the floors in the common area. The benefits of a job are; you earn a pittance, time is subtracted from your sentence, and you get to participate in both rec periods of the day. The latter is an incentive, because I'll have greater access to the telephone. It also means that I'll be locked down only 19 ½ hours a day and get relief from the monotony.

Sentencing + 36 days. No sunrise and I haven't had my coffee yet. Blood pressure 138/82. I had a good talk with the black male nurse about staying here and getting a job with a lot of walking. They are anxious to keep me here. Why?

I finished reading Carlson's book that you sent, "You Can Be Happy No Matter What." I feel as if I've lived my life according to his principles and they have worked for me. I wish we were together with Auslese in front of a fire so we could talk about the book. I, as I read, wanted to turn to you and say, *"When he says X, that's why I do Y."* I, for example, have refused to dwell on the acts that led to my arrest. I acknowledged them, pled guilty, and will seek therapeutic help as soon as possible, but refuse to bear relentless guilt and negativity. To some, my attitude is evidence of denial. Not true! No good can come from continuing to beat myself. What is done is done and reparation and restorative justice to the extent possible should be made and life must go forward. I have many good qualities and, now especially, I focus on them to draw self-esteem. I have to believe that I'm worthy of your love and worthy of a good life after this or I'm doomed to a downward spiral of depression and degeneration. We'll get through this and life will be better than it ever was. Does the chocolate I'm eating spur my optimism? ☺

I like the way Carlson attacks—and makes his case well—traditional methods of therapy wherein the negative is explored *ad nauseam*.

Carl sent me an article for "Sports Illustrated" about basketball. The other inmates lusted for it. Information starvation.

The inmate who "borrowed" the popcorn was shipped out. I suspect that he was aware that he was a short-timer and tried to take advantage of me to the extent possible. I'm glad I didn't "loan" him more than one bag. Lesson learned. I'm glad he's not around anymore. He had the most terrifying eyes. I wonder to what extent one's countenance dictates life's role. If you look like a criminal are you more apt to become one? I've certainly known executives whose only qualification was that they looked like executives.

To dream (as Carlson says to do): I'd like to get an assignment to a pre-release center and a internal job as a teacher.

Sentencing + 37 days. For breakfast, I got grapefruit juice. It's been over a month since I had any. I have four packets of coffee to last three mornings—I get to have two cups on one of the mornings. When do I need a lift? I will have the ultimate lift tomorrow when you visit. The day after that I will get a commissary order so my supply will be renewed. Yes, today is the day to have two packets! (Talked myself into that, didn't I?)

Do you know yet what the telephone calls cost? Other inmates say they are expensive. I assumed they were the same rates as outside. Wouldn't the penal system want to encourage the inmate to maintain family ties?

I had a weird dream last night. I was young—about twenty—and living at home. The family had just moved and Mom had invited the new neighbors in for an afternoon party. The house was a mess, however, and I was appalled about the untidiness. Mom was uncharacteristically sanguine about it. The difference in our reactions caused me to decide to move out—to finally go out on my own. Not much sense to it.

Sentencing + 38 days. When I returned to my cell I watched you drive away. It was a good visit.

I'm glad you received an answer from the warden even if the news isn't good. I assume he never sent you a copy of the Inmate Handbook. I would bet that the system doesn't want to set a precedent of selling copies and then having to deal with indigent inmates.

There was a large demonstration against the death penalty this afternoon. From the cell window, I could see six police cruisers and a paddy wagon. The state—via the death penalty—says it's OK to kill a human.

Sentencing + 39 days. I got a cellmate named Willie. He moved in about midnight. He's been through the system eleven times, he says. On the street he's known as the 'Pill Man,' he says. He forges prescriptions apparently. He swears that the cops use him. According to Willie, the cops put him under surveillance after he is released and when his criminal behavior is profitable enough for him to buy a luxury car—which he cannot resist—they arrest him and seize the car. He has bought, using cash, and lost—according to him—three new Cadillacs and two new Lincoln Continentals. He says the Mayor's car used to be his.

I was talking to another inmate who has been here for over two months—a gruesome prospect! Willie says that he has spent no more than four weeks here before being transferred.

The cops are still outside *en masse*. I understand that the inmate to be executed is to be transferred to the execution cell today. The execution is discussed a lot in here. The most frequent question is *"Is he black or white?"* I understand the jaundiced view of the system implied by the question.

I get a commissary order today. It will be awkward to have a supply of snacks and supplies while Willie has none. I feel vulnerable and worry that any generosity will be interpreted as weakness or fear, but I don't want to be viewed as penurious. A dilemma. Life is full of dilemmas.

I'm happy you're having a therapy session today. I, too, have wondered about your lack of expressed anger, but was thankful for it. I assumed you had migrated beyond anger and if you felt it, you would've expressed it. You have never been reticent before. ☺

Willie insists on teaching me pinochle—a game I have no interest in, but he's keen on it and it does pass time. He plays a poor game of chess, but at least I can insist that we alternate games.

Willie, after learning that I knew something about computer technology, asked me questions about scanners and laser printers, especially in relationship to blank prescriptions forms. My career possibilities have widened.

My weight continues to drop. Blood pressure is OK. No commissary next week. I have $33.18 in my account. Should be enough. I have to remain sane. When I get out of here, I want to be someone you can continue to love

Sentencing + 40 days. A fantasy: We drive to the river and find a light breeze blowing white caps on the waves. We park and walk along a riparian path. We hold hands as bicycle riders pass us in each direction. Other pedestrians are walking dogs, pushing baby buggies or jogging. The birds prattle in the trees. A frog jumps into the murky water. We squeeze each other's hands and don't have to say a word. We walk off the path and sit on a log to watch the motorboats dart beneath hanging gulls. An army of termites works beneath us as we pass a water bottle back and forth.

No wait! That's not a fantasy. We've done that. It's a memory.

Sentencing + 41 days. Four weeks here today. It has been tolerable—reasonable cellmates, commissary orders, window view, and the nexus of mail deliveries, phone calls, and contact visits.

I haven't heard from Bud. I hope he's OK—and OK with me. I got one supportive letter. I'll bet he's just busy (trying to remain positive).

I appreciate Barbara's efforts to get the church to change its stance, but I'm not optimistic. Others have tried before her. The Minister—in spite of the Unitarian-Universalist principles—must play congregational politics.

Rochelle State Prison, Housing Unit 1, Tier B, Commons, Bunk 4A.

Sentencing + 42 days

Dearest Wife,

Well it happened; I was moved. Hopefully, you have received word. I was transferred from my cell yesterday afternoon about 1:00PM to the transition tier where I spent a night incommunicado. My personal belongings were packed, and thus I had nothing last night and still don't, but expect to receive them tomorrow. No medication here, yet. We were supposed to be able to make a telephone call upon arrival, but the CO "forgot" about it. I have learned that I'm required to supply a visitor's list and a telephone list.

I'm in an area that has been transformed from a common area into a dormitory. They have put four double bunks, a large wooden table, a TV, a commode-sink, a hot water pot, a microwave and eight lockers into an area that was formerly recreation space. The Commons—as it is officially designated—is a temporary staging location. From here, as space becomes available, one migrates to a cell. At Rochelle, there are seven housing units (HU), each with four double-decked tiers arranged as arms radial from a central hub. The populations in the tiers and the housing units are independently controlled. Each tier has 98 cells, four showers, a rec area, a washer and a dryer. There is much to learn about the routine.

Meals are served cafeteria style at the "chow hall"—our Amaltheia—to which we must walk (thank goodness!). Copies of newspapers are delivered to the Commons and circulated among the eight of us. Only three of us read them. I have seen chess being played.

I expect to be able to arrange the visit you had planned for Classification.

I'm told—no official information—that I can receive a box of personal clothes within the first month. Other inmates tell me there is a list of allowed items.

Inmates—I understand—at specified intervals, are allowed to order from catalogs and can received approved radios and televisions.

When I told Willie that I was being transferred and where I was going, he said I'd be OK, but advised me to buy all of the guys on the tier a TV (!). He said they'd treat me OK if I did that. I figure that would cost in excess of $20,000.

The other seven guys in the cohort seem to be OK. I've had a couple of good interactions already. I'm OK and hope you are as well.

Sentencing + 43 days. I was able to place a telephone call to my brother, David, when I retrieved my personal belongings. I gave him a message to relay to you and I left messages on our answering machine and Phyllis's. I've done everything (oral request, written request) I can to pave the way for your visit, but I'm not sure permission will be given, although I'm led to believe that visits are encouraged.

I learned more, officially, about the initial package and will detail later about suggested contents. I've gotten a batch of clothes from the State.

Money can be sent in via certified check, but stamps are not allowed in incoming mail. I have sixteen in my cache and will use them to write only you until the commissary process starts working smoothly for me. Let the others know so there's no concern about the lack of answers to their letters.

Have you been reading about the Smyth case—similar to mine? I wish I could talk to him, poor soul. I know what he's going through. I hope he has a wife and a family like mine to support him.

I've watched chess games. Looks like the competition will be adequate.

Apparently when my telephone list is implemented, I get access to the telephone every five days. There is much competition for access.

A target range is apparently next to the prison. Often, as I lay on the bunk, I hear the staccato shots. I picture the COs shooting at human silhouettes, knowing that they are practicing to shoot me.

I see us. The alarm goes off. The aroma of cinnamon coffee wafts from the timed coffeepot. Sunlight beams come through the Venetian blinds making a mosaic on the tossed bed covering. You turn off the alarm. My arm snakes around your waist.

Hope to see you tomorrow.

Sentencing + 44 days. What a great visit!

Items allowed in the initial package—two pairs of trousers, two shirts, sweat pants and shirts, two athletic shorts, six undershirts, six pair of shorts, six pair of socks, two pair of long johns, six handkerchiefs, one hat, three towels, three washcloths, one jacket, one pair of athletic shoes, a pair of winter boots, a pair of shower shoes, a deck of cards, and a belt.

Barry, a fellow inmate, has been here about two weeks longer than I have. He was a roofer in the construction business, white, and affable. He fell from a roof, damaged a hip and now needs a cane to walk. He's well built and is vane about his appearance—especially his hair. He fancies himself a lady's man.

He brought me an orange from breakfast. I didn't go (who can rise at 5:00AM for reconstituted scrambled eggs?). He lives in Damlier and once a month his family drives over a thousand miles to visit him. His family raises and sells German Shepherds. He has no tattoos, a rarity herein. We play gin rummy but only after we sorted out our difference in rules.

Additional thoughts about the initial package—the shirts can be colored, but avoid clothing with logos. Barry says they rejected his Harley shirts. Logos may signify a gang allegiance that I'm unaware of.

Sentencing + 45 days. I've learned there is an honor tier, the A tier, that is much less confining. The inmate has a key to his cell (but not to the tier, housing unit, nor prison ☺) and can come and go in the tier except for lock-down periods. There is open access to the telephones, showers, rec room and the laundry. I understand that you have to establish a record of behavior for six months before becoming eligible. I'll apply immediately to get on the waiting list. All of this I learned from other inmates. There is no official information.

I've asked Barry to borrow some commissary items until I can order from commissary. He's agreeable. I'll limit my requests to stamps and coffee. There are inmates who make a business called "3-for-2"—you borrow two items and repay three. I refuse to participate.

A CO reprimanded me last night. During the rec period (when the inmates from the cells are allowed out into the floor below us) an inmate tossed me a plastic jug and asked me to fill it with hot water. We, in the Commons, have our own hot water heater—in fact a large coffee maker with the internals gone—and frequently the hot water downstairs runs dry. I did so and dropped it back down to him. At the end of the rec period, after the inmates returned to their cells, a CO came from the bubble and asked me if I could read. He then pointed out a list of rules posted, one of which prohibits inmates from exchanging items. I apologized and said I was new and just learning the rules. I was "Sir'ing" at every possibility. He nevertheless loudly warned that the next infraction would lead to being put into isolation. I felt it was ironic that I, among the population in the Commons, was the first to break the rules. I was the "bad" guy.

Fantasy: It's about 4:30AM. You and I, dressed in our housecoats, have been up since about 2:30 attending our female sheltie, Queenie, who is whelping her first litter. She awoke us by whining. We've been stroking her head, petting her, and being there for her. We, of course, have been anticipating the birth. Queenie and her five puppies are lying on a large soft dog quilt. Queenie has cleaned the puppies and they blindly nuzzle her for nourishment. They yelp weakly as they grope with their bobbing heads. The last puppy was born about ten minutes ago. The mother gets up and licks them in turn. They bump into each other in their aimless crawling. The second one is a beautifully colored male, slightly larger than his brother and three sisters. Queenie drinks some water and lies back down beside her litter. You and I sip our cinnamon coffee as Queenie sleepily looks at us. We turn out the lights and return to bed. Thirty minutes later we get up to "check on things." We have to start thinking of names.

Sentencing + 46 days. I got Procardia and Zoloft today—my first medication since arrival. I suppose the Zestril will show up sometime.

The food is better than I expected, but the service is rushed. At a signal from a CO, one has to take his plastic glass and metal spoon, deposit them in a washtub, leave the chow hall, and return to the housing unit. Since all housing units use the same chow hall, the COs have to expedite the meal. Knives can be made from the spoons so they are monitored carefully

I spoke with a young white guy, Tony, who works in the Education Department. The Education Department is exempted from the requirement to hire in sequence from a waiting list. They can hire whom they wish. Tony is halfway through a six-year sentence. Tony is on A tier. He doesn't have a college education, but is a teacher's aide. I'll apply. Tony also says they have three bridge players on the honor tier and need a fourth. Good things can happen.

Barry says that some of his outgoing letters disappear. Strange.

Sentencing + 47 days. I got Carlson's book that you mailed! Thanks. Paperbacks are allowed in—a bit of heaven in comparison to Classification. Spread the word wide and far! I got a blank commissary order form. I can buy large manila envelopes so you don't have to worry about sending anymore. I can also get grapefruit juice. I may confuse this place with a four-star hotel. The wine list however is short.

The paper this morning contained a review of a relevant article from the "Atlantic Monthly" concerning the prison-industry complex. Profit motives encourage harsher treatment for inmates.

Barry is going to commissary and will get me ten stamps.

I was called to the dispensary. My blood pressure was 126/72. The nurse made sure I was on the 8:00AM medication list for Zoloft. I have to go to the dispensary, adjacent to the chow hall, to receive it. She said I should get the Zestril and Minoxidil today.

I applied for a position in the Education Department.

I hope you have sent money. I want to buy a hand held stereo radio—a Walkman—with a headset that I can use here in Commons. When I am transferred to a cell, I'll order a radio with cassette and/or CD capability. I understand that you can send CDs if they are still in the original wrapping.

Barry did buy me stamps and coffee

There has been a transfer. One of the guys moved into a cell and a new guy, Morton, has moved in. He was in Classification for three months! I feel like an old-timer telling him how things work here. He, like Barry, has a limp from a recent injury. A knee pains him and he massages it. He's requested a brace. I asked if the injury was a result of his apprehension. He said, "No," and didn't elaborate. I suspect it was a drug-related infliction.

I'm beginning to hate gin rummy. Barry wants to play incessantly and analyzes each hand after it's played. It's also true—to be fair—that he is winning most of the games. I had thought my strategy was optimal. Have to rethink.

Scene: You and I wake up—ten inches of snow has fallen. We drink a cup of cinnamon coffee, change into winter clothes, fill a thermos with the remaining coffee and venture into the white outside. We're the first to walk on the unsullied path in the park. There is no wind and the temperature is bearable. We stop at a creek and watch water flow between the ice-encrusted banks. Birds chirp from among the crystalline tree branches. Steam wafts upward as we refill our cups. A squirrel scampers along a limb and knocks snow onto us. We return home to uncover the cars.

Sentencing + 48 days. I was awakened this morning at 3:00AM (!) to give blood and a urine sample. Had a nice stroll across the cold prison compound. The sky was clear and the stars were twinkling.

At 8:00AM the tier CO calls "medication" and those on the morning medication list are released to walk to the dispensary. I go for the Zoloft. I'm not getting any Minoxidil and Zestril, but am assured that I will. I believe it, but in any case my blood pressure appears to be OK.

Today is my bunk's turn to clean the Commons—sweep, mop, and clean the toilet. The duty, done three times a day, rotates among the four bunks.

Later: Mail delivery included ten letters, most forwarded from Classification. Three of the letters were from you and included the money. They still haven't transferred the funds from Classification.

I'm reading a borrowed mystery, "All that Remains" by Patricia Cornwall.

Scene: Shortly before sunrise, we're together at the bow of a Caribbean cruise ship. Broken clouds ahead promise to provide a palette for the sun to paint a spectacular phantasmagoria. From the coffee bar, we have hot cinnamon coffee. From time to time, the reverie is disturbed by passers-by. Dolphins race ahead of the bow wave and arc glisteningly over the sea's surface. The sun slowly rises and fulfills its duty of decorating the sky—just for us. The horizon shows the emerging silhouette of an island.

Sentencing + 49 days. Went to "yard" today for an hour and a half. It's an outside exercise facility within the prison compound, surrounded by a razor wire fence and two guarded locked entrance gates. One can see the surrounding weald. It has an oval track for running or walking, basketball courts, softball fields, handball walls, and benches for gathering to talk. Wispy clouds were chilling until I started walking, so I walked and walked—as fast as I could around the track. Two or three housing units are there simultaneously. Barry walked with me, but his bad hip forced him to quit after a while. I needed the exercise so continued without him. Apparently, during good weather, we go alternately to yard and to the gym. The outside exercise will be positive.

Once a week they distribute toilet paper. Two rolls per inmate.

I was told today that they're not going to give me the Zestril or the Minoxidil. I could view this negatively and perceive them as bastards trying to save money and screwing around with a proven regime. Positively, I could adopt the attitude that it is a worthwhile experiment to see if the Procardia alone can be effective. Since I can't affect the medication, I might as well be positive.

Barry's success at gin rummy has led me to play a different strategy. I am winning more—if not most—games. During our games, we talk. Barry claims to be a survivalist and a member of a militia. He says, *"With the government going the way it is, you just never know."* He says that he was a Marine who served in Laos. He got into an argument with co-workers on a job site that led to a fight. He pulled a gun and shot wildly. He didn't have a license for the gun. This is his first offense and at times, he is more naïve than I am about the system. I trust him and he seems to be a nice guy. He has done me favors and helps when he can.

Next week the commissary is closed. I hope my coffee lasts. I'm sharing with Morton. The "start-up" times, from my experiences at County and Classification, are aggravating, but fade in the memory.

Sentencing + 50 days. An inmate was caught yesterday receiving a piece of candy orally from his wife during a visit. He was handcuffed and taken to isolation for three days. He loses his visitation rights for six months. He was probably testing the system as a prelude to smuggling in contraband.

I will—in a week or so—submit a sick-call request (the only way to talk to a medical person) to wean myself from the Zoloft. I can, of course, refuse to take it, but I'd rather do it under supervision so that I can resume quickly if need be.

Our library day is Wednesday, but next week it will be closed for inventory.

Later: Just had a visit with Elgin and Kathy. I enjoyed seeing them, however the COs limited the visit to one hour, which I don't understand, and they didn't deign to explain. I thought that weekday visits could be longer.

Scene: Dressed in our sweats, we're sitting on a porch of an isolated mountain cabin. We're immured in an early morning fog. We sip our cinnamon coffee and listen for a break in the silence. We munch on small blueberry bagels. The shroud of haze slowly lifts at the beckoning of a veiled sun. The bases of massive pines become visible. From the edge of the forest, a doe with twin fawns step through the mist. The dappled Bambis rambunctiously play and feel no fear. The world was made for them—and for us. Love.

Sentencing + 51 days. I walked fifteen laps at yard. Took an hour and half. A cold wind was blowing. I wore my heavy state denim coat. Barry and Morton walked with me for a while, but found my pace too arduous. I need the exercise and prefer to push myself than to slow for companionship. They understand.

I've taught Napoleon—a simple five-card game—to Barry and Morton. At least it's a break from gin rummy.

Morton awoke the tier in the middle of the night screaming. He was asleep and remembers nothing about it. What demons lurk within him? I imagine him reliving the breaking of his knee by a drug enforcer.

I'm doing laundry tonight in a *real* washing machine—not in a sink. No bleach allowed.

I've put in a request to exchange my size 42 denims for size 38. I brought both pair from Classification. The 38s fit fine. They're the only trousers I now have.

Sentencing + 53 days. I had orientation this snowy morning. It was routine—until I asked about non-smoking housing. I was told that all housing was non-smoking because of the requirements of state laws. However only a pretense is made by the COs to enforce the non-smoking regulations. If you smoke during inspection or outside your bunk area (cell, commons), you are punished, but you can have a pile of cigarette ashes and butts a foot high beside your bunk and it goes unnoticed. Hanging tobacco smoke is ignored. I was further told that the largest profit for the commissary comes from the sale of tobacco products. The profit from the commissary supposedly goes into the "inmates benefit fund" from which Christmas treats are bought. I wanted to retort, *"So to get chocolate, we suffer lung cancer!"* but did not because of the fear that I'd be viewed as difficult. Tolerance of smoking by the system is counter-productive since DOP is responsible for medical treatment at the taxpayer's expense. Is DOP's flouting the laws concerning smoking in public places in accord with a mission to punish those who break the laws? Does it instill a trust in the system?

In orientation, we were able to sign up for a variety of support groups. I did sign up for an Alcoholic Anonymous group. Given the judge's admonition and the need to relieve boredom, it's a choice without risk. After I signed up, the social worker told me that my choices might be moot—no new groups are forming. Why give us a choice that doesn't exist? But, all I can do is what I can do.

The two blank cards you sent were delivered. WHAT ARE THE RULES?

The sun came out and the light snow melted. We had yard. I had a good walking partner, Don Miller, in yard this afternoon. He's about my age, white, well educated, but guarded in his conversation. He's halfway through a two-year sentence. I don't know his offense. He has a job as a tutor in the Education Department and has a supportive family.

I enclose a draft of a letter to the Governor. Love.

Dear Governor;

Inmates are in prison because they broke the law and it seems as if the administration of the prison system should also obey the law. The current law of the state is that no smoking is allowed within state owned buildings, and yet, Rochelle State Prison openly and blatantly chooses not to enforce that law. The housing units have ashtrays and cigarette butts inside the cells and indoor recreational areas. All inmates suffer from the clouds of second-hand smoke, but it is particularly offensive for non-smoking inmates. Since most prisoners are smokers, I'm writing this letter anonymously to lessen the probability of retaliation by inmate or CO smokers.

I'm being discrete and sending this letter only to you. If the situation doesn't improve, I'll be forced to seek a wider awareness of the problem.

Some prisons, Classification for example, is totally non-smoking, however if non-smoking laws are impossible to enforce in prison then that fact should be acknowledged and the non-smoker be catered to. The best solution may be to allow, through legislative means, some housing units to be designated as smoking and enforce non-smoking rules in the remainder.

The taxpayers bear the burden of medical care for the problems incurred from smoking. My health should not be endangered more than that of the citizen outside. Respectfully yours. A Rochelle inmate.

Sentencing + 54 days. My blood pressure this morning was 144/90—a bit high. I've lost twenty pounds in two months. The medical staff enrolled me on a special cardiovascular diet. I'm not sure what that means, but hope it designates, steak, cherry pie á la mode and Auslese.

I'm concerned about my supply of stamps so may limit my letters.

Later: The new diet may be OK. For lunch, instead of bologna I had fish finger. For dinner, I had an orange instead of cake and a hamburger patty instead of meatballs.

I finished the Cornwall book and am starting "Spencerville" by Nelson Demille.

Sentencing + 55 days. I met with my case manager, Ms. Keenan. My first parole hearing will be in six months! I asked what I can do to affect a positive outcome. I suggested that I document that I have a home, a job to return to, letters from neighbors welcoming me back, and a therapeutic plan. She didn't express any particular reaction.

Sentencing + 56 days. It was a great visit! You looked great and your radiant smile shone. I went to the library and got a couple of non-fiction books. I called Bud and Carl. I wrote Phyllis and Dianne and have three stamps left until commissary, next Tuesday.

One of the inmates on the Commons, Charles, chided me for calling the COs "sir." He told me that I was older than the COs. I didn't deign to argue with him.

Sentencing + 57 days. Writing you is a special part of the day. I played Morton a game of Scrabble. He's an excellent player and makes good use of the special squares. He had another scream last night. These screams are not whimpers—they are loud blood-curdling shrieks. I suspect they have something to do with his busted knee.

The only dictionary on the tier is a small paperback. Could you send the Scrabble dictionary we have? My words, "KIVA" and "QUO," were successfully challenged and I suspect they are in a better dictionary. The calendar you sent will be useful. I can note letters received and answered and daily events. Thanks as well for the book of chess games. I've played two of them already. Some other inmates, even chess players, deem it strange to play chess with one's self. I get the cloying question, *"Who's winning?"*

Scene: Our cruise ship, amidst icebergs, has docked at a small Alaskan town. The clear blue sky is festooned with ribbons of black smoke rising from dilapidated chimneys. We join others on a tram that takes us to a vast glacier that fractures into the sea. A chilly breeze blows from the frigid sea forcing us to wear our hooded coats although it's spring. The tram stops at the glacier's edge where a small shop serves hot drinks. As we enter our glasses fog over. We remove them, order cups of steaming cinnamon coffee, and return outside replacing our glasses. There's excitement among the tourists—a whale breaches in the bay, expels a fountain of mist and flops backward into the water. The bell rings on the tram recalling us to the ship.

Had a good yard exercise. I walked with Don who gave me a lead to a job in the Education Department.

The money from Classification was transferred—the money from County has yet to find me. The policy herein is that an inmate has a "flex" account into which one can transfer money from one's "regular" account. The flex account is used for commissary and to send money home, but not for catalog orders. In the regular account, a reserve is accumulated for the inmate upon release. It is excessively cumbersome and was probably born from a long forgotten swindle that enabled an inmate to misappropriate an extra dollar or two. It does have the benefit of having a few more COs employed.

I have a case of diarrhea—no stomachache or nausea. Have gone to the john four times today. With that romantic thought, until later.

Sentencing + 58 days. Stomach is better, but I have a runny nose and sore throat. My diet substitutes pineapple chunks for cookies and hamburger patties for macaroni and cheese. I had a nice apple today.

Another inmate on the Commons is Mr. John. He and I are the oldest inmates in Commons. He's a large stout black man with gray at the temples. He's old enough to be immune from testosterone poisoning. I'm not sure of his offense. Several of his and my habits—time of rising, TV preferences, time to sleep—are similar. He speaks a lot of his granddaughter from whom he has pictures and receives letters. For my cold, he gave me a mentholated cough drop and a tea bag and told me to make a hot toddy from them. Although he serves as a father figure for the younger black guys, he is irritated by their antics at times. Mr. John has external money and, thus, has an ample supply of tobacco, which he doles out to the younger guys eliciting their deference.

I asked the psychiatrist about suspending the Zoloft. He told me that if he suspended it, then the resumption would take six weeks or so. Inane. My plan is to continue to go to medication and get the pill, but not consume it. I'll toss it on the walkway. If I, then, have problems with the withdrawal I can resume immediately. Why does the system promote waste?

Each housing unit goes, tier by tier, to chow as an entity. When a housing unit is finished eating and returns, then the next housing unit is released. There is minimum opportunity for contact between the inmates from the different housing units. As the inmates walk to the chow hall, they have to stay on the sidewalks or be cited for being out of bounds. The COs, spaced twenty yards apart, stand back from the sidewalk on both sides along the entire path from the housing unit to the chow hall. On the return trip, inmates spit and toss empty milk pint cartons, crusts of bread, apple cores and other garbage on the path. Each day there is a cleanup of the grounds, but the return from the evening meal involves navigating an obstacle course of dross.

There is a small tree denuded of leaves about thirty feet from the entrance of the chow hall. In the evening flocks of sparrows gather in the tree to feed on the discarded garbage. The sparrows chirp and fluff their feathers giving the tree the appearance that it's in bloom with spherical sepia blossoms fluttering in a breeze. It enthralls me.

Sentencing + 60 days. I was pleasantly surprised that Walter accompanied you for the visit. I noticed that you lingered after our visit. Did you get a chance to speak to Don's wife? Seems as if mutual support and sharing would be possible. At least you know who my walking partner, Don, is.

I interviewed at the Education Department and was told, nicely, that "preferred" jobs are given to an inmate only after they have been here for 180 days, so nothing is likely to happen there for awhile—but I tried. My cold is gone (perhaps due to Mr. John's elixir?) and I feel much better.

I could tell you have lost weight—no doubt due to the lack of my cooking.

Sentencing + 61 days. I had a confrontation with another inmate, Charles, one of the eight on the Commons, last night while doing laundry. Yesterday was my bunk's turn to do the cleanup of the area. With the responsibility comes the privilege of having first access to the laundry facilities. Barry, Morton, and I have been including each other's laundry with our own when convenient—it's just as easy to do three pairs of denims as one. Charles saw Morton's denims and thought I was abusing my priority privilege and tried to put his load in before mine. I explained, but he retorted, *"Pops, Yuz jus' fuckin' mit me, man."*

Charles is a small middle-aged black guy with prominent buggy eyes. He has no teeth. The prison regime for dental repair is tooth removal so he's no stranger to incarceration. He speaks in a loud expectorating lisp. Even the black guys and the COs, whom he plies with blandishments, see him as a nuisance. When it's his turn for cleanup duty he often disappears or has an excuse. He's a devout Muslim and warns us not to touch his religious material, which he leaves scattered on the game table.

I felt I had to hold my ground or be labeled as a wimp—how quickly one is imbued with the ethos.

Rain shut down the yard, but I walked for an hour inside the gym.

I received lots of mail today and will make telephone calls tonight. Tomorrow is commissary day, which is a highlight. I'll get mustard packets. So many small things can ease and vary the day-to-day routine.

Sentencing + 62 days. A down day. The damn system screwed up and only transferred $3 into my flex account instead of $300 so I could only buy a few stamps and nothing else at commissary. I could become paranoiac and ascribe these "accidents" to deliberate acts meant to bedevil the inmate. Once a mistake is made there is no process for succor. I just have to wait until the next cycle of money transfer and commissary shopping. On the "Request for Transfer," I probably wrote "$300" instead of "$300.00." I sent a request to repair the error, but the chances for redress are nil.

To add to my misery, I got no mail. I don't know if my languid mood is a result of the events of the day or the deletion of Zoloft. If I don't feel better tomorrow, I'll resume the medication. The frustration builds and one becomes a ticking time bomb ready to explode at another inmate or a CO. I probably shouldn't be writing today.

Sentencing + 63 days. Mood is better. Blood pressure was measured—150/90. The doctor didn't seem concerned.

I thought I had lost my hat—significant because I have no idea how to replace it and my balding head would've suffered in this cold season. However, I found it in my coat sleeve where it had remained even after pushing my arm through.

I slept from about 6:00PM until 11:00PM, awoke, played chess (5 games, won all), went to breakfast. We were served a grapefruit half. I brought it and sugar back to the housing unit where I ate it slowly and with savor.

Barry is fighting a mail policy. They wouldn't allow him to receive photos of his gun collection. He's worried about retaliation and being taken to isolation. I think he just testing the system to relieve boredom. He and I agreed that if something untoward should happen to either of us, that the other will contact the wife through our own wife and let them know. I enclose Janice's telephone number if that were to happen.

Sentencing + 64 days. What a great visit! We're becoming acclimated to the environment so the visits are more natural. As you saw, my dandruff problem is bad. Might be a combination of the low humidity, stress and ineffective shampoo.

I ordered a pair of "boots"—water tight Oxfords and a combo AM/FM cassette player. It's a Walkman made of clear plastic (so no drugs can be hidden inside). Total cost—$120. I'm allowed eight cassettes, so I get to play the "marooned on a deserted island" game.

Below is the draft of a letter. Could you do what editing you think will help and mail it for me? Thanks. Love.

Chief of Security
Rochelle State Prison

Dear Sir:

I have a cardiovascular problem and second hand smoke is harmful to my health.

The housing units, I understand, are by law to be smoke free. However, it is widely acknowledged by the inmates and the Rochelle professional staff that this law is ignored. The inmates openly and blatantly smoke without interference.

I understand the problems associated with the enforcement of "no smoking"—indeed, I believe, based on my experience at County and Classification, it is folly to try to enforce them. Ideally, the state legislature should accommodate the prison system's unique problem, but in the absence of such recognition, I think it is possible that Rochelle can establish an acceptable environment for all. Suppose that some tiers in all seven housing units were designated by internal policy to have non-smoking enforced. The inmates who feel strongly about the issue, like me, could then opt for those tiers.

I'm somewhat anxious about raising this issue. Some inmates could consider my efforts would deprive them of smokes—an action they would not view favorably.

It's not an easy problem, but we can do better.

Sentencing + 67 days. Wet and warm outside. They increased my procardia dosage.

Four of us on the tier play chess well. I organized a double elimination tournament. Tonight "Shrimp" and I play for the championship. Shrimp is a young black—perhaps twenty years old—with cornrows. The rumor grapevine says he was sentenced to 25 years for a drive-by shooting. He affects an unconvincing tough attitude. I suspect that the prospect of spending his youthful years in here prompts a survival strategy. He seems a decent guy. He and I share a fragile mutual respect that is born from our chess games.

Many inmates choose to talk about their offense, but there is no peer pressure to do so. No inmate asks another about his crime. An inmate can tell any story about his offense and background. Some inmates, I'm sure, embellish their offense to appear to be "a bad dude." The true official rendition is apparently carefully guarded. I don't believe even the COs know. My story is that I'm in here for a computer related securities violation-giving financial advice and soliciting investment money without the proper credentials and registration. The inconsistency arising from that I'm in a state prison for a federal crime isn't probed.

Charles—from the laundry confrontation—and I are treating each other with respect during unavoidable encounters. Our enmity is repressed. I did laundry last night and included stuff from Barry and Morton with no problems.

I borrowed medicated aloe lotion from Barry for my scalp. My request to exchange the oversized denims from Classification for a pair that fits was refused. Wanting a different size is not sufficient reason to disturb the system.

Later: Won the chess tournament. I've started reading "The Richard Trilogy," by Paul Horgan. Phyllis sent me "The Emperor's New Mind" by Roger Penrose and "The Mind of God" by Paul Davies. Take care of yourself.

Sentencing + 68 days. I spoke with the prison chaplain. I can receive materials from *The Church of the Larger Fellowship* (CLF), but it will be counted against my limit of four subscriptions. I hadn't known that there was such a limit. A religious medallion—such as a Flaming Chalice pendant—can be no larger than one inch square and has to be sent directly to the chaplain. I also learned that I can list only one person as a religious counselor. I wonder if there is <u>one</u> UU minister who would assume that role.

I played two games of gin rummy, a game of Scrabble, and two games of chess. Won them all. What's a smart guy like me doing in a place like this?

Sentencing + 69 days. I have a bunch of correspondence to give to you tomorrow—letters to be mailed for which I have no stamps and mail I have received—to be saved. My request to return stuff to you has been acknowledged but the morning tier CO has to sign off, so there is always an element of uncertainty.

Later: I got the bank statements you sent—and the six stamps cleverly attached on the back. I rationalize the circumvention of the rules—if the system hadn't screwed up the transfer to my flex account, I wouldn't need to have stamps smuggled in.

Sentencing + 70 days. I got a pass today to pick up my medication refill at the dispensary. I was one of a dozen or so inmates with such a pass and we formed a line at the nurse's station. When I was next to receive my refill another inmate came in, and instead of getting at the rear of the line, started chit-chatting in an "old-friends" manner with the CO on duty. When I gave my pass to the nurse to identify myself, the newly arrived inmate shoved his pass in before mine. I said I was next in line and shoved his pass back towards him. He said, *"Oh, OK, Pops,"* and picked up his pass and went to the back of the line. I responded automatically. I hope I haven't created animosity that will haunt me.

Sentencing + 71 days. They passed out the holiday candy today. Each inmate got a box of six assorted chocolates. Wages of smoking.

My weight continues to drop. Perhaps for each month I'm in here, my life will be extended for a year. While waiting to have my blood pressure measured in the dispensary, the medical staff received a call that an inmate had drunk the disinfectant used to clean shower stalls. Judging from their lack of concern, this happens frequently. The response was, *"Put him in his cell. He'll be sick for four or five hours and then recover."* I wonder about the mental health issues. Will the inmate receive any counseling?

I asked about receiving over-the-counter shampoo from the outside. No outside toiletries are allowed.

I'm on page 71 of the Trilogy and am enjoying it. Some books are a chore to read, e.g., "The Iliad"—others, like "Cold Mountain" are a joy. The Trilogy is akin to the latter.

Sentencing + 75 days. The commissary order went OK! I got everything I wanted and paid Barry everything I owe him. I bought cigars. The other inmates were amused when I got a cup of coffee, sat on a plastic chair, propped my feet up on my cot, lit a cigar, and leaned back. It did taste good, but I'll make it an infrequent treat. Helps me affect a persona. ☺

I have written the State Transportation Department to see how to renew my driver's license. The timing is such that my current license will expire before I get out. The worst-case scenario is that I take the driving test again.

I am on the waiting list for the honor tier. The notification could be pro-forma, but it's better than being refused. Also in the mail was the application information about *The Church of the Larger Fellowship*.

I got a chess set at commissary. I have a lot of nostalgia for the old paper one. Spent many hours with it. I'll keep it in case I punch a CO and am sent to lock-down. ☺

Later: Confession time. From my newly acquired commissary supply, today I have consumed one cigar, one Baby Ruth, one roll of Life Savers, one bag of potato chips, one small can of grapefruit juice, three cups of coffee, and one bag of microwave popcorn.

I am a good listener, which has pluses and minuses. Mr. John will talk to me for long periods of time. When the background noise is maximum, I hear about one word in every five, but I nod, shake my head, and laugh at what I hope are the correct moments. I may say one word to his two hundred. He's happy that someone is interested in his stories. My fear is that he'll discover that I haven't the vaguest idea of what the hell he's talking about. Luckily he never asks, to my knowledge, questions such as *"Has something like that ever happened to you?"* I'd be at a loss to know what "that" was.

Sentencing + 76 days. Morton (of all people) has complained because I tear the crossword puzzle out of the paper, so I'll abandon that pastime. He doesn't work them, so I don't know the cause of his complaint. He did tell me once that "misery loves company," so maybe he, like the dog in the manger, doesn't want me to have that iota of enjoyment.

Jose is the only Hispanic in the Commons. His ability to understand English varies according to his wish to understand. He is short, stocky and mustached. He is taking an ESL course. I understand that he shot a guy who was having an affair with his wife. In his native country such machismo would receive praise, I suspect. He is quiet and reclusive. I explored the idea of improving my Spanish with him, but I determined that he has no academic understanding of language. When I spoke about the "future tense" he had no idea what I was talking about.

Remember—storms make trees develop deeper roots.

Sentencing + 77 days. I think I've fixed the broken nose pad on my glasses with a bit of glue and string. Time will tell. Mr. John was told this morning to be ready to move to a cell. He wasn't happy about it, but has no choice. Thirty minutes later they told him to forget it.

After the last in the package of five cigars is gone, I'll buy no more. I don't want to develop a nicotine addiction. The popcorn addiction is bad enough!

Morton got his initial package today and his sister bought him all new stuff instead of sending him his older stuff. The denims didn't fit. He was irritated at her. *"Why didn't she just do what I asked?"* I pointed out that his sister went to a lot of trouble—shopping, etc.—and that it was a sign of support rather than being a negative. It's his fourth time in prison. He was also depressed.

Played seven games of chess today and won them all.

I bought a small sewing kit from the commissary. I have small mending on my trousers—torn seams.

Sentencing + 79 days. My Walkman came! No batteries were included, but I borrowed a set from Manny. The Walkman works great. I can receive two classical stations, an "oldie-but-goodie," and, of course, a slew of country and westerns.

Manny is on the top bunk next to mine. He's a muscular, middle-aged, soft-spoken, black man—several inches shorter than I am. He keeps his head clean-shaven. He has an impish smile and I like and trust him. He's quiet and his circle of friends is small. He doesn't affect an attitude.

They limit the number of batteries one can have, so he took a risk in loaning me a set. The story—true or not—is that he was a "mule" in the drug trade. He transported large quantities, but was not involved in the selling, buying or use. He has done me a favor and I will reciprocate when possible.

Manny reminds me of the beneficent character, Arnold Jackson, an ex-con, who appears in Somerset Maugham's story, "The Fall of Edward Barnard." In that story, in speaking of Arnold, the question is raised, *"Is Arnold Jackson a bad man who does good things or a good man who does bad things? It's a difficult question to answer. Perhaps we make too much of the difference between one man and another. Perhaps even the best of us are sinners and the worst of us are saints. Who knows?"*

Sentencing + 80 days. I listened to "Car Talk" on my Walkman. I have also been listening to classical stations. I'm worried about battery life, but it's nice while they last.

Could you buy earplugs and send them to me? They don't sell them in the commissary. I'd also like to get a copy of "The Official Rules of Chess." It's not a big book and I remember seeing it in the bookstore. There tends to be discussions about the "subtle" rules. Some inmates get more enjoyment from arguing about the rules than fun from playing the game—any game.

Smoked my last cigar.

Sentencing + 82 days. I got my beard trimmers this morning. Fortuitously, they use AA batteries just like my Walkman. An inmate is allowed to have two sets of batteries per appliance and you get a chit that entitles you an initial two sets. Since I don't use the trimmer much, I'll essentially have four sets of batteries for my Walkman. To buy a new set from the commissary, one has to turn in a set. As I write, I'm listening to the "Peter Gynt Suite" on the PBS FM station.

My medication prescription got screwed up. Since I'm to take 30mg Procardia, three times a day, I have separate prescriptions for 20mg and 10mg pills. I asked for a renewal for the 20mgs and they gave me 10mgs. When I pointed out the discrepancy, the medical staff was defensive and affected ignorance and innocence. I didn't make an issue of it.

Mr. John is being transferred to a cell. He says—and who's to know—that he's in here because of a technical parole violation (his original offense was arson) and has a hearing in two weeks. If the hearing goes well, he'll be back on the street. If he's retained he says his life is over. He was released on parole after serving twenty-five years. I will miss him when he moves out. We shared much.

Went to the dispensary and was told to take three of the 10mgs and forget about the 20mgs. The damned nurse treated me like I was a troublemaker and gave no explanation. She made me feel that my concern was ill founded and I was being obstreperous. Someone made a mistake, but the admission would burnish the shine from a perfect system.

Sentencing + 84 days. A young white man, Luke, moved into Mr. John's spot. I loaned him a stamp and gave him a candy bar. He appears a bit slow.

Smoking on the Commons has decreased significantly since Mr. John—the benefactor of impecunious smokers—moved into a cell.

I've enjoyed the packets of commissary mustard more than expected.

Sentencing + 85 days. Enjoyed your visit. I can't imagine maintaining a relationship in this manner for five years, can you? Your warnings about excessive optimism about an early release were sobering, but necessary. It's better to be down a bit now and avoid a crash later, so keep me realistic.

Manny got transferred—perhaps temporarily—today. He had a sore on his leg that wouldn't heal so they sent him to the hospital unit. The doctor suspected diabetes. Manny asked me what diabetes was and appeared fearful.

I've entered a malaise engendered by the lack of novelty. The personalities, interesting for a while, wear thin and I must work to curb my acerbic wit that could be interpreted as disrespect. I retreat into laconism. If this feeling continues, I'll resume the Zoloft. The inhumanity and absurdity of this system can only exist because those who have created it have never lived in it.

I think I will order a television, so that when I get transferred to a cell I'll have it as soon as possible.

There is a common psychological trait in here—the need to talk. There are three or four inmates in my small circle of acquaintances who search me out to talk. They talk about nothing specific—their lives, their family, this and that. The conversation borders on a monologue. I nod, shake my head and contribute wisdom such as, "hmmm," "wow," "gosh," from time to time. They just keep talking. Inane crap. They feel comfortable with me, I guess, because I don't challenge their assumptions, argue or play I-can-top-that games.

Played a bunch of gin rummy with Barry. I've noticed a puzzling thing. One is much more likely to have, when ginning, three of a kind (e.g.,7,7,7) than a run (e.g.,7,8,9) even though the latter is more favorable because you can extend the ends, whereas with three of a kind, one is stymied after adding the fourth.

Sentencing + 86 days. I won the chess tournament last night (that I—hmmm—organized). This morning, Shrimp, who I consider the next best player, was transferred to a cell. I'll miss his competition. Charles—the arrant SOB with whom I had the confrontation about the laundry—was reprimanded by the COs for causing trouble. He has had verbal matches with two other inmates beside myself.

I heard a piece of music new to me—Grieg, Opus 51, "Old Norwegian Romance." The batteries in the Walkman are holding up well—still on the first set.

My mood is better this morning so I'll continue to throw the Zoloft in the grass. Not having to go to morning medication is nice. Mustard is nice. Coffee is nice. Mail is nice. Life Savers are nice. Popcorn is nice. Crossword puzzles are nice. Reading is nice. Music is nice. Chess is nice. Being able to write you and having you there are nice.

From time to time, I reorganize my storage space. I have a shelf for my writing materials, mail and books. Another shelf for personal hygiene and medicine. Food and clothes occupy the remainder. Stacking clothes causes them eventually to spiral into chaos.

Sentencing + 87 days. My mood continues to improve. I believe my blue funk was caused by the realization that even with the trivial accouterments—coffee, Life Savers, music, etc.—life wasn't good and not going to get much better. Your words—*"It could be much worse"*—and just your voice make me feel better. I have to be more pro-active in establishing a positive relationship with the other inmates. Try not to be reclusive. It's true, however, that the time I have to myself—reading, playing book chess, listening to the radio—is the time I enjoy the most. Maybe that's an argument for a cell.

Many inmates engage in a primitive interaction. Two guys will behave as if they are angry at each other. They mouth threats, square their shoulders, pick up a chair or whatever, approach each other and glare. After a moment, they break down in giggles and slap their hands together. For all appearances, the antagonism is real until the dissolution into camaraderie. Whites and blacks are participants. An anthropologist could probably explain it.

Later: Another great visit. When I got back to the Commons, Barry had been transferred to a cell. I'm the senior white guy in the Commons now. By universal acquiescence, whites and blacks don't share a cell, so I'll fill the next opening in a "white" cell. Another inmate, a young white guy, Phil, already fills Barry's bunk.

I played—and lost—a chess game with Morton. He gloats so much it's hard to be a good winner or loser with him. I'm glad he wins occasionally so I can maintain an interest in the game. I wish that winning wasn't everything with him, but that is the way he is. I should be thankful to have a chess player available of whatever disposition. I miss Shrimp.

Charles—thank God—is being transferred into a cell. The Commons cohort is changing composition. I hope someone more compatible will move in. Soon I'll move. I'd worry about who my cellbuddy will be, but there's so sense in doing so. I have no control.

Inmates here do not use the term "cellmate"—probably because of the subtle sexual innuendo—and use "cellbuddy" instead.

An example of paranoia. I started to play a game of chess with Luke. Two pawns were missing. I had last used the set in playing a game from a chess book. I tore my bed apart, but couldn't find the pieces. I keep the set underneath my bunk, accessible by all. I thought another inmate (Morton?) was playing a practical joke on me. I kept my cool—continued to ponder—and checked my locker, coat and pillow with no luck. I paused for a moment and remembered that I had been absent-mindedly playing with the set and sticking the pieces inside each other. I re-examined the set and found the missing pieces.

A new guy, Ron, has moved onto the tier. He is obese, white and middle-aged. He asked me if I had been using his ID card. When I answered, "No," he said that over two hundred inmates were using his ID number to buy things at the commissary and to place telephone calls. He further explained that the head of the FBI personally directed his imprisonment in Rochelle. The Attorney General is a personal enemy. I don't know if he's faking a mental illness or is really deranged. He seems harmless.

Sentencing + 88 days. Jose has moved into a cell. Hispanics are placed with a black or a white. I suppose they could make a preference known.

Morton had a physical confrontation—pushing, angry words—with one of the new black guys. The COs didn't see it—at least they didn't intervene. I have a tendency to step in and try to be a peacemaker—a dangerous course in this environment. I must stay out of it. Ron—the new obese guy—intervened and

told the black guy that if he had to hit someone, to hit him. Morton's psychological state has deteriorated. I wonder if he's missing medication.

Luke had a court date yesterday that he didn't know anything about and,
apparently, his lawyer failed to do anything about. The date will be rescheduled,
but the delay means that his release date is pushed further into the future. Luke is
angry with his lawyer for not staying on top of his case. I know only Luke's side
of the story. Nevertheless, a slight procedural mistake—beyond the inmate's control—can have drastic consequences for the inmate.

Sentencing + 91 days. Turned in my dirty linen and went to the commissary.
I bought two bags of coffee, but loaned one to Mr. John. He had a snafu in his
financial account (sound familiar?). Mr. John has done me favors so I was glad to
help. Even if I don't get the coffee back it's OK.

One serendipity—when I received my trimmers they gave me two sets of batteries (the maximum allowed per appliance), but didn't mark my property slip.
So today, at the commissary, I bought two more sets. They marked my property
slip, but now I have an ample supply. As one set becomes drained, I can trade it
in to buy a new set. I don't have to worry about being without the Walkman. I
heard a Copland work, "Prairie Journal," last night that was new to me. Typical
Copland.

Today is library day but it looks like I can go to gym <u>or</u> to the library.

Later: I was able to get to both the library and to the gym. I checked out "Life
on the Mississippi" by Mark Twain and "The Sea-Wolf" by Jack London.

You'll laugh, but it has been a busy day: 8:30, commissary; 10:00, lunch;
noon, dispensary to pick up pills; 12:30, library; 1:15, gym; 3:00, mail; 5:20, dinner.

In the mail I got your letter, but not your package with books and the earplugs.

Sentencing + 92 days. I'm about to finish "The Richard Trilogy." I find a
parallel between Buz, the murderer in the last book, and some of the guys in here.
Especially the way Buz manipulated Ritchie and was able to rationalize his treatment of other people.

Sentencing + 93 days. I was notified of a $3.75 charge to pay UPS. There was
no explanation. I suspect it was to pay to send the earplugs back to you. I wrestle
with the question of how much to push the issue. I'd like an explanation of why
and how they spent <u>my</u> money. As it stands, I don't even know if my suspicions
are valid. If I gripe by making the earplugs an issue, they could respond by moving me into an undesirable cell. Harassment by information control. I also was

notified that I will be trained to work in food services. I understand that I will be taught how to wash my hands.

Finished "The Richard Trilogy." I've started reading "The Mind of God" by Paul Davies.

Later: I may be completely wrong about the $3.75. When contraband is returned the inmate gets paperwork—which I haven't received.

Received my food services training. Besides proper hand washing technique, I also learned how to put on a hair net. While I was in the dispensary being trained I asked for a blood pressure check—140/88.

There was a fantastic sunset—a phantasmagoria of blue and gold. I've also started "The Sea-Wolf." I've signed up for the 50+ gym session. I understand bridge is played there. It's not mandatory that I go. The more options, the better.

Sentencing + 94 days. "The Sea-Wolf" has some parallels to my own situation. A young man, as result of a ship collision in the San Francisco Bay, is "rescued" by a seal hunting ship. He is "enlisted" by the captain (the Sea-Wolf) to fill a vacancy. So, this young gentile intellectual is forced to be in the company of a rougher side of life that is alien to him. I identify strongly with his reactions.

At commissary, I bought jalapeño cheese spread. A welcomed respite from blandness. I just heard "Morning Has Broken."

A Unitarian miracle. Remember me telling you about the card game "Napoleon" that I taught to Barry and Morton? Guess what game is played in "The Sea-Wolf?" Yeap—"Napoleon." That two such events—teaching an obscure game and then reading about it—happen so closely in time amazes me. Of course, if I hadn't taught the game, I wouldn't've paid any attention to it when I read about it. It is only because the first event happened that the second is noticed. There must be many such potentialities in each day, so at a rational level, it's not that amazing.

Sentencing + 95 days. I just listened to a Bach concerto for oboe and strings in D-minor. An oboe in D-minor is a haunting voice.

I'm enjoying "The Sea-Wolf." Have you read it? I doubt that you would enjoy it. I find parallels between Richard of the Trilogy in New Mexico and Humphrey of the Sea-Wolf aboard the ship, "Ghost." Both came from privileged backgrounds and are thrust into the "real" world. Since both books were placed within a decade or two of the turn of the century, I wonder if that theme had a particular appeal at that time?

I spoke with Don about being cellbuddies. He likes the upper bunk—I like the lower, so no problem there. He has been told that he is the next to go to the honor tier. I'll write the tier sergeant and suggest that moving us both simultaneously might make sense. See what happens. Can't hurt.

Later: Got your letter with the legal letter from Herb about the appeal. I'll return it to you. Would rather not have it lying around.

Morton is a pain in the ass. He's like the typical schoolyard bully. Since he has become acclimated to the environment his true nature manifests itself. He tries his best to irritate me (and others) and make my life miserable. His primary motivation is jealousy. He's envious of the quantity of mail that I get. He's jealous of my ability to buy at the commissary. He's envious of my ability to listen to a radio. He resents my ability to win at chess. My best reaction is not to show irritation and hope he gives up trying, but so far, he has only increased his efforts. Misery loves company and he does his best to enlarge the circle. After the mail delivery today, he commented that for all the letters I write I don't get many in return. He had just gotten his last letter to his "girl friend" returned unclaimed. I'd like to terminate all contact—chess, scrabble, whatever—with him, but worry that it would just prove to him that he has "gotten to me" and would spur his perverse behavior. I tread a middle ground. One of us will soon go into a cell.

Sentencing + 96 days. Finished "The Sea-Wolf." It is not only a great sea story, but also a stark study of human nature. Jack London was a Marxist at one time and it shows in his story. It has quite a bit of gore and inhumanity. I don't think you'd enjoy it, but it is an poignant study of good and evil. I've started the Mark Twain book.

Sentencing + 97 days. I taught myself a new solitaire game, "Canfield." It is interesting and doesn't take much space. After the play, all the cards are face up and thus it is easy to reassemble the deck.

In our calculation of incarceration time, we overlooked the "good conduct credit." I could be out in fourteen months from now.

Just heard Haydn's "Concerto #2 in D-major for Cello" and his "Symphony #7 in C-Major." I escaped into each of them.

Rochelle State Prison, Housing Unit 1, Tier B, Cell 15.

Sentencing + 98 days.

Dearest Wife,

I was moved into a cell today and so begins a new phase! Moved in with Barry. I'm happy with the move. The cell is ten feet by six feet, eight inches. It has a bunk bed, two lockers, a small desk and a combo sink/commode with a metal mirror above. There is a single wastepaper basket and a solitary chair. I suppose the person assigned to the lower bunk is expected to sit on the bed. The sliding door, like those in County, is solid metal with a small square window. It is closed, opened and locked electronically from the CO's bubble. On the outside wall, there is a thin vertical window with a screen inside and bars outside. We can open the window by a crank handle. There is one enclosed fluorescent light in the center of the ceiling and a smaller one above the sink. They can be turned on and off by switches inside or an outside master switch adjacent to the door. There is a cable TV connection and a dual power outlet, but no telephone or wet bar. ☻

We're without a TV and I'm without a newspaper. I miss the latter, and a TV would relieve the boredom when confined to the cell, even more so because of the luxury of being able to choose the program. Barry's former cellbuddy, Andy, (they were together for 10 days) had a black/white TV, but it went with him of course. Barry is interested in buying a TV. I told him I'd pay a portion. I don't think I'd buy one just for me—the future is just too uncertain. I have the upper bunk, because of Barry's hip injury, but ascend and descend without difficulty by using the chair as a ladder.

The move from the Commons into a cell is a blessing!

Sentencing + 99 days. What a great visit. Good news—Barry has arranged with the COs to "borrow" the TV from Andy. The cell into which Andy moved has a color TV and Andy is willing to loan his black/white unit to us.

We're allowed out of the cell in the evening to go into the rec area (downstairs from the Commons) where there is a TV for viewing by all, several card tables, a hot water pot and a microwave. The schedule appears chaotic. Perhaps, a rhythm will become apparent.

I understand the $3.75 UPS charge. It was to return the boots to you. If the boots have metal in the sole they are not allowed because of the possibility of making a shank.

Sentencing + 100 days. Don tells me that one can subscribe to a newspaper. That would be a godsend.

The TV deal is iffy. I'll believe it when it happens. The transfer was to happen this morning. There was an excuse. Tomorrow is now the target date.

Phyllis wrote me that she is mailing the Chaplain—as has to be done—a flaming chalice religious pendant designated for me. The Chaplain is the resident arbiter of what is and what is not a religious icon. Is there a religion that has a hacksaw blade as an icon?

Sentencing + 101 days. Barry and I talked about religion. He's a regular attendee at the Protestant services and Bible studies, but he's an adherent—although he doesn't realize it—to Pascal's argument about the existence of God, so his heart is not really in it. He's out of the cell now and I'm alone—the first privacy I've had since Classification. I had a good exercise period—walked over three miles. I'll be glad when this is all over.

Sentencing + 102 days. I'm in a blue funk today. There seems to be an letdown after a major transition—when I moved from Classification to Rochelle, when I moved from Commons to a cell. I feel I'm in nothingness.

Any person who is sentenced to more than fifteen (say) years in prison should have access to state assisted suicide. Life in here is so meaningless that the quality of life is on par with the Kervorkian infirm. Doing away with oneself should be an option—not mandatory, of course. Inside this fantasy, would judges cluster sentences at fourteen years, eleven months to deprive the inmate from the option? Would the public applaud or lament when an inmate chooses the option? Would the prison administration better the environment to promote the "life" option? What chance is there for an inmate, after fifteen years of this benighted existence, to lead a meaningful life upon release? Are we, as a society, going to praise him for paying his dues, and make sure he has a job and a place to live? Or are we going to label him as a "dangerous felon" (are those two words ever separated?) and place Herculean barriers to a successful reintegration? Getting rid of a few inmates would save the state money. Getting rid of malcontents would improve prison life for those who wish to live, and, by relieving suffering, would be a beneficence for the inmate. Perhaps my thoughts are too gloomy to be sharing. I'll brighten them.

A popular diversion is preparing a "cook-up." The idea is to combine ingredients that one can buy at the commissary and cook them in the microwave during rec period. For example, one can mix "Ramon noodles" and "beans and franks" and heat them. Another praised dish is the crumbling and mixing of BBQ potato chips into spaghetti. The attraction is a different taste, an outlet for creativity and an alternative to the chow hall. Barry wants to take turns in making cook-ups and sharing the results.

No further news about the TV.

Tomorrow I can change my visitor's list (I've been here sixty days!). Any ideas on additions or deletions? In two more months, it's conceivable that I'll be out of here if the legal petition is successful.

Sentencing + 103 days. Commissary went OK, except they didn't have any batteries. Luckily, I have a stockpile. Barry has a good plug-in stereo radio, so I'm not using the Walkman as much.

I witnessed an example of typical prison behavior. When an inmate returns from commissary shopping, he is to take his purchases to his cell. An older inmate, Arnie, with two bags of items, for some reason, returned to the rec area where a bunch of us were assembled waiting for gym exercise. Arnie sat at a table, set his bags on the floor beside him and started talking across the table. His bags gaped open with candy bars lying on top. Damion, one of the more obnoxious, belligerent, and aggressive inmates, sneaked to beside Arnie and with exaggerated movements took one of the candy bars. By purposefully being obvious Damion could, if Arnie detected him, affect an attitude that it was all a joke and return the candy while laughing and thus avoid any confrontation. Arnie was unaware, so Damion pocketed the candy bar, walked away for a moment, passed the candy bar to a "homeboy," returned to Arnie's side and repeated the act. Damion did this four times stealing all the candy bars. I was watching and Damion knew I was watching. After the last candy bar had been successfully passed off, Damion came to me and said, *"He was lucky, 'cause I left the chips."* Damion relied on my silence because of the inviolate rule against snitching.

I woke depressed again. I dread being put to work in the kitchen. I would like to get a subscription to the newspaper.

Your package came in the mail—thanks! The earplugs were refused, but I'll file an appeal. I can make a good case. Carl had sent a cassette tape that was returned as well. I'll not appeal that since I can order tapes and I'm becoming convinced that just the radio will be sufficient and less consumptive of batteries.

I'm earning good conduct credit of ten days per month. An eighteen-month sentence would be reduced to twelve if I behave myself.

Sentencing + 104 days. The television—true to my prediction—is still a no-show. Lots of mail. The State Transportation Board, in response to my letter, replied there is no way I can renew my driver's license by mail unless I am out of the state for an extended period. I'm tempted to concoct a story and use the out-of-state address of a friend. Trying to outwit the system is a slippery slope. The worst-case scenario is that I'll take the driving test again. No big deal.

Some aspects of cell life are less desirable. To shower, one goes to the down-stairs rec area (with about sixty other inmates) and waits for one of the four shower stalls to become available. The longer the wait, the colder the water. An older white dude ain't gonna be near da fron' of da line.

I don't deal well with uncertainty. It creates anxiety. I don't want to worry about being able to shower. At County, in Classification, and in the Commons I knew when I could shower. The same uncertainty exists concerning access to the telephone or to the microwave. I much prefer a guaranteed access—even at an inconvenient time.

Listened to Mozart's "Symphony #40."

Sentencing + 105 days. Great visit! From the visit, I went to the gym for a good walk. I go around and around the basketball court, trying to dodge the bodies flying from the basketball games.

On the way to the chow hall I walked briefly with Arnie and confided that he needed to watch his commissary stuff while in the rec area. I didn't mention Damion. Arnie just grunted. He's an old-timer, he should know better.

I was called to the Chaplain's office and received my flaming chalice necklace. I'm not sure he knows what a Unitarian Universalist is.

Sentencing + 106 days. Had a visit from Walter, Harry and Brad today. On the trip here, they were engrossed in discussion and passed the exit by twenty miles! Walter asked about future appeals, etc. I told him about the parole hearing in four months and said our attorney is trying other things.

I played chess with a new opponent and was beaten three times. I'm not sure if that's good news or bad. I want good competition, but want to win. I want to play Bobby Fischer and "barely" win each time. ☺

One benefit of cell life—my laundry is done for me. Two inmates have the job of doing all the personal laundry (not linen) for the tier. The "customer" has to furnish soap and softener. Today was my first use of the opportunity and it came back in good shape. One typically "tips" the laundry man with a candy bar.

Tomorrow, it's my turn to clean the cell—sink, toilet and floor.

Sentencing + 107 days. I managed to win one of three games with my new opponent. I wonder if he let me win?

The cleaning of the cell took ten minutes. On cell-cleaning day, soap and toilet paper is distributed.

Had to renew the batteries in the Walkman.

Have you heard of a "summer-sausage?" It's a new term for me. Barry knows of it. Apparently, it refers to a pre-cooked hard sausage. One can buy them (a popular ingredient in cook-ups) in the commissary.

I've formed a theory about the sparrows in the tree outside the chow hall. They're so happy because they've been eating the Zoloft I've been discarding on the grass!

Just heard a "Concerto for Bassoon" by Vanhal—a new composer for me.

Sentencing + 108 days. Enjoyed the telephone call last night. It's excellent news about the newspaper subscription. It will be great!

I also think that continuing my participation in our book club is a fantastic idea. I can read the books, write my comments and mail them for you to present. It's generous for the other members to lend support in this way. I'll read "American Pastoral" as quickly as possible.

I had a minor incident in chow hall today. Those of us on special diets (cardiovascular, vegetarian, diabetic, etc.) have a window at which we must present our diet card. To get to the window one must pass along the line of inmates waiting for the normal serving. As I passed between the inmates and the wall, Damion (remember him—the guy who stole commissary items from Arnie) backed up suddenly and we collided. I don't believe he knew I was there, but who knows. I apologized but he accused me of deliberating running into him. I explained that I was just trying to get to the diet window. The COs were watching us, so I said nothing further and moved up the line.

An oddity: Even though the majority of the population is black, the majority of the inmates in the diet line are white.

Sentencing + 110 days. I got the book yesterday and am on page 71. I'm enjoying the book. I also received the information from *The Church of the Larger Fellowship*.

I have an appointment with the psychiatrist today—four weeks from the last one. I want to talk about my blood pressure measurements, earplugs and medication. Not any mental health issues.

I read the article in the newspaper yesterday about marriage and teasing. Their conclusion was that the marriage that included teasing, *"…is the only kind we found that remains romantic and passionate after 35 years."* So, don't give me grief for teasing you. I'm just keeping the passion in our marriage. ☺

"Bolero" is on the radio. I heard Joshua Bell playing Mendelssohn's "Violin Concerto in E-minor."

Catalog ordering is in two weeks, so it's not too early to send the money needed to buy the TV. I feel like a college kid writing home and asking for $5 (although I suspect that figure dates me).

Later: Just saw the psychiatrist—a disappointment. He wasn't affable. I said nothing about discontinuing the Zoloft. I talked to him about the blood pressure measurements. Nothing he could do about it—*"Different department."* I griped to deaf ears, I'm sure, about the long waits to shower. I didn't mention the earplugs. He asked the standard questions: *"Visitors?" "Suicidal thoughts?" "Hallucinations?"* There is no group therapy or counseling available herein. He'll see me again in six weeks.

Sentencing + 111 days. A fantastic sunset last night—gold, reds, gold, purples, gold, yellows, gold and pinks. Gorgeous. Did I mention the gold?

My blood pressure was measured—158/88. The nurse said the 88 was the important number and since it was less than 90 it was OK. Their aim is to get the inmate out and not to find a problem. She also told me that I was completely out of line asking for a biweekly measurement. Standard operational procedure is to take a measurement every three months and it was not my place to "dictate." Their coffee breaks mustn't be disrupted. These insentient nurses and doctors must be the dregs of the profession. They don't even pretend to be concerned. Why would anyone work in a prison if they had any other option? They are bitter at life and spit their venom at the defenseless inmates.

I'm on page 87 of "American Pastoral" (=AP). This had better be a hell of a story—Roth is certainly building up to it.

The monotony, the endemic stupidity, the mindless routine, the lack of intelligent and humane interaction wear at my psyche. I fight against it and am sure I can win—but would I know if I lost? If I—in a fundamental way—changed atavistically, would I recognize it? If you saw a difference in me, would you tell me? Far greater than any fear about rejection by community or church is the worry that I will emerge from this Hades mutated for the worse. The letters, visits and telephone calls are important because they provide a nexus to reality and to my past. My morale is mercurial. I want to remain the person whom you loved. I want to remain the person I was.

There is a creeping crud in here. Under the pressure of the milieu, one begins to believe that "in-here" is "normal," the people herein are "normal," the manners of interpersonal interaction are "normal." I have to keep reminding myself that this is *not* normal. Compassion does exist. Altruism does have a place. Forgetting about the good is a cancer that overcomes you if you're here for a long time. Your worldview is sacrificed for psychological survival. This sacrifice undermines the return to a normal life upon release. You wonder what swindle everyone is pulling. You can't take people at their word. You look for opportunities to further yourself at the expense of others. After fifteen years, you are not fit for any meaningful existence.

Sentencing + 112 days. My laundry is done. I have fresh linen. I've been to the library. Does life get better? At the library, since I have a collection of reading material, I wasn't too fussy. I may not even be able to get to them. I got a Star Trek book, "Probe" which is "...the spellbinding sequel to Star Trek IV." Have you read it? I also got "Trader" by Charles de Lint, "...a novel of identity, an adult coming-of-age story." I have a noon appointment to pick up medicine. Got five letters in the mail!

The opening of a new maximum-security prison in Moretown is rumored. Sixty inmates from here will be transferred there.

Sentencing + 113 days. What a nice visit! I love to watch your eyes. They completely give you away! I can tell if you agree or disagree with what I suggest.

My catalog order will include the TV, a headphone extension cord and an AC adapter for my Walkman. Total—$265.43.

I believe that filing the appeal before the parole hearing is the correct tactic. If the parole hearing goes badly, I fear the judge wouldn't want to be perceived as overruling the parole board.

In one week, I'll have been incarcerated for four months—halfway through. The light at the end of the tunnel! I know that this isn't a sure thing, but the hope is better than nothing. Imagine how we'd feel if the appeal had been refused to be heard. Life is good. We love and have each other. We have family and friends. We have a home. We have most of our health. We have cinnamon coffee!

Barry has written his attorney to start divorce proceedings against his wife for the stupidest reasons, born of paranoia—he *thinks* she may be seeing someone else. I don't understand the enmity between the two. I'm trying to argue him out of it.

Sentencing + 114 days. I got the package with the boots! They fit fine.

No newspaper yet, but I don't know how I'm to get it—through the mail?

Barry is doing better and hopefully won't mail the letter. He's going to try to call his wife today. The personalities are so volatile anything can happen.

Had a good piece of chicken breast for dinner. Pineapple chunks, rice and BBQ beans. I finished "American Pastoral" and include my comments for the book club. Love.

Dear Book Club:
Re: "American Pastoral" by Phillip Roth.

Thank you for letting me participate in this manner. It is a privilege to be able to express my thoughts and not have to defend them against your insightful rejoinders. I'll pay homage to that favor by brevity.

I finished the book in six days—a testament more about my surroundings than the quality of the book.

My discussion will be divided into two spheres—technique and purpose.

I liken Roth's technique to that of an impressionist painter who creates an image by combining a multitude of seemingly disconnected brush strokes. Each individual stroke is unimportant in that it could be eliminated without destroying the rendition. However, the representation depends on the sum of the strokes. Roth uses a palette of paragraphs to create a montage of allusions which, in his view, combine to make a novel.

I noticed a peculiarity. The vocabulary that Roth uses in the first 100 pages is much more robust than that used in the rest of the book. I suspect that he started the book with an intense desire to create a literary work and kept his lexicon at hand. As the work progressed, he cloyed from the effort.

What was Roth's purpose? Teach us how to make a glove? What role in the book did the discussions of the minutiae of glove making play? Perhaps to illustrate the consumptive power of life's trivialities?

Is the book about the Vietnam War? Or about the difficulty of parenting? Or about the great American struggle for prosperity and comfort? Is there more to the book than a collection of clichés—beauty queen marries sports hero—a daughter's rejection of her bourgeois family—the Jewish heritage? Or are these banalities the brush strokes composing a story?

Why, in the invidious confrontation between sixteen year-old Merry and her mother, was there no mention by either of their previous sharing and mutual enjoyment of cattle rearing? Such a strong nexus between the two would've attracted *some* vituperation, I suspect. Perhaps Roth wrote the facets out of order.

If the book is to be taken as a serious statement, I found two poignancies that provide the thread holding the book together. *"What kind of mask is everyone wearing?"* Roth asks. He further observes, *"Without transgression there is no knowledge."* The book illustrates the impact of those two aphorisms in the form of Seymour Levov's life.

However, I think Roth intended the book to be a joke. In the same way that Ravel wrote "Bolero" as a joke (and was surprised to have the monotonous music taken seriously), Roth penned "American Pastoral." The mordant title and the disjointed enigmatic ending—as if he just gets tired of writing—give support to this interpretation.

If I were with you I'd ask about the religion of Jain—and probably be justifiably shushed because of the diversion that would tempt the discussion. Is the religion real? Is it as austere as indicated?

I welcome reaction. Thanks.

Sentencing + 116 days. Good news! I got the newspapers from the last two days. They lifted my spirits! The routine, as explained to me, is that each morning I will get a pass to the admin building that enables me to retrieve the paper. Another chance to get out of the cell and get exercise—a double win! What a luxury to be able to read the paper—unrushed by other inmates wanting sections. It's all mine. I can tear it apart as I wish.

When I went for my afternoon medication a new policy was announced. We have to combine our trip to the dispensary with our afternoon chow hall trip. In fact, most of the guys were already doing that, but I had made a habit of returning to the housing unit after the dispensary because that's what the Inmate Handbook says to do and I enjoyed the walking. So having lost one jaunt, I hope to gain its replacement in picking up the newspaper.

Sentencing + 117 days. I didn't get a pass this morning for my newspaper (arghhh), but I did get a morning gym pass to join the 50+ period and found it much more accommodating—fewer people.

I asked the CO about my newspaper. He'll look into it.

My Procardia ran out without a refill. I sent a querulous note to the Medical Department and CC'ed Herb. I'm told that the system treats you better if you have an attorney's attention. There is no excuse for their negligence. The vitriolic Medical Department is the least effective group in the infrastructure.

I haven't heard from the warden concerning my request for earplugs. According to the protocol in the Inmate Handbook, he has five days to respond. That period elapsed fourteen days ago. No explanation—no nothing. The inmates are to follow the rules, but the system is exempt from such an inconvenience.

I'm about two-thirds of the way through "The Mind of God" and am enjoying it.

Barry didn't mail the "divorce" letter. Maybe I've done good in helping keep a family—they have three small children—together. Barry has an arrogant misogynistic view of women. Any sign of independence by his wife roils him. How he expects her to cope and remain completely dependent while he is locked up is beyond comprehension. I told him that I was blessed by having a beautiful, independent and intelligent woman who <u>chooses</u> to be with me.

Sentencing + 118 days. Heard Copland's "Hoe-Down" this morning. Looking forward to your visit tomorrow. No news about my medicine yet. I wrote the health services supervisor. Got my newspaper this morning so maybe a routine is in place.

We had a fire drill this morning at 2:30AM. All 500 of us in the unit had to dress and stand in the rain. Luckily, it wasn't cold.

Listening to Beethoven's Ninth as I write.

Sentencing + 119 days. I did get to commissary after our visit. Mr. John paid the coffee he owed me. I was called to the dispensary and received a refill of Procardia. No explanation of the problem. The orthodoxy is that the system never explains their mistakes or failures.

In the mail, I got "A Distant Trumpet." My laundry is done. My bed is made. Had a good exercise period and shower. Played four games of chess against some of the better players and won all!

When I finished the paper today, I passed it to Manny. I know him from the Commons. He did me a favor by loaning me batteries for my Walkman before I had a chance to go to commissary. He said it was the first paper he had seen since he was transferred into a cell from the Commons. He, however, has no interest in "Newsweek," which I'll pass on to Don.

Just heard Nat King Cole's song "All I Can Offer is My Love, Forever." Goodnight, Love.

Sentencing + 120 days. I had to ask the COs for a pass to get the newspaper so it's not routine yet.

Morton has been transferred to another prison—thank goodness. He was OK when he first arrived in the Commons, but transmogrified. I wonder if the change was due to suspension of his psychosomatic medicine.

The mail brought an unexpected and surprising response from the medical service supervisor. She wrote a note, at the bottom of the form I sent her, curtly stating that I should have my medicine by now. No explanation of the disruption. I sent it to Herb Diamond.

The procedure for evening medication has changed again. I go to chow with the tier and after the meal go to the dispensary instead of returning to the housing unit. So, I've lost the advantage of another walk.

Sentencing + 121 days. I got my newspaper at 8:00AM. Enjoyed the walk and the leisurely reading of it.

I've ordered sermons from *The Church of the Larger Fellowship*. I've created an ersatz religious ceremony. Instead of lighting a chalice, I light a match and let it burn out. I include an opening reading, a written sermon and closing words. The opening and closing I read aloud in Barry's absence. The last sermon, which I enjoyed, was by Rev. Gilbert of Rochester. I imagine the chalices burning—or about to burn—in all of the churches, congregations, and fellowships and feel a kinship with others of our denomination. I wonder if they would reciprocate?

Sentencing + 123 days. I had a nice visit from Elgin, Kathy and Mary this morning. Elgin wants to mail me books to maintain my technical skills. I talked to him about letters he could write in support of the appeal and the parole hearing.

Heard Beethoven's "Symphony #1 in C-Major." I wonder what proportion of first symphonies are in C-major?

You like the artwork on the envelope? Some inmates do the artwork and sell them for a "noodle" (cost 14¢)—a package of Ramon Noodles. The envelopes are a bit hokey, but show initiative.

Two "friends" are being transferred to Moretown. One is Mr. John from the Commons. The other is Papa Doc—an older (65?) white man who had said he was going to start walking with me. Both don't understand why they are being transferred and are upset. There is no explanation from the system, of course—information control. I hate to see Mr. John go. His situation is lamentable because he was to have a court hearing tomorrow that could significantly reduce his sentence. Apparently, they postponed his court date to be able to transfer him. That's his story.

I had my blood pressure measured by an automatic machine, whose dial I could see. It read 172/78. The nurse said, after seeing me reading the results, *"This machine is all screwed up."* She then read it manually in a manner that I couldn't verify and proudly announced, *"136/82!"* Why am I suspicious?

Sentencing + 124 days. I think of the torment I've subjected you to. I think of the dismay, the silent suffering and the pain that you're going through—and yet, you're still there for me. Does anyone else have the deep bonding that I feel between us? I have faith that you feel this nexus as well. It goes beyond love, but includes all of love. We're sharing spirits. Each of life's pleasures is magnified when I share it with you. Each of life's disappointments is diminished when you're there. Could I live without you? Could you live without me? Yes, of course, but the tragedy of not having you would bring darkness through which I would have to fight to find value in the empty days and nights. We're both strong individuals. We choose to be with each other. Each of us, I feel, would lose a tremendous part of our life without the other—but we'd persevere and continue to contribute to the world what we could.

Sentencing + 125 days. I got two long nice letters yesterday from Brad and Jessie.

I got a notice that I've been accepted into an AA group starting next week. Should I go? My going could be interpreted as an admission on my part that I acknowledge the need. But I can argue that the judge ordered it. I don't want to create a situation, when I get out, where I can't have a glass of wine with dinner without breaking parole.

Newspaper retrieval is routine now and a blessing. I do the crossword puzzles and read virtually the entire paper.

Played chess—won some, lost some. I'm making more friends from the population of the tier as a whole. These guys are NOT the embodiment of pure evil. I find some of them interesting. I can easily see them—if they had been born into a different socioeconomic situation—being successful. Some are the victims of their origin. But in the back of my mind always is the nagging caveat that I'm seeing them in a controlled environment. If the chains of restraint were absent, would they be as affable?

During rec period, the white guys gather in one spot—the stairs leading to the upper tier. We sit and chat. It's not an enthralling discussion. I miss *your* discussions and insights.

Sorry about the telephone calls last night. You probably have a half-dozen empty messages on the answering machine. Uncharacteristically the phone was free, so I just stood there—imagining you entering the house and rushing to the telephone. I hope you didn't interpret the number of messages as an emergency. If I had wanted to contact you, I would have—as I've done in the past—called someone to relay a message.

Sentencing + 126 days. No medication refill! I've written the nurse supervisor again and CC'ed Herb. It's either unbelievable incompetence or retaliation (against what?). I had a nice morning walk to get the paper. The sky was spectacular. Went to the library last night. I returned the two books unread that I had checked out. I checked out "Oliver Twist." Shamefully, I must admit I've never read it.

I got a letter from Bud with the results of a web search on the recommended frequency to measure blood pressure. If the condition is controlled and the dosage stable, then a measurement every other month is sufficient. Less frequent than I would've guessed.

Sentencing + 127 days. Thanks for the visit! I certainly enjoy them, but you have enormous demands on your time to maintain a life to await us after this hell is over. So if you can't come on the weekend, I understand.

I will forgo buying cassettes. With the newspaper, the TV, and the Walkman I have enough entertainment. I compare what I have here with what I had in Classification and feel rich!

Barry is morose. I've suggested getting counseling and anti-depressant medicine if possible. He has huge mood swings. He's reverted to seeing only negative in his relationship with his wife. She's taken a part-time job at a restaurant and that has upset him. I subtly preach Carlson—our perception of things can be dictated by how we choose to see them. I may be making progress that is not immediately obvious.

I've sent Herb Diamond a rendition of the blood pressure and medication saga for possible use during the appeal.

Sentencing + 128 days. Still no medication. Had a good shower this morning. In fact, it was so accessible I may change my routine of evening showers.

I played three games of chess last night against one of the better players. Won two, so my mood is up! Drat, I don't want chess to affect my moods.

Barry is in a better mood. He says he appreciates my advice and views. I'd be more flattered if I had an effect.

Sentencing + 130 days. Still no medication. I submitted an Official Complaint Form (OCF), which according to the rules cannot be ignored. The system must pay attention to them, but also gives inmates grief if they abuse their use.

Had a nice visit from Sam and Lucy. Thanks for acting as social secretary.

Barry has ordered his TV. I offered to share the $20 charge for express handling. I'll order mine in the next couple of days and indicate routine handling.

Tomorrow is commissary and early morning 50+ gym.

Sentencing + 131 days. I was called from my cell last night at 3:00AM for blood and urine work. I mentioned that I have been without hypertension medication. They'll "look into it."

It's commissary morning so things are chaotic. I did not get the gym pass, nor was I called to pick up the newspaper. The system can only handle one activity at a time.

I find getting to the telephone is stressful and letters are adequate communication. I may not make the effort for the telephone regularly. An additional benefit will be the cost savings since the calls are so expensive due to the state's surcharge. Better telephone access will be a blessing of the honor tier.

Later: I got my medicine! Enough for ten days. They said the delay was caused by a supply problem with the pharmacy and thanked me for my patience. Ha! When I got the medicine, I also got my paper. Because of the busy day, I missed the exercise period in the yard.

Sentencing + 132 days. Ordered my TV today. I'm on page 113 of "Oliver Twist." Although it's going slowly, I'm enjoying it.

Tomorrow is the first meeting of the AA group. Maybe I'll just say what is expected to be heard and thereby be acknowledged as cooperative and redeemed.

Sentencing + 133 days. The COs comment about the quantity of mail I get. The letters, magazine articles and cards are welcomed. I snacked on chips and salsa and awoke dormant taste buds.

Went to the AA meeting and was disappointed. It was simplistic, and theistic. It opened and closed with a prayer. The sharing among the participants was nothing beyond self-serving claptrap. I didn't say anything. Everyone introduces himself as, *"I'm Joe and I'm an alcoholic."* I did not introduce myself in that manner and was the only one not choosing that avenue. The group is entirely voluntary and meets once a week. At the least—as with the retrieval of the Zoloft—it's an outing from the cell.

Sentencing + 134 days. Had a good visit with Walter, Brad and Harry this morning. The direction of the conversation falls upon me. I'm at ease in the role, but wish it were less one-sided. The conversation is a full dialogue, but the topics originate with me, and, of course, I can't ask about what I don't know. Do I make sense? Maybe they don't want to ask uncomfortable questions.

I'm making better progress with "Oliver Twist" and want to finish it so I can read the next book club selection, "Snow in August."

We should prepare ourselves for a postponement in the appeal date. Happens frequently, I understand. Each month seems like an eternity.

Evening. I got to the telephone and called Carl. Had a good conversation. When I told him I was reading "Oliver Twist," he asked if that was part of the punishment. I love that kid. I then called Bud. He wasn't there, but I spoke with Jessie. I'm glad Bud found her. She's as supportive as a daughter could be. I called you, but the machine answered (as I knew it would). I heard a few words of your voice.

Sentencing + 135 days. I'm in a good mood this morning. I practice Carlson's art of positive thinking and psyching myself up. It works.

I had my religious service. My chalice lighting words this morning:

May the light we now kindle
inspire us to use our powers
to heal and not to harm,
to help and not to hinder,
to bless and not to curse,
to serve you, spirit of freedom.

These words comfort me and especially provide guidance for my actions herein.

I'm on page 295 of "Oliver Twist." The poor little boy is subjected to powers and evils that he has no control over and survives. He keeps his benefic spirit and willingness to do well. To be trite—there's a lesson there for us all.

Sentencing + 137 days. The telephone was free this morning except I couldn't take advantage of it—I was *en route* to get the newspaper. It's cold today. I'm wearing long johns. I'm submitting my medication refill requests today. I have enough medicine for four more days. The 10mg tablets—which I've had to use because of the lack of 20mg pills—have been refilled so often that my last supply says "No Refill." I predict problems.

On the Walkman last night, I heard a 20th century piece on the PBS station. I thought Stravinsky—no, Bernstein—no, Copland—no. There were bits of all three in the music. I was baffled. It turned out to be "Catfish Row Symphonic Suite" from "Porgy and Bess" by Gershwin. I enjoy such discoveries.

I finished "Oliver Twist" and made a discovery. It is far better and more informative to read the "Foreword" or "Introduction" (which are not written by the author) *after* reading the book. Irving Howe wrote the "Introduction" to the edition I read and, lo and behold, I agree with his critical comments. Howe makes a couple of startling remarks. First, he says that "The Adventures of Huckleberry Finn" is a far greater book. Secondly, Howe says that "Little Dorrit" by Dickens is a more meritorious book. Forsooth, I must admit I've not heard of it. I'm anxious to see the film version of "Oliver Twist" with Alec Guiness as Fagin, the Jew. Now, on to "Snow in August."

Sentencing + 138 days. I did have 50+ gym this morning. It's great to have the additional space.

On the return from chow after lunch, two inmates got into a fight. It was fifty yards or so behind me. One of the inmates had a shank and stabbed the other. The COs constrained them quickly. Both inmates will be treated by the system as equally culpable. Both will be put into isolation and eventually transferred to another prison. They will lose "good-time." The one with the shank may have additional legal charges.

I received the material from *The Church of the Larger Fellowship*. They apparently sent four sermons in a three-ring binder inside a zipper bag—both of which are contraband. I have to pay to have them returned. The CLF must not have experience in dealing with inmates and prisons.

I'm on page 69 of "Snow in August" and enjoying it.

Sentencing + 139 days. I listened to a recorder and bassoon double concerto. An odd combination but it worked nicely. Isn't a bassoon a much more modern instrument? A harpsichord was present, as well. The composer? Telemann, of course. I hope I can still play the recorder.

Sentencing + 140 days. I went directly to chow after our visit and then returned to the housing unit. As I waited for the tier door to open, a CO asked me why I was in prison. I answered that I had broken the law. I suspect the COs don't know the offenses of the individual inmates.

The AA meeting went OK. I didn't say anything. Members spoke about trigger words, e.g., "anger," "guilt," "recovery," etc. and then chose the next person to speak. Luckily, I wasn't picked. When I returned to the housing unit from the meeting, huge snowflakes were falling. I tried to catch them on my tongue. I must've appeared to be crazy.

Sentencing + 141 days. I'm waiting to be called for the newspaper. Today is inspection day and trivial things like newspaper retrievals tend to be forgotten. However, I can remind them later. I have a pass for 50+ gym and the tier has afternoon exercise during which time I can shower. Ain't life great?

Your life sounds harried. I wish I were there to share the load and not be part of the load. I certainly have let you know of ways to help me and you have. Let me know of ways I can help you. One way I know I can help is to keep myself as fit—physically, mentally, spiritually and psychologically—as possible. With your help, I'm working on all of them. For physical fitness, I exercise regularly using clothes you furnished. For mental health, I read and play games with materials you have given me. Spiritually, I use inspirational materials and have meaningful rituals that you support. Psychologically, your visits, letters and acceptance of telephone calls are nonpareil.

Another way I can help is to do what is needed—cooperating with the system and staying out of trouble—to shorten the incarceration time as much as possible. Luckily, because of my personality, this is easy for me, as opposed to some inmates I see.

I'm on page 265 of "Snow in August." Michael is recovering from his beating. I find pages that are dog-eared, meaning that your fingers have touched those pages—your eyes have scanned those words. I feel closer to you.

Barry is anxious to get his TV. I must be a boring cellbuddy!

Sentencing + 142 days. I finished "Snow in August" and will send my book club report. I've been at Rochelle for 100 days! How many more? Soon the nightmare that began 142 days ago will be over. It will always be there—in our history and in our memories—but we will be together and that will make all other problems insignificant and manageable.

I received a set of four sermons from *The Church of the Larger Fellowship* by Rev. Robin Gray, the Minister at Milford, Massachusetts. Titles are, "On Being Forgiven," "By Faith Alone," "I am, I am," and "Living Dangerously"—all relevant. ☺

Sentencing + 143 days. My chosen sermon today was "By Faith Alone." A nice metaphor—*"People are like teabags. You never know how strong they are until they're in hot water."* My ersatz services help. They force me to focus on our religious principles and reinforce the imperative that doing well is the <u>right</u> thing. For example, it is correct to give the newspaper to a kind and interested person and not to sell it (e.g., for a candy bar per week).

There is a break in the water main so no showers or laundry today.

It's nice to hear your voice. You must be lonely. Should you call your family more often? Take the initiative. You're wise—you know what should be done.

Sentencing + 145 days. When I returned to the cell after our visit I had a lunch of Vienna sausages. I made telephone calls as well—Phyllis and Troy. Troy tells me that Sue may have to have her neck vertebrae fused as mine were.

Barry and I are planning to get up in the morning for breakfast (oatmeal and French toast)—as a break in the routine. If I make it, it'll be only my fourth breakfast in Rochelle.

In the mail, I got a formal reply to my OCF—no new information.

I enclose my notes on "Snow in August."

Dear Book Club:
Re: "Snow in August" by Pete Hamill.

"Snow in August" was an enjoyable read. Compared with "American Pastoral" it is a much simpler story.

A slight diversion before discussing the book itself. I have just read "Oliver Twist" and it struck me, as I was reading "Snow in August" how similar

Michael Devlin is to Oliver Twist. Both were boys of unbelievably good character, both lacked adult protection, and both won against enormous odds.

I was warned about the strange ending of the book, however I found the ending to be a resolution, somewhat akin to the ending of a mystery, and not strange.

The mystery, to me, is did Hamill intend to write a novel or a fairy story—a fantasy? The early descriptions of Jewish life in Prague, wherein Michael seems to be totally absorbed, could be interpreted in either of two ways, and thus, the mystery. The first interpretation is that Rabbi Hirsch was such an accomplished storyteller that Michael was transported into the time and place—but only in his imagination. The second possibility is the simpler one in which the depiction of Michael's involvement is to be taken literally.

Thus the mystery restated: did Michael imagine the scenes in Prague or did he participate in them? The ending resolved the issue.

The story is a fairy tale with Golem as the hero. It is more cleverly written than, say, "Cinderella," but belongs to the same genre. This type of fantasy—having an all-powerful ally—is a common one among young boys based on my own experience and raising of sons.

The book renders a useful insight into Judaism. Coincidentally as I finished the book and started on a crossword puzzle, the clue for 17-down was "Automaton of Jewish legend." The forces of the supernatural are awesome! ☺

Sentencing + 146 days. My medication problem seems to be solved for the present.

I've been to two AA meetings. I don't feel as if I belong, but will continue to go and keep an open mind.

Barry's alarm didn't work so we missed breakfast. He is still fantasizing about a rapid receipt of his TV. From my experience with the system, I don't share his optimism.

Some tier cohorts moved onto the honor tier this morning.

Sentencing + 147 days. The snow was a surprise this morning. A few forlorn and lost seagulls were fortunate because the blanket of fresh snow highlighted scrapes of food thrown by inmates.

Did you read the newspaper article about the "After Prison Ministry" run by a local church? It was reported that the recidivism rate among released inmates is 80%! If true, how can it be claimed that the penal system works?

I'm not going to gym or AA today because I have a hold-pass for the heart clinic. A hold-pass means they can call me at any time and I have to be available to respond. I have to prioritize and I don't want to provide an excuse for not monitoring my blood pressure. If I miss two consecutive AA meetings I'm taken off the list, so I have to go next week.

Later: Just returned from the heart clinic—140/90, if I believe the results. I talked with the supercilious physician about my hypertension medication and the difficulty I had on the outside achieving a witch's brew that worked. He maintained that physicians on the outside are pill-pushers who are paid by the pharmaceutical companies to prescribe their products—*"If a doctor writes a hundred prescriptions, he gets a golden pen."* I complained about the infrequency of measurement and quoted the recommended schedule. The conversation became acrimonious and I left him holding the field when he declared, *"In here, I make the rules."*

I signed off on the Zoloft—I will no longer receive it—so the sparrows will have to look elsewhere.

I bought Tang for the vitamin C. I enclose a copy of a letter.

Dr. Goldstein:

Thank you for your professional help, understanding and sensitivity immediately before my sentencing for crimes to which I plead guilty. The judge sentenced me to nine years—all except 2½ suspended. My whole family and a large cadre of friends have been supportive and I will weather this ordeal. I will also control my behavior in the future and anticipate getting therapeutic help.

I have an appeal and a parole hearing soon and hope for a reduction in my incarceration time. Currently, I expect to be released in ten months.

I'm in prison at the Rochelle State Prison. The quality of medical care herein—purported to be the best in the state penal system—causes me concern.

I self-terminated my anti-depressant medication and feel fine.

My hypertension medication is currently 30mg of Procardia three times a day. I don't know if it is working or not. Presently they measure my blood pressure every three months. I asked that they monitor more frequently. When last measured, an electronic sphygmomanometer indicated 172/93. The nurse immediately proclaimed the instrument defective and used a cuff and stethoscope and reported 138/88, which I couldn't verify. I confess that the environment promotes paranoia. This incident also convinced me that requests for more stringent monitoring would not yield credible results.

> *Do you know of any external monitoring of penal medical services? When I attempted to discuss the quality-of-care issue with the physician herein, he demeaned my previous medication regimen and stated that outside physicians were pawns of pharmaceutical companies.*
>
> *He also asked me what symptoms I had from hypertension. This must have been a trick question. At any rate, I'm stuck with what I have and I hope it won't last much longer.*
>
> *I'm sending a copy of this letter to my wife and to my attorney, Mr. Herb Diamond, with whom you may correspond as you wish.*

Sentencing + 148 days. I'm fighting to keep my spirits up. I'm winning the battle, but the war takes unexpected turns. I sometimes feel like a cornered animal. I want to scream about the injustices and inhumanity. I want to write vituperative letters and file complaints—and this predilection is increasing. Yet, I fear that any action will redound. All of the grievance procedures initially rely on the local system—the very system that is being accused. Why should it be trusted?

Hope and optimism flows from the image of the future—the good times to be shared. When those times come, these times will seem a distant nightmare. I think of extremes—the Holocaust and its survivors. Did the victims have hope? Can they get beyond what happened to them? How did they survive and live from day-to-day?

Some inmates immerse themselves in religion. The Christians have Bible study sessions and engage in endless argument about the meaning of obscure scriptures. The Muslims gather around a local guru for enlightenment. I will admit that they gather hope. They believe they are saved and their life has a purpose and meaning. They get what they need to survive the day. If for no other reason, religion is valuable for them for that alone. I envy them for the ease with which they garner hope and peace.

Sentencing + 149 days. Miracles! I was called to the dispensary and 1) given my medication <u>without</u> asking for it and 2) given an EKG. I don't believe either was a response to my tête-à-tête with the physician. I would like Dr. Goldstein to have the results. I enclose a medical release form. Could you please duplicate it and send me as few copies? They would give me only one. I, in theory, could get copies made at the library, but access to the library is so problematical (canceled the past two weeks) that I'd rather not rely on that avenue.

I had a good exercise period followed by Tang. My mood is good. Strange how it varies. Up for three days and down for one. Played chess. Won some—lost some.

Sentencing + 150 days. The sermon I read this morning was "On Being Forgiven." This title was the cause of my selection of Rev. Gray's packet of sermons. Wife—do you forgive me?

Sentencing + 151 days. According to my calendar, I'm to see the psychiatrist tomorrow. I hope it doesn't interfere with my 50+ gym. The gym is more important since I'm no longer taking the Zoloft and thus don't need the periodic evaluation as a justification.

The system is forcing all the cells to have a uniform furniture arrangement. Reason—who knows? For Barry and I, the new policy means we have to move a locker from the head of the bunk beds to the opposite wall. We'll lose storage space.

Sentencing + 152 days. I did get a hold-pass to see the psychiatrist, but I went to gym anyway. I either missed the call while I was in gym or the call never came.

No TV yet.

Sentencing + 153 days. In preparation for the parole hearing, could you please write the Parole Administration Department and state that I have a place to stay and financial independence? Before they issue a favorable opinion, I understand they check those details. Might speed the process. Should CC Herb to keep him informed.

I enclose a copy of a letter I wrote to Herb.

Dear Mr. Diamond:

Another update.

I'm off the anti-depressant medication and feeling fine. My hypertension medication supply problem seems to be solved. They did an EKG on me and I've taken steps to get a copy to my physician, Dr. Goldstein.

What is the probability of the appeal date being postponed? I'm preparing myself for such an eventuality.

I'm attending AA meetings here, but missed the last one because of a conflict with a medical appointment.

Regards,…

Sentencing + 154 days. When I returned to the housing unit after our visit, I was "interviewed" by the senior trustee, Andy, who has a cell on the honor tier and is looking for a cellbuddy. He's a middle-aged white man who's in for life.

I've told Barry of the possibility. I don't know much about Andy, but the allure of the honor tier is powerful. We'll see what happens.

I went to AA and picked up literature. I had not realized that AA is much more than a program of alcohol abstinence—it's a way of life. For example, they proselytize positive thinking and the worth and dignity of each human. What they preach, I've been doing—but I'll keep going.

Sentencing + 155 days. We still are upset about the proposed mandatory furniture arrangement. The arrangement makes access to the commode particularly difficult—the locker crimps one's knees during defecation. It must seem very insignificant, but it is so unnecessary that one believes it's merely harassment.

Retribution against complainers may or may not be real, but the fear of retribution is real. In order to circumvent the system, suppose I send you my letters of complaint. Outgoing letters are not read. You could then type them and mail them anonymously. The letters could not be traced. One could also CC various authorities and media. I need to fight against the insipience and cruelty and yet I worry about reprisals. The letters may not accomplish anything, but, at the least, they will help keep my spirits high. Outside attention to an issue is anathema to the penal system. What do you think? I enclose the first such letter.

To: Warden, Rochelle State Prison

The inmates in HU1 (and perhaps others) are being forced to adopt a furniture arrangement that has two major problems. An alternative arrangement addresses the expressed concerns of the COs and eliminates the problems with the proscribed arrangement. The problems are:

1) Most importantly, access to the commode to defecate is severely limited and requires awkward placement of knees and legs. This is inhumane.

2) The lockers completely cover the single AC power outlet.

By moving one locker next to the bunks, all problems are solved—including the stated need to have visibility into the cell from the outside.

Respectfully,…an Inmate.

Sentencing + 156 days. I had my pro forma interview with the psychiatrist this morning. Nothing new.

I'm not optimistic about the move to the honor tier. Andy's body language tells me that he's still looking. It doesn't bother me. In a relative sense, I'm comfortable and have a good cellbuddy. The possibility generated a flush of excitement, but I'm OK where I am.

Barry and I have rearranged the furniture for the third time in an effort to satisfy the COs and still have access to the commode. I expect that the new arrangement won't pass muster either, but we're trying.

Barry has a temporary cash-flow problem. I'll loan him money—as he did for me once.

A hundred and fifty-six days! Looking backwards, the time has passed fast. The appeal is in two months. Hopefully something good will happen. But, there could be a postponement—or a refusal. Played chess. Won all the games—boring! ☺

Sentencing + 158 days. I read the sermon, "I Am." It was the third of four and I've ordered the next set. I told them not to send the set in a three ring binder.

Sentencing + 159 days. No mail today, as is often the case after a weekend. I suspect the lack has something to do with the dynamics of sorting the larger volume.

Had morning 50+ gym. Besides the advantage of fewer people during exercise, I also have more options in showering

Sentencing + 160 days. I had birds come to the cell window this morning. They were obviously familiar with the geometry of the window and looked for crumbs at the base of the screen. I pushed bread through the screen, but not before they flitted away for plusher pastures. Other inmates must feed them as well.

The mail brought the receipt for the order of the TV and six other letters! Barry is upset because he ordered his TV before I ordered mine and we split the cost to expedite delivery and, yet, his TV is not yet ordered. I suspect that it has been ordered, but the receipt not delivered. We'll see.

Sentencing + 161 days. Went to the library. I returned "Oliver Twist" and checked out "The Great Gatsby" by Fitzgerald and "The Trial" by Kafka. I turned in my request, with trepidation, for a refill of my medication as well.

The birds have not returned. My breadcrumbs lie ignored. "The Birdman of Rochelle" is stillborn.

Sentencing + 162 days. A busy day. It started when I thought I heard myself being summoned, *"Report for TV test."* Wow, my TV is here, I thought, and it needs to be tested in my presence before delivery. I was excited. I reported and was told to roll up my sleeve. It was a TB test. Arghhh.

Brad and Harry came for a visit. I told them about the appeal hearing in two months and possibility of parole. I spoke about the spectrum of outcomes and indicated I was steeled for whatever would happen. I hope I believe it myself.

I walked across the compound four times—medication refill, newspaper pickup, visit and lunch. I'm on page 91 of "The Great Gatsby."

Sentencing + 163 days. For my sermon this morning, I read "Living Dangerously," the fourth and last of the packet. I'll return the set to you so you can return them to *The Church of the Larger Fellowship*—OK? The logistics of mailing packages is difficult herein. You will also have a chance to read the material if you wish.

Hope to have yard exercise this afternoon. The weather is unseasonably nice. My left knee has a throbbing pain—probably a mild ligament inflammation. I have so many restrictions on exercise; I hope my ability to walk isn't curtailed.

Finished "The Great Gatsby" and have started "The Trial" by Kafka. Have you read much of his stuff? I remember "The Metamorphosis" vividly.

Later: Had a great pain-free yard exercise period. I bought an ice cream bar with canteen tickets (available from the commissary).

Sentencing + 165 days. Kafka is a slow, but fun, read. For the past two nights, I have listened to the Walkman as I fell asleep. The headphones mute the ambient tier noise. I awake about 2:00AM and turn the radio off and remove the headphones.

Since I couldn't exchange the over-sized jeans for a pair that fits, I requested a replacement pair and alleged, on the advice of other inmates, that the zipper on the fly had broken. For each pointless rule, one must find a work-around.

Sentencing + 166 days. The result of my TB test was normal. No mail today. I'm surprised I haven't received the copied medical release forms. Did you mail them or are they caught in a mail problem? Did you send them with anything else?

I am on page 102 of "The Trial"—what a weird author. I had a hold-pass this morning and, hence, wasn't allowed to go to gym. The pass was to sign a release form to send the medical records to Herb. The system makes sure you are punished for each undeniable request.

Sentencing + 167 days. The mail today included the copied medical release forms. Thanks! Dianne sent me "Memoirs of a Geisha." Carl tried to send me sports cards, which are contraband. Inmates have been known to escape by building ladders from sports cards and then hold up liquor stores by flinging sports cards at the clerk. Does the Constitution say anything about the right to have sports cards? Anyway, the sports cards were returned.

Sentencing + 168 days. I'm sorry that our visit ended the way it did. I had to urinate. The rule that the visit ends if the inmate goes to the bathroom is, of course, a response to illicit drugs. Hopefully you can use the extra time. Some nights I have to get up five or six times.

Finished Kafka and started "Memoirs of a Geisha."

Sentencing + 170 days. The days are routine. Not much to distinguish one from another. I'm more depressed than I have been in a long time. Our short-ened visit initiated a downward spiral. I suspect the medication is causing the uri-nation problem. I'll take the last pill of the day earlier.

I've lost most chess games recently. I'm sure my malaise is to blame, but the direct connection is not obvious. I seem to concentrate and focus as well as when I'm in a good mood. In the midst of a game, I don't think of much else than the game—yet, I lose. The human mind is unfathomable.

No TV yet.

Sentencing + 171 days. Last night I took my last medication before 6:00PM, and I reduced my nightly forays to two. I'll continue the experiment.

Did you read about the killing of the policeman who was acting undercover as a drug dealer? Of course, the killing of a cop is a cynosure and the full police force is mobilized to catch the culprit. Can you imagine the angst of the killer who thought he was shooting an obscure churl only to discover he had killed a cop? If the police had a reputation of pursuing the killers of a drug dealer with the same relentlessness as they do a murderer of a cohort, would last night's shooting hap-pened?

Sentencing + 173 days. My mood is improving. Lots of mail today. No TV yet, but it has to come soon. Had yard exercise today and I wore my Walkman. Wild onions are popping up. The birds flock overhead.

I appreciate your reluctance to participate in the anonymous letter stratagem and you've expressed your reservations well, but—(you knew there had to be a "but," didn't you? ☺)

As you say, the issues that concern me are miniscule compared to inhumane conditions of medical care, rehabilitation and job training. But those issues require changes in societal attitude and can only be affected by a lengthy political campaign. Immediate concerns to me, such as secondhand smoke, inability to receive earplugs, and placement of lockers in front of the commode are local and could be solved by the decision of a single administrator. Perhaps the results, even if the efforts are successful, are trivial, but there is the side benefit of having spirits lifted by having been engaged in a righteous cause—of being a paladin—of hav-ing a purpose in the day-to-day existence herein.

I'll give you another example of inane harassment. Each day, immediately before dinner, the COs conduct a "bar-check" of all cells. The inmates have to lie on their bed while a CO comes into the cell, checks that the bars are secure in the window, that the light fixtures haven't been dismantled, and that the lockers are in order. Barry and I usually have the lights turned on as we read. Some of the COs—not all—insist on irritating us by turning the lights off as they leave the cell. One of us then has to get up and turn the lights back on. The COs may excuse their behavior by attesting that they have to check that the switches work and haven't been tampered with, but if that's the case, wouldn't a more complete security check be made by returning the switch to its original position? We've also purposely had the lights off; pretending to nap, and the misanthropic COs then turn the lights on before exiting. It's a childish pitiful power play that takes advantage of inmates. I feel sorrow for the personality that must indulge in such puerile escapades.

Sentencing + 174 days. I have asked permission for you to mail me my prescription sunglasses. Don't send them, however, before the internal paperwork is completed.

I also need a catalog with men's summer clothes. If the appeal doesn't go well, I'd like to order walking shorts, a summer hat, light weight socks, and a couple of short sleeve shirts. I received notice that in three days I must start working in the kitchen on "sanitation." I must help keep the food preparation area clean.

I'm enjoying reading (on page 78) the next book club selection, "Waiting" by Ha Jin.

Sentencing + 175 days. Went to the library and got "The Gentleman in the Parlor" by Maugham. I thought I had read everything he had written so the find was a pleasant surprise. I'm almost finished with "Waiting" and will send you my comments.

No TV today.

I'm enclosing another anonymous letter. I hope you mail it, but your judgment, perforce, rules.

To: Warden, Rochelle State Prison

The Inmate Handbook dictates the rules for inmate behavior and states that if the inmate shows respect for the staff, the staff will return respect. CO Collins, who mans the reception desk in the dispensary during most dayshifts, capriciously disregards this dictum. (I may be mistaken about the name. The CO usually has his nametag hidden. He's white, middle-aged and bald.) He plays bestial games when doling out toilet paper to inmates who have to use the restroom during the long wait.

Without provocation, CO Collins accuses inmates of being malingerers and any innocuous question is met with inappropriate and unnecessary invective.

Respectfully,...an Inmate.

Sentencing + 176 days. I received another set of four sermons without any contraband. I also wrote the County Detention Center asking how to receive credit for the time served there. Any extra days at the end of the sentence will seem an eternity.

I'm not looking forward to the kitchen job. It will give me work credits that shorten my incarceration, but I worry about my ability to meet the physical demands of the job.

Sentencing + 177 days. The TV arrived and works! There is one cable outlet in each cell so if each inmate has a TV then a splitter is needed. Barry and I had bought the splitter and coaxial cables at commissary so we were ready. The AC adapter for the Walkman has the wrong connector, but I may be able to jerry-rig it

Later: It has started. I was walking in the yard when they called me to go to work. I went to the chow hall—six hours of mopping, wiping, mopping and wiping in the kitchen. My back is hurting and my left side is cramping. The motions are the ones the surgeon warned me against. I feel trapped and helpless. If I refuse to work, I'll be sent into isolation and receive no work credits.

On a happier note, I'm watching "Frasier" (a program of *my* choice) and it's quiet enough to hear without maximum volume. The Walkman AC adapter can't be made to work. I must've ordered the wrong one and will try again on my next catalog order.

I have finished "Waiting" and include my notes. The next selection, "Charming Billy," by Alice McDermott is a good choice. This job is a downer. Prison shouldn't be permanently debilitating.

Dear Book Club:
Re: "Waiting" by Ha Jin.

Achieving critical acclaim because of its depiction of life in Chinese society, I found "Waiting" to be notable for the depiction of masculine angst. The protagonist, Lin Kong, is caught between responsibilities to his wife, Shuyu, of an arranged marriage and his real love, Manna. Lin, in the face of the inability to resolve the pulls of his heart and the legal and cultural obligation to his wife, does his best—year after year—to do the least harm and achieve the best compromise in the emotional conflict for his persona. He continues to provide material support for Shuyu and their daughter, while he continues to share a modicum of life with Manna. His lack of love for Shuyu prevents him from sharing her bed. His love for Manna remains chaste since he refuses to risk sullying her reputation. The book illustrates the moral incubus faced by the archetypal knight-on-a-white-horse. If he strives to do well for all of the females to whom he owes an obligation, emotional or historical, the inevitable result is dissatisfaction for all. To achieve a degree of meaning and tranquility, emotional ties have to be cut else one form of waiting is transmogrified into another. The book teaches this lesson.

Sentencing + 178 days. I read a sermon "Loneliness" by Rev. Walker-Riggs. One great aphorism—*"The difference between solitude and loneliness is whether you like yourself."*

Had my second day on the job. Because there is no effective way to make an inmate take initiative or to have pride in their menial duties, there is a lot of goofing off. Consequently, there are many more inmates assigned to a duty than are required to do the job. The biggest spur is peer pressure, which works both ways. If you don't do your perceived minimal share, fellow workers castigate you. If you do more than is needed you are seen as soliciting special treatment. Thus, the lesson taught to the inmates by the penal system is *"Don't work hard."* Prison converts many who had a correctable transgression into persons unfit for a responsible role in society. It pushes people down further rather than lifting them up. Should the lust for vengeance create more victims? To paraphrase Trotsky, *"The vengeance of history is more terrible than the vengeance of a bureaucracy."*

Sentencing + 181 days. I respect your decision to rejoin the church. Their reaction to me will be interesting when I get out.

I've been on the kitchen job for four days. My physical reaction is not abating. In response to a sick-call slip, the nurse's aide said that the pain is probably due to inactivity since incarceration and offered me aspirin. She said there was nothing in my medical file concerning a back operation! I thought the process at Classification was to document all relevant medical factors.

I wrote the CO in charge of the kitchen and suggested I be given a job consistent with my physical condition. I enclose a note I sent to my case manager concerning the job assignment. The only explanation, I believe, for having me do sanitation work rather than helping teach is for punishment. However, many inmates would like to have my current job, whereas there are few who have experience teaching. It does not make sense that they can force me to do a job that causes permanent physical harm when there are others who want the assignment. In response to my complaints, I expect action soon. Perhaps they will put me in isolation and rescind my visiting privileges. If I am transferred to isolation, I can manage that. I entertain myself and can read books. All of this is a downer.

To: Ms. Keenan:

While at Classification, my history of a back operation and fusion of vertebrae was verified. The Medical Department here says that no such operation is documented in their records. If necessary, I can retrieve records from my physician, Dr. Goldstein, to further document this condition.

My current job assignment involves six hours a day of mopping, sweeping, lifting, scrubbing and overhead cleaning of oven hoods and is causing great pain, numbness, and cramping.

I respectfully request a job assignment consistent with my physical limitations and medical conditions.

Sentencing + 182 days. No news about the job situation. It is depressing.

Another inmate today told me a story. A few weeks ago, he believed that he was due for a parole hearing and eligible for a transfer to minimum security. He hadn't heard anything so he made inquiries of his case manager. He was informed that the parole process was backed up and no transfers to minimum security were being made without a psychological evaluations, for which there was an eight month (!) waiting period. In response to this information, he wrote letters complaining that the system was denying him timely process, etc. Today he had another meeting with his case manager and was informed that the parole process was caught up and that the psychological testing backlog was mistaken information. The case manager, whose job is follow the processing of each inmate, told him that <u>he</u> should have been more vigilant in following his own parole process.

Everyone in the system blames his or her own job performance inadequacies on the inmate. The inmate is an easy scapegoat because they are unsophisticated, uneducated, powerless, not credible, and, in the view of the public, ogres.

I enclose a copy of a letter I wrote to Herb.

Dear Mr. Diamond:

A situation has developed here that is troubling that may require legal intervention.

I've been assigned a job that involves lots of sweeping, lifting, and mopping for six hours per day.

They have scheduled a medical evaluation by the same medical staff who were responsible for the lapses in my hypertension medication. I have acrimonious interactions with them and this provides them a perfect opportunity to retaliate.

I fear they will judge me fit for the job—a job I may have to refuse to do because of the possibility of injury. I will then be subject to discipline.

What should I do?

I have indicated I will do any job within my capacity and have interviewed for a teaching assistant's job. I worry that the situation will degenerate in a way deleterious in the appeal hearing. Regards,...

Sentencing + 183 days. About the job, I've decided to do whatever is necessary to shorten my time in here, whatever the physical risk. I have heard inmates, most with long sentences, speak of escape and I understand the allure, but the inmates who escape go, perforce, to an entirely different life—a life of running, paranoia, hiding and looking over his shoulder. When I get out, I want the life I had.

I was called to have an EKG again. I asked the nurse, whom I hadn't seen before, if having an EKG every month was routine. She said that the last one was done badly by an inexperienced technician. She disparaged the medical staff. I talked to her a bit more about my hypertension medication and my back problems. She was quite affable and sympathetic, but said she's on a call-in basis, comes in rarely, and couldn't help.

Sentencing + 185 days. I wrote Health Services a letter. I enclose a copy.

To: Health Services Administrator

I was recently assigned a job in the afternoon kitchen sanitation effort. I have tried to do the job for four days and I cannot do the job. The job produces neck pain, muscle spasms and numbness of my left arm.

Twenty months ago, I had an anterior cervical fusion of vertebrae C5, C6 and C7. My physician advised me to avoid the use of shoulder strength—lifting, overhead work and repetitive motion because of the possibility of additional damage to neighboring vertebrae. My physician, Dr. Goldstein, can collaborate and provide X-rays, MRIs, etc.

I wish to appeal the initial evaluation that deemed me fit for this job. I'm CC'ing my attorney, Mr. Herb Diamond.

Sentencing + 186 days. A great visit! Now we know that the parole hearing will be in five weeks. No medical evaluation yet, which I interpret as a positive sign. Hopefully it means that they are not taking it routinely. It also gives the head of the Health Services Department more time to intervene.

Lots of mail today—five letters.

Sentencing + 187 days. The medical evaluation has not yet happened so I'm still obligated to go to work and things did not go well today. Today I was told to do mopping and I refused. I talked with a senior CO who told me that I had to do the work or be transferred to isolation. Life is hellish now. Lots of stress, anxiety and pain. So senseless.

Sentencing + 188 days. Some good news! I had a meeting with my case manager, Ms. Keenan, this morning. The parole hearing will be next week—not in five weeks! Maybe it will provide the solution to the bad job situation. Ms. Keenan said she had received your letter and described it as excellent and supportive. I am anxious to get Elgin's letter, detailing employment possibilities, in the file as well. Ms. Keenan said she'd call you to pursue that possibility.

No medical evaluation yet. Ms. Keenan said she'd try to get me out of the kitchen job. Surely, with all of these possibilities, something good will happen.

My mind is in turmoil over the parole hearing. Ms. Keenan was taciturn about her recommendation although other inmates have known beforehand the recommendation of their case manager. What does her silence mean? If the parole hearing goes badly what effect will that have on the appeal hearing? I understand that the parole board could recommend a transfer to a minimum-security facility. Should I welcome that outcome or will the judge, during the appeal, think I've received sufficient succor and not provide further relief?

I must not count the chickens before they hatch. The most likely result is nothing.

Sentencing + 190 days. Because of our visit, I missed the "MMPI," (a psychological evaluation test, one and a half-hour long) given no doubt in preparation for the parole hearing. Visits are given the highest priority. I'm not sure of the implications for the parole hearing.

Sentencing + 191 days. Barry got his TV! Ironic that we paid for the expeditious delivery of his and mine arrived first. For Barry it means that he can now watch Jerry Springer—which I can't stomach.

I couldn't get to the telephone or shower this morning.

Rochelle State Prison, Housing Unit 1, Tier B, Cell 33.

Sentencing + 192 days. Egad, they moved Barry out of the cell and into the medical unit. I suspect the move was in response to a slight fall, observed by the COs, that Barry had on the stairs. His hip gave way, but he caught himself on the railing before collapsing. After Barry moved out, I was told that my new cell-buddy would be a young black man. The clerk of the housing unit (another inmate) told me was a "nice guy." I inquired if it was possible that Sam, a white middle-aged guy, from the Commons could be moved in. I don't know Sam and my only rationale was that the demographics were better. The clerk said he'd check on it. Ten minutes later, after a presumed consultation with the COs, he returned to say I could move into cell 33 with Ben Watson, if I wished. Ben is a quiet hippie looking white guy. I have spoken to Ben twice and certainly don't know him well. Ben's cellbuddy was moved to segregation yesterday because he had filed an OCF against the tier sergeant. I knew little about Ben, but I knew nothing about Sam or the young black guy, so I opted to go to cell 33.

I got the lower bunk. Neither Ben nor his previous cellbuddy had a TV so Ben welcomed me. Cell 33 is further away from the rec area and so is much quieter. It is also closer to the telephones.

Barry was unhappy at being forced into a different cell. We had a good routine worked out and were compatible. However, in the medical unit he has freer access to telephones and showers—a major plus for him as he tries to keep his family together.

There is such enormous turmoil in my life at the moment—the horrid job, the parole hearing and the cell change—that I'm surprised I'm still sane (or am I?). I'll see Barry seldom now. He's in a different housing unit and our paths will cross infrequently. He and I shared several months. In this hostile environment, he was someone I trusted. I'll miss him.

Sentencing + 193 days. No medical evaluation. I enclose a copy of another note. Do they go into a black hole?

The lieutenant CO in charge of the kitchen sanitation detail has told the other COs not to force me to mop or sweep. Of course, the other inmates will think I have received special privileges because I'm white or politically connected or rich or educated or older or whatever their imagination can conjure. If the system had never put me into this situation, it would've been easier for all concerned. I now worry about being set-up.

Ben is quiet and easy to get along with, however he does smoke. He asked me if the smoke bothered me. I indicated that it was not pleasant. He smokes by the door so that the breeze, when present, blows the smoke out into the tier hall. I hope I'm not here much longer.

Ben attends GED classes all morning and I work during the afternoon, so we don't interact much. Barry and I poked fun at each other, which helped relieve the tension of cell life. I don't think Ben and I will be able to do that—different personalities.

I'm still not sure when the parole hearing will be—sometime this week. The parole hearing is the light at the end of the tunnel—even if it is a mirage.

To: Health Services Administrator

Following the process that is recommended on page 43 of the Inmate Handbook, I recently submitted an informal request. I have not received a reply nor have I received an evaluation of my physical fitness to do my assigned job. My file, as substantiated by my case manager, Ms. Keenan, clearly indicates a history of back and heart problems.

My assigned job causes me great pain and discomfort and has the potential for causing permanent physical harm. I have volunteered to furnish x-rays and MRIs. I can also furnish statements from my physician, neurosurgeon and orthopedic surgeon. I am quite willing to do a job I'm fit for.

Sentencing + 194 days. I had the parole hearing. Only one commissioner and my case manager, Ms. Keenan (who remained silent), were present, beside myself. The overweening commissioner directed the hearing in a sardonic tone. Surely a sham. They are legally required to hold the hearing, but they don't have to make it relevant. I'm glad I didn't get my hopes up. I do have the right for an appeal.

I got a reply from the director of the Medical Department in response to my request to be medically evaluated for fitness for the sanitation job. His reply was,

---

"I have reviewed your letter. Unfortunately, once you have been medically cleared to perform a job, that status remains unless there is a change to your condition. There is no documented change in your condition or any indication by you stating any change in your condition. Consult with your case manager to resolve this issue."

In other words, if they make a mistake, that mistake must manifest itself in injury or harm before any corrective action will be invoked. Unbelievable, *"…absolute power corrupts absolutely."*

So, nothing good happened today and a couple of edifices of hope proved to have false foundations. I must work on my positive thinking exercises.

Sentencing + 195 days. The parole hearing—being asked all of those questions again—and then having the door slammed shut caused resentment, frustration and anger. If the appeal goes as poorly, then I'm only a third of the way through. All until now has been prelude. The real imprisonment, with this debilitating job, has just started.

I miss Barry. I didn't realize how much of a friend he had become. I trusted him and we had cell-life worked out. Things were comfortable. Ben will be OK, but the whole relationship has to be worked out. I fear that he doesn't have outside support and will be "borrowing" all the time. Maybe not.

Sentencing + 196 days. I'm sorry for the weepy visit. You were a tower of strength. Had exercise in the yard. I was able to walk and think. One can see deer in the distant forest. Large cumulus clouds threatened from the west. Saw Barry.

Other inmates tell me that when I go for the appeal hearing that I will leave here at 2:00AM and be taken through Classification with no hot meals or sleeping space. If true, this will double the length of the trip. Sounds horrid.

Rumors. I hear that my cellbuddy, Ben, wants to move in with a friend. I'm trying to locate someone to move in with me if that happens.

Sentencing + 197 days. Negative feelings and thinking have flooded me. Things like the job, the polemics with the Medical Department, the failed parole hearing and the cell changes are dark clouds. When I am open to the positive, I find it. I now have the TV, which is a godsend. I have adequate reading material—which seems trivial until I remember Classification where there was none. I have a deck of cards and a chess set. I have the love and support of you, our family and most of our former friends.

Another positive is the shortness of my time remaining. I'm starkly reminded of that when I talk to another inmate who has 8, 15 or 25 years to go. My worst-case scenario is another year. If I had a large amount of time, I'd minimize contact with the outside world, as many herein have done, and build a life in prison.

Cell 33 is close to the telephones and I can't avoid eavesdropping on many conversations. There's an enormous amount of misery and tragedy revealed. Some inmates, using the power of their personalities, try to force love to continue, force others to visit, force money orders to be sent, and so on. Can't they realize that a relationship can't be forced? Barry falls into that error.

Sentencing + 198 days. I'm feeling better and recovered from the depressed emotional state you saw me in the day before yesterday. Sam and Lucy were here yesterday for a visit. I managed to keep my composure. I asked them to tell you I was OK.

After work today, I showered by myself and the water was hotter than the usual tepidness. Having better access to showers is a benefit of the job.

I heard that Barry has been transferred from the medical wing to HU3. This makes no sense. In terms of medical accommodations, HU3 is identical to HU1, from which they transferred him. Was the whole move a ruse to get him away from HU1? If so why?

Sentencing + 199 days. I read a great sermon this morning titled "The Imperfect Life." The advice is given, *"If you can't fight and you can't flee, then go with the flow."* Boy, do I take that to heart!

As we walked to the chow hall for lunch today, there must've been a fight in HU2. Most of the CO's who monitor our progress on the sidewalk rushed off to HU2. One CO—short and a bit roly-poly—tripped and fell as he ran across the grass. He got up and took another five steps and realized he had dropped his baton and had to go back to retrieve it. Most of the inmates laughed and pointed. The scene was akin to the Keystone Cops.

Sentencing + 200 days. Lots of mail and a good walk in the yard. It's getting hot! I wore my Walkman and heard Beethoven's "Symphony #7." To add to the good, I beat Canfield for the first time in a long time.

Sam—the inmate who I had considered inviting into cell 15 with me when Barry was moved out—was put into "protective custody." Apparently he had borrowed from many people and owed too much. He feared retribution so asked for protection. I dodged a bullet.

Sentencing + 201 days. I had a meeting with Ms. Keenan this morning. She will get me out of the kitchen job, but stated that I must work at some job. I said, *"Of course. I have been trying to get a job in the Education Department."* I explained that I had a life waiting for me on the outside and I wanted to stay healthy enough to enjoy it upon release. She also said that the process to transfer me to minimum security has started. What job do they have for me? Which minimum-security prison?

I saw Barry today. He was some distance away and we didn't get a chance to talk, but he did indicate that he didn't understand the move to HU3 either.

A criminologist, in an article in the newspaper concerning supermax prisons, stated, *"There is no magic wand that makes decent people while incarcerated."* Why is it anathema to believe that most inmates *are* decent people who made a mistake? The characterization of people as decent or not is too simplistic. The stark division eliminates the need to think about each as an individual.

Sentencing + 203 days. No real news. Things to happen—the end of the kitchen job, the transfer to minimum and the MMPI test. Nothing has happened, but they will. If my sentence was longer, I would have to accommodate myself to the surrealism herein. The news that the appeal hearing will be in two weeks is welcome. I hope it isn't postponed. I'll try not to build up my hopes.

Ben is OK as a cellbuddy. He's not as articulate as Barry and is more of a recluse. Ben is tall—over 6'3" and thin. He's in his mid-forties, has a handlebar moustache and sad eyes underneath bushy eyebrows. His hair is often tousled. He doesn't interact with most of the inmates, whereas Barry liked the jiving and the bs'ing. Ben never asks for anything, and when I offer candy or stuff, he generally refuses. He hasn't had a visit since I moved in and has gotten no personal mail. He'll watch whatever is on the TV. He smokes by the door and does his share of cell cleaning. His offense was aggravated assault. He, while drunk, apparently beat someone. Banged their face into a car's bumper until it was pulp. I suspect that the tranquil exterior of many inmates disappears when booze or drugs hit their body and changes their personality and demeanor.

Sentencing + 204 days. A day off from work. What do I do? Play chess? Stay in the cell and read and write? Watch TV? Some or all of the above?

I had a good talk with Don Miller—remember the older educated white guy whom I hope to share a cell with? He's about eight months from being released and was offered a transfer to minimum security. However, he refused. He said it's like a dormitory and he prefers his current privacy. The transfer would also disrupt his job and he'd lose time credits. He may have a point. So many rumors—so little information.

Sentencing + 205 days. I got my monthly paycheck stub—$20.75! As I was being frisked as I left the kitchen the CO said, *"I guess you'll soon be going to another job."* Maybe something will happen.

Sentencing + 206 days. I intended to go to yard exercise today, but when I got to the rec area (where we assembly before being leaving the housing unit) I discovered I had left my ID in the cell. The rules state that you must always have your ID with you, however if you're merely on the tier it is never enforced. So, I missed exercise on a beautiful day because I couldn't leave.

Sentencing + 207 days. An inmate in HU6 overdosed last night. He was found dead in his cell. The rumors are that the COs bring in the drugs and are paid by outside contacts of the inmates.

How is a warden evaluated? How would you rank the following criteria: 1) the recidivism rate of those released, 2) the level of violence inside the prison, 3) the number of inmates enrolled in educational or job training courses, 4) the number of escapes, 5) the cost per inmate of the incarceration, and 6) the number of suicides? These criteria are not independent. Cost per inmate could be minimized if starvation was the norm. I suspect that escapes are the most egregious blot on a warden's record.

Recidivism, no doubt, depends on the education and job training. The level of violence depends not only on the inmates, but also on the "triggers" that the system supplies (remember Attica).

What changes to the current system would ensue if wardens were evaluated solely on the recidivism rate? Such a policy should enjoy public support. With a low recidivism rate, the penal system could be viewed as producing productive members of society and therefore having a positive role. Allowances would have to be made for the different security levels (minimum, medium, maximum, etc.) of incarceration. I found out that Barry was transferred out of the medical unit, which also houses inmates held in isolation, because his cell was needed to house an inmate caught selling syringes. There are a limited number of medical/isolation cells and they prioritize their occupancy. The inmate had a job in the dispensary, stole the syringes and resold them for $10 each. So the rumor goes.

Sentencing + 208 days. I got your lovely card yesterday. This experience has made us realize how much our relationship means. It has been strongly tested and has endured. My most anticipated event when I get out is being able to be with you—in our home, going out to eat, grocery shopping, walking in the park. Each moment we will spend together will be precious.

I've sent notes to both the Psychology and the Education Departments stating that if I know when the next MMPI test is scheduled I'll make sure that I have no visitors that day.

The weird routing of your last letter through the Midville prison might be an indication that my next destination will be—however Midville is also a medium security site—not minimum, so I have no explanation.

I entered the Rochelle chess tournament, but hope I'm not here long enough to participate.

I got a pass to pick up a refill of my Procardia. That process seems to working OK. I wonder what my blood pressure is?

Sentencing + 209 days. Good news! I'm no longer working in the kitchen. I'm on a standby list for tier sanitation. I continue to be paid and earn work credits but don't actually work until there's a vacancy. Tier sanitation is not a difficult assignment.

Barry hates HU3. He says there is lots of racism and hatred. He'd like to come back to HU1. I'm not optimistic about his chances. Inmates can move from tier to tier within a housing unit with the permission of a single sergeant, but from housing unit to housing unit requires the approval of two lieutenants.

The yard was closed today for maintenance, so exercise was in the gym. It had been awhile since I had a good walk, so I went. I wore the Walkman. I listen to music at every opportunity.

Sentencing + 210 days. I learned that the MMPI test will be given tomorrow. I've called Phyllis to get word to you so that any planned visits can be curtailed. I want to get the test done so that there's no impediment to a transfer if offered. One more week to the appeal hearing.

I finished "Charming Billy." My notes are included.

Dear Book Club:

Re: "Charming Billy" by Alice McDermott.

My biggest difficulty with the book is illustrated when I try to state what I learned from the book. (One is supposed to learn something from a book, right?) Among candidates are:

1. It's bad to be an alcoholic.

2. Being jilted by an early love affects your life.

3. Most Irish are alcoholics.

4. Alcoholics affect all around them.

5. White lies are unproductive.

Each of these candidates is trite. Where's the profundity in the book? I view it as a personal failing when I don't appreciate a book that has garnered much acclaim.

On the technical level I found two irritations:

1. A mish-mash of characters is thrown at the reader in the beginning at the wake, with no character development.

2. The voice of the book—indeed the gender of the voice—isn't identified until after page 42. Rather late for the reader to form a connection.

Sentencing + 211 days. I took the MMPI test this morning so that is done.

I'm watching a travelogue about an Alaskan cruise—Ketchikan, Juneau, Sitka, salmon bakes, gold mine tours, and helicopter trips to glaciers. I imagine us there.

Sentencing + 212 days. My current insouciance attests to the oppressive nature of the kitchen job. I'm relieved to have escaped that hell.

Ben and I are going to switch laundry days next week, so that my clothes will be clean when I pack for the trip for the appeal hearing—assuming the appeal happens. Jose—the friend from the Commons—had an appeal hearing last month. His result—no reduction at all—is a warning. Apparently, there is no opportunity to sleep during the night before the appeal hearing. The trip starts at about midnight and the inmate is bussed to Classification where he waits until buses leave for the various counties. No hot meals, showers or beds are provided. The inmate must appear to be a bedraggled bum to the judge. No wonder so few hearings are successful. The same process on the return journey.

In the afternoon before the trip, an inmate's personal property is inventoried and boxed to prevent pilferage. When he returns, the sealed boxes are returned.

Is the trip purposely made arduous to discourage actions that result in court hearings? I've become very cynical about the system.

I missed yard exercise again because of a forgotten ID. My subconscious—anticipating the possible release—is playing tricks on me. I also patted my hip pocket twice in the last week checking for my wallet, which I haven't carried in seven months.

Sentencing + 213 days. I saw an inmate smuggle a spoon from the chow hall today. Because of the possibility to create a shank from a spoon, a CO dispenses them individually and each inmate must deposit one when exiting. The smuggler merely rose from the table after having gone through the line once and went through the line a second time. Thus, he had two spoons and after depositing one, had one left.

I watched "Pretty Woman." Nothing like a romance story to make me think of you.

If the appeal hearing goes poorly, I suspect I won't get a chance to speak to you. I'll be hustled in and out.

Sentencing + 214 days. A great visit. We lack something to talk about at times, but we never fail to fill the time. I've started reading "The Chamber" by John Grisham. Seems appropriate. ☺

Sentencing + 215 days. You will get this letter after the appeal hearing and as you read these words, you'll already know the outcome. Whatever the outcome, I'll be OK. If there's no action, I'll be disappointed, but the worst part is over. I have a good cellbuddy and feel safe. I'm out of a terrible job. I know the routine. I have books, crossword puzzles, chess games, a newspaper subscription and a TV. My medication seems finally to be in order and I have opportunities to exercise. I can telephone and exchange mail. Things could be much worse. If the outcome is good then I'll be with you sooner and that will be infinitely better than the best herein.

Sentencing + 219 days. Thanks for the beautiful visit yesterday. It was the only good thing about the last two days. Your are a stalwart of understanding and support. I now have to accommodate myself here. The parole hearing—the appeal hearing—both proved to be barren hopes that are now behind us. Nothing remains before us except to let the sentence run its course. Even though these "lights-at-the-end-of-the-tunnel"—while portentous—gave something to live for—a reason to get through the next month, the next week, the next day—the crash after the refusal is devastating. I feel that both hearings were pro forma required by law and no other outcome was possible.

I received my medication refill—the 10mg tablets, but not the 20mgs. They may come in tomorrow. I doubt it. I predict another snafu.

I played chess against "middle" players. Won all. There are three of us at the top and, depending on moods, each of us is capable of winning against the other two. The three of us generally win the vast majority of the games against the middle strength players. It passes time.

Tomorrow is the start of catalog ordering. Since I will be here for a while, I'll order clothes.

I received my boxes, and unpacked them. The TV works! ☺

I got beautiful letters from Jessie and Dianne. My chin quivers and my eyes weep at the thought of their effort to help and support me.

Sentencing + 220 days. I heard the rumor that Ms. Keenan, my case manager, has been reassigned to HU4. I don't know if that's good news or bad. She knew me. Now, I must get to know her replacement. I don't know what this does to the possibility of transferring to minimum-security. I've written her a letter—a copy enclosed. My current plan is to accept the transfer if offered—let a miracle happen, but I view it as a risk because I'm comfortable *in situ*.

I got the rest of my medication refill.

I finished, "The Chamber." It gives a good feeling of the issues of capital punishment. Its depiction of prison life is realistic.

Could you send me a good paperback dictionary?

I've written the Education Department stating that I'll be here awhile longer and would still like to have a job.

Exercise in the yard today. I need it. Till later.

To: Ms. Keenan:

First, thanks for your help in the transfer from the kitchen job. I feel much better.

Second, no change was made at my appeal hearing, so I'm here for the duration.

Third, I've heard that you have been transferred to another housing unit. If so, I hope you'll forward this appropriately. If so, I regret the loss of the ability to talk to you. I feel that a trust was developing between us—a rare commodity herein.

I know that you were working on a transfer to minimum-security for me. After talking with other more experienced inmates, I have several questions and concerns. I understand that some inmates have opted not to go because of concerns of personal safety and property security. Any insight?

Also, how long does one stay in minimum-security before being released to a prerelease center? I was also told that having an outside job is a possibility while in minimum-security. Is that true? What is the relationship of "prerelease" and "work-release?" I'm trying to inform myself so I can make the right decision. Thanks for any help.

I'm also applying again to the Education Department to be a tutor/teacher's aide. Even if it's on a volunteer basis with no pay or good time credits, it's something I'd like to do. I believe I have the ability to help other inmates and would like to do so.

Thanks for your time and attention.

Sentencing + 221 days. I have about 30 minutes before yard rec period. Walk my three miles again.

I heard a nice piece of music by Franz Schubert—the "Guitar Quartet" with a flute, viola, guitar and cello. The announcer said it's the only piece Schubert wrote for such a combo. It almost qualifies as a flute concerto, the flute having the melody and theme.

Could you please send me my prescription sunglasses?

My new case manager's name is Ms. White.

Sentencing + 222 days. I've caught up on my letter answering. I asked CLF for more sermons.

Sentencing + 223 days. I have a surprise for you tomorrow when you visit. I got a drastic haircut and trimmed my beard. I should appear less shaggy.

I heard Dvořák's 12th string quartet, the "American," last night—familiar and lyrical.

Sentencing + 224 days. Another great visit. The parole pass was just to officially inform me of the result and appeal process. I do plan to appeal since there's no harm in doing so, but have no hope of any change. I want to make two points. First, they cite judicial leniency. My retort is that the judge knew more about the case than they know and he is in a better position to determine what is fair. Second, they suggest I continue the therapy sessions. What therapy sessions? There are no therapy sessions. There could be if I was released to the community. I don't know the basis of this dictum.

I got a note from Barry. He's been moved onto the honor tier, and is much happier.

Played three games of chess against a strong player and won all. If chess is a litmus test for Alzheimer's, I'm OK.

Sentencing + 225 days. I had a talk with my new case manager, Ms. White, this morning. After a favorable psychological report a committee of four (case manager, housing unit lieutenant, work supervisor, and case manager supervisor) decide whether to recommend a transfer to minimum-security. The recommendation then goes to the commissioner for approval, which takes about a month. The transfer is to the next available bed—no choice is possible. She also said that she couldn't help the application to the Education Department.

I don't want this episode to be the leitmotif of my life. I've done much good—fathering, all the volunteer work for the church, the professional achievements, the help given to friends—and I don't want it to be forgotten. It is sad that those few friends who abandoned us overlook so much of my life. It is hypocritical for the church to distance themselves from us given that when they had a need, we were there for them. Now that the situation is reversed and we need them, they are remote and standoffish. Maybe it's a church only for saints or for those who don't want to be bothered by intramural failures. Perhaps they are capable only of providing lip service or money to noble causes and don't want to get involved in the nitty-gritty. I acknowledge there are supportive individuals whom we have met in the church, but they have acted as friends independent of the church.

Sentencing + 226 days. A rare event—I got up for breakfast! Pancakes and oatmeal. I'm going to skip lunch. The menu is not a favorite. A telephone was available this morning, but both you and Carl weren't home.

Sentencing + 227 days. When I awoke this morning, my left big toe was sore as hell. I suspect it's nothing other than an inflamed tendon. I'll take aspirin.

Sentencing + 228 days. I got a letter from the County Detention Center stating that to get credit for the time there, the judge would have to modify the sentencing order. I suppose that Herb, as my attorney, has to write the appropriate motion. It's only a few days, but a few days delay in being released will seem like an eternity.

I got a note from Barry. He is depressed and going through hell because of the turmoil with his wife and kids. I urged him to seek counseling. I wonder if I should alert the psychological staff?

Sentencing + 229 days. Mood is good. The days seem identical. I got "three-hours" worth of mail today—took three hours to read it. My catalog order has been mailed. I got the notice of the withdrawal from my account.

I notice, from a review, that Etzioni discusses "personal privacy" in his latest book. Barry and I once discussed the inherent right to privacy. We went into the rat hole from an argument about gun control. To Barry, the right to privacy was as natural as the sun rising. I grant that our culture has made privacy an inalienable right, but I can envision a culture where a desire for personal privacy was anti-social. Anyway, I'm glad that my skepticism wasn't sophomoric.

Sentencing + 230 days. Don Miller has been moved to the honor tier. My (our?) plans to share a cell never come to fruition. We also have never been able to develop a camaraderie that I had hoped for. The demographics seemed right. I sense that he has his guard up against any form of familiarity with any inmate. Perhaps there is a well-founded reluctance to forming what could be perceived as a clique. I would like to be his friend. I'm happy for his move.

I'm on page 123 of "Necessary Losses." A welcomed break from fiction. I wish I could discuss certain points with you as I read them.

Sentencing + 232 days. Thanks for the visit. I love our time together—the hugging, the talking. Do you worry about us learning to live together again? Will you tolerate another invading "your" space?

I'm at page 205 of "Necessary Losses." The author is regurgitating sophomore psychology. What did you think of the chapter on marriage? A deficiency of many psychological treatises, that develop a technique for discovery of the origin of a problem, is the lack of guidance for reparation. Is there a theorem that the understanding of the genesis of a problem is tantamount to curing it? I'm reminded of the brouhaha when Hillary offered explanations, in terms of childhood experiences, of Bill's behavior only to be castigated for making excuses. The soft sciences are so soft.

A friend received notice from the parole board that he'll go to prerelease in six weeks on a "delayed release"—a stratagem that is not documented anywhere that I can find. Information control.

Sentencing + 234 days. The days are the same—one to another—each to the other. I had a good walk in the yard today. Walking, under the sun, around the path is similar to being on a rotisserie. I'm getting a good tan. I have finished Judith Viorst's "Necessary Losses" and include my comments.

Dear Book Club:
Re: "Necessary Losses" by Judith Viorst.

I find it surprising that the author, who had a successful writing career, embarked on a new trek and studied psychology for six years. I suspect underpinnings of a midlife crisis.

The unique perspective offered in the book is that the stages and relationships of life are a sequence of losses that are endured to grow emotionally and psychologically. The author does a good job in developing that perspective while regurgitating "Psychology 101."

A few chapters offered me clearer insight while others seemed mundane. The chapters I enjoyed were those on marriage, aging and dying.

Chapter 13—Love and Hate in the Marriage State—was good. I wonder if all of the significant relationships we have in life—siblings, parents, spouses and children—have a hate/love component? I'd vote "yes."

But the hate facet is wrongly assigned. One loves one's spouse. One needs one's spouse. The "hate" however is not directed at the spouse, but rather at the incompleteness of one's self. One hates the "need" for another. Similarly one loves one's children, but hates the impact that the children bring with them—the demands on time, the expense, the loss of freedom, etc. But, I digress.

The chapters on aging were especially relevant. I'm beginning to recognize new limitations. I can walk, but not run. I can no longer play tennis. I anticipate the day when my opinions will no longer matter because I'm "old."

I found the chapters on gender, identity, sibling rivalry and Oedipus complex to offer nothing new. Maybe this is a statement of my age.

I enjoyed the book and I know that in the future—as I face developments in my life—I will ask myself, *"What herein are Necessary Losses?"* We can't keep everything. To move on, we have to let go.

Sentencing + 236 days. The psychologist has been on vacation so there have been no transfer interviews.

They transferred an inmate off the tier to suicide watch. Some of his anti-depressant medication had been stopped. His family became concerned because of a telephone conversation and called the authorities. I knew him and played chess with him. I believe him endowed with a hair-trigger temper. He seems permanently angry.

He once told me that he didn't want to play chess with anyone else except me. My manner when playing chess is atypical herein. I don't brag or play verbal games. Most often, I play the whole game without saying a word. If I lose, I find something good to say. If I win, most often I say nothing. If I have played the opponent several times and feel comfortable, I may try to indulge in mutual analysis. This most often goes nowhere.

I finished another book, "Neanderthal" by John Darnton. It is unbelievable and farfetched at the end. The author was clearly in a hurry to finish the book. Events happen faster and faster the nearer to the finish.

What about visitors this summer? We could pay the airline tickets for your daughter—or any of the kids or your sisters. Would that appeal to you?

Sentencing + 237 days. I won't be able to return the books to you tomorrow during your visit. One learns to hate the system. Lazy bastards. I had submitted the paperwork in plenty of time and got no response. *They* blame everything on the budget—the perfect excuse. If there was enough money, someone could be hired to do the job *they're* supposed to do. I realize I'm irrational. It bugs me when I follow the rules and the process and because of *their* failure, it doesn't work. I'll try to cool down.

I received five letters today and had a good three-mile walk. Heard good music on the Walkman. There is good to be found.

Sentencing + 238 days. Thanks for the visit. I know you are busy and appreciate the time and effort you made to be with me.

My blood pressure was measured—133/88. While in the dispensary, I asked about receipt of prescription sunglasses. The doctor told me that the medical staff must first examine me for "light-sensitivity." Unbelievable. I've submitted the sick-call slip for such an examination.

I asked the doctor why two EKGs had to be done. He spent a moment flipping from one to the other and then, rather than admitting that the first one had been done wrongly, said that they were being extra careful with me. I have yet to hear anyone in the system admit that any mistake is ever made within or by the system. It's endemic. I wonder about the genesis of this attitude.

Sentencing + 239 days. I finally had the psychological interview. The psychologist was pessimistic and again claimed that the judge had been lenient. It amazes me that people—without the knowledge that the judge had—second-guess him and then feel it's their vigilante duty to do what the judge failed to do. The psychologist has invited me to join an ongoing informal weekly group therapy session. The MMPI results show minimal correlation to an alcoholic.

I also was called to the Medical Department to discuss my prescription sunglasses. Nobody knows what to do! The crotchety nurse asked me why I turned in a slip to receive a pair of sunglasses. I replied, *"Because the doctor told me to."* She said that that's not the way they do it. I pointed out that a normal-sighted person is permitted to buy plastic sunglasses from a catalog, whereas those of us that must wear glasses have no recourse, since clip-ons are not allowed. I'll, no doubt, have another meeting soon with them.

My weight is staying steady—in spite of the commissary junk food. I'm feeling well. My mood is good. I've resigned myself to spending eleven more months here. It could be much worse. Good things—honor tier, tutor job—can happen. I'm lucky in many ways.

Sentencing + 240 days. Looks like I will be able to return books and old letters to you on the next visit. The process is the one that the housing lieutenant said wouldn't work. The left hand doesn't know what the right one is doing.

Sentencing +242 days. A good visit. I'm glad I was able to return the books and stuff to you. I'm sorry that I had to tell you the bad news about the transfer. I'm always a bit down after a visit—anti-climatic reaction, I suppose—but it was a bit deeper today. The only remaining scenario is the worst case. Eight months have gone by and eleven remain. The past eight had many transitions—from County to Classification to Rochelle, from the Commons to cell 15 to cell 33, onto the kitchen job and off—that have helped the time pass. I worry that the next eleven will be filled with nothing except stagnation.

I just talked to the doctor's assistant about the sunglasses. I must be the first inmate ever to make such a request. The assistant is perfectly willing to grant the medical permission, but wants me to write the lieutenant in charge of the Receiving Department. So, the Receiving Department has referred me to the Medical Department who has referred me to the Receiving Department. I'm doing all that they ask. We'll see what happens.

In the mail today, I got a note stating that I can't return stuff to a visitor. So, I not able to do what I was just allowed to do. The lesson for the inmates is that chaos reigns.

Sentencing + 243 days. Had a good walk in the heat today. Felt good. I'm reading "The Client." Grisham has a knack for legal thrillers. They showed "Moll Flanders" on PBS tonight. I had started reading it at one time, but was interrupted. It has a shipwreck in it. DeFoe must've been obsessed by shipwrecks.

Sentencing + 244 days. Had a conference with the case manager this morning and found out that the psychologist recommended against a transfer to minimum. This surprises and shocks me because during the interview the psychologist indicated that <u>the system</u> would most likely prevent any transfer. He didn't at that time hint that he, himself, would be the agent of the system. Duplicity. Shortly after the interview with the case manager, I was called to the psychologist's office as a preliminary to joining the informal group therapy group. I told him I felt he hadn't been up-front and that I felt betrayed. I feel a breech of confidence in the psychologist and question his motives and his character. I don't believe he expected me to learn of his lack of a recommendation. I questioned him about the confidentiality within the group. He has no way of enforcing it. I opted not to join the group. My joining or not joining doesn't affect the worst-case scenario.

The mail was good to me. Three letters and a permission slip to receive the prescription sunglasses. Will wonders never cease? I'll forward it to you so that you can include a copy with the glasses when you mail them. Don't mail the original. It could "disappear" too easily and be impossible to replace.

I wrote Barry another note to raise his spirits, although, I must admit, if I were facing years instead of months, I'm not sure anything could prevent depression.

Sentencing + 245 days. After sleeping on it over night, I feel good about not joining the informal therapy group. I guess that you have reservations about the decision. We can talk about it.

Sentencing + 246 days. The visit was nice. Your disappointment in me for not joining the group was more than I anticipated. However, I still believe I made the right decision. You have to make decisions—and I have to make decisions.

I, too, was disappointed when you chose to shoot down the "blind-letter" idea, but I reconciled myself to your decision because 1) maybe I was wrong and 2) I can't dictate what you do. We are two individuals and part of our mutual attraction is that we don't always agree. We've disagreed in the past and we will in the future. We deal with our differences responsibly and in a mature manner. If either of us could completely control the other—we'd both be unhappy. I may be wrong in this decision. I don't think so. I believe I acted in our best interests.

I'm accepting that I will be here for another eleven months or so, and if I squint and focus, I can see a flicker of light at the end of the tunnel.

Sentencing + 248 days. I wonder what you are doing at this moment. Sipping coffee? Watering the plants? Stuffing laundry in the washer? Cleaning the birdcages? I talked to my brother David last night. Troy has sold his house in LA and will be moving to Wisconsin. David's son, Junior, and his wife, Marsha, are expecting a baby in six months. David will be a four-time grandparent and I have none. Troy and Sue haven't even had a kid yet and probably won't.

I listened to Saint-Saëns' "Violin Concerto #2" (in C-major, again!) and Haydn's Symphonies #6, #7, and #8 ("Morning," "Noon," and "Night"). I enjoyed them, but not enough to buy them.

I have yet to receive any more sermons from *The Church of the Larger Fellowship.* I'm disappointed. Maybe things just get slower this time of the year.

Sentencing + 249 days. I may have a problem with my catalog order. There is a limit to the number of trousers, shirts, etc., which one may have. They have an inventory of what one came in with and what one has received and if you go over the limit one must return some. This may just be inmate gossip. Nothing I can do about it now.

I received the dictionary. Thanks.

Sentencing + 250 days. An insidious part of being incarcerated is not being able to give in a relationship—only take. I feel that I'm taking and taking. I want to give. Not only to you but also to all who have supported me. Most inmates, who have a long sentence, have no outside contacts. I suspect that the inmate, himself, cuts the ties because the relationship is so one-sided. For example, I think Barry may be subconsciously sabotaging his marriage. It wasn't strong to begin with and he makes irrational demands—perhaps designed to drive her away.

I may have a self-induced lapse in my medication. I waited too late to request the refill.

Sentencing + 252 days. I discovered another benefit at the library. They have a variety of magazines. I had been so busy perusing the books that I hadn't explored further. I may try to get to the library weekly just to read the magazines, if for no other reason.

I got a note from the mailroom saying that my sunglasses are being refused because I didn't get prior approval! Arghhh! I wrote them back saying I had prior approval and the approval slip is in the package. Is this the system that is just and fair? They can't get even the trivial things right. Anyway, I mustn't let these things upset me. I worry that our only copy of the permission slip is in the package and will disappear. I worry that if, indeed, the mailroom finds a copy of the permission slip that retribution will be forthcoming. How dare I expose their ineptness? What—me paranoid?

Sentencing + 253 days. A cool night. I didn't sleep well. I wrote the lieutenant in charge of the mailroom asking for help in getting the sunglasses. He was the one that originally signed the permission slip.

I talked to the tier clerk. I'm 20th on the list for a tier sanitation job. He says it will take almost six months to get that far. I'm suspicious that a bribe is being solicited to accelerate the process. Hopefully I'll get a tutor's job before that. A tier sanitation job is not a difficult assignment—thirty minutes work each day. It does have privileges such as easier access to telephones and showers.

Sentencing + 254 days. I got my sunglasses and case! You were right in calling for instructions before mailing them. I must learn not to listen to other inmates. I find it extraordinary how small things can acquire an exaggerated importance herein. I remember Solzhenitsyn had a similar reaction. A button in the gulag was a treasure.

When I was returning from the mailroom, I met Barry on the walk. He had gotten his haircut and was on the way to a visit with his wife and kids. I hope he allows them to love him rather than trying to force the love.

I watched the movie, "The House of Yes" last night. Sort of a film noir. Ben couldn't understand it at all. Watching "Searching for Private Ryan" now.

I'll put this letter back in the locker and add words later. Then I'll mail it. Then you'll hold it in your hands—hands that I wish I could hold now.

Sentencing + 255 days. A boring day. Watched "Nuts" starring Barbara Streisand.

Sentencing + 256 days. There was a nice analysis of church attendance in the paper. I cut it out and mailed it to the Minister. It studied the demographics of congregations through history in America. Even mentioned Unitarians.

I watched "America's Most Wanted" last night. John Walsh became the paladin of the public effort to catch criminals because of the brutal death of his six-year old son, Adam. I am bothered by the polarization that the show engenders. Does Walsh ever consider that those he denounces and loathes—the scumbags, the cowardly creeps, the sleaze balls and the "bad" guys—were once a six-year old like his son? He and probably most police and prosecutors see only the absolute worst in people. I see inmates, some of whom must have done horrid deeds, doing admirable things. I question if Walsh and his cohort have any more compassion than those they condemn. I wonder what my attitude would be if one of my sons, Bud or Carl, when young had been murdered. I don't know, but I'd hope I wouldn't dive into the cesspool of hate and venom that Walsh lives in. Walsh rationalizes his vehemence as helping justice. I speculate that if the same efforts were made in preventing crime that is spent in catching the criminals that there would be fewer victims. As Thoreau said, *"There are a thousand hacking at the branches of evil to one who is striking at the root."* Is my view from behind bars clouded? I'm sure many would say so.

Sentencing + 257 days. I guess I have to ask you to e-mail *The Church of the Larger Fellowship* and check on my refill of sermons.

I've ordered an electric fan. One can get them through the commissary.

A sunny day for my three-mile walk. Made use of my sunglasses.

Carl would like to come out for a visit. Seems as if coordination with your vacation plans to Pinesburg would work. He could ride with you going one way or the other. I need to change my visitors-list to accommodate him.

A couple of new chess players have moved onto the tier. They play with their minds and not their mouth.

I enclose a copy of a letter to the editor.

To: Editor

Your story concerning home detention programs repeats an oft-made mistake, i.e., only reporting failures and not mentioning successes. What percentage of the sentences to home detention end favorably? No program is perfect and by concentrating only on the failures your reporting may do great harm.

In a bad airplane crash, many innocent people are killed, yet planes continue to fly and often, statistics are offered to demonstrate the safety of air travel. We should not expect greater perfection from social programs than we tolerate from technological ones. The failure of one individual or one plane should not condemn all. For many, home detention is appropriate.

Disclaimer: I am incarcerated and, if offered home detention, would be one of its successes.

Sentencing + 258 days. It was good talking to you on the telephone. I also called Bud, but he was on a business trip so I spoke briefly to Jessie. Tried to call Carl and got an answering machine. Same with Warren and Phyllis.

Sentencing + 259 days. Got my fan today. I also got a dispensary pass and a library pass. Busy day. The library pass is at the same time as yard exercise.

I've started reading Upton Sinclair's "The Jungle"—to fill a gap in my literary education. I worry that it will be depressing—the last thing I need.

Barry wants me to write Janice, his wife. I don't know why she's more apt to believe me than to believe him. He wants to forbid her to go to a nightclub with her friends. Control freak. I'll talk to you about it when you visit.

Sentencing + 260 days. I'm listening to "Scheherazade"—dreamy, ethereal and spirited. When I was young, it was the first piece of classical music that I thought was better than Hank Williams' crooning.

I'm enjoying "The Jungle." I like the sardonic style.

Sentencing + 261 days. I enclose a note from Barry to assure you that upon release you'll be getting a great cellbuddy. ☺

Ben has made a card that I'll mail to you. He's put a lot of effort into it. I think he wants to repay me for the popcorn and other stuff that I share.

Sentencing + 262 days. So many guys are in here because of bad decisions. Isn't the most important thing a parent can do for a child is to teach them to make good decisions? Seems as if that is a universal truth regardless of the talents and abilities of the child.

A popular view of child raising is to instill strict discipline and under that umbrella all the decisions are made for the child. When the kid eventually leaves home, they have no experience in deciding matters for themselves. How can a kid make a good decision at 18 (say) if they haven't made a decision at 16? A parent needs to start at an early age—say, 8—in letting the kid make decisions. The mistakes that a kid makes at 8—and mistakes will inevitably be made—will have much less significance than those made at 18. Making decisions is like bicycle riding: You can't learn by watching. You have to try it.

I've been trying to write poetry. Fills the time.

Sentencing + 263 days. Good morning. (I originally wrote "God Morning"—an interesting typo for a Sunday morning.) I tried to call you, but I bet you were showering. Hmmm, let me dwell on that image for a while.

My efforts at poetry induced thoughts about poetry. I remember classical poems from early classrooms such as Poe's "The Raven" and Tennyson's "The Charge of the Light Brigade." I compare them with modern offerings in "The Paris Review" and the literary supplement in the newspaper. At the risk of being plebeian, I detect a qualitative difference between the impact of the "old" and the "new." The older poetry was written for everyone—the shoe-salesman who read "The Raven" could be emotionally moved, be appreciative and, reflecting on his own ability, concedes being incapable of similar creations. The newer poems have evolved in quality to the extent that only other poets and literati can appreciate them. The shoe-salesman is largely unaffected by them and, upon perusal, sees no reason that he couldn't create something similar. Art has traveled an identical journey. Great representational pieces of the past such as "The Night Watch" by Rembrandt and "Morning in the Tropics" by Frederick Church were universally admired. The shoe-cobbler appreciated the art and acknowledged his inability to create such beauty. On the other hand, the significance of modern masterpieces such as Rothko's "Yellow Band" and Mondrian's "Composition in Red, Yellow and Blue" completely escape the grocery store checkout-clerk. The clerk sees the blotches of colors and feels perfectly competent to make similar arrangements. But, to the academically trained, modern art may represent an evolutionary step to be greatly admired.

To a lesser extent, there are traces of this tendency in prose as well. Michael Downing in "The Perfect Agreement" refuses to paragraph. Cormac McCarthy in his trilogy uses no quotation marks. Would such flaunting be tolerated in a manuscript submitted by a waitress? The unwashed believe they could also write, if unbounded by the rules of composition. The point I'm making is that the greatest difference between selected acclaimed past and present renditions of poetry, art, and prose is the impact on the hoi polloi. Today, poetry, art and some prose are created only for other poets, artists and authors. All of this has been said before. The thoughts fill the hours.

Had a good session of chess last night. My sunglasses were a welcomed relief during the walk yesterday. I enclose a copy of the letter I wrote to Barry and his wife, Janice. I hope it helps.

Dear Barry and Janice,

What a tough time you're going through! My wife and I have it easy compared with you. Our kids are grown and we live close enough to Rochelle to have frequent visits.

I wish I had magic words that would make it easier for your marriage and relationship to survive this ordeal. I know from our cell-talk that Barry wants it to endure. He sees a life together to be the goal that would enable him to get through the incarceration ahead.

The understanding couples share in a marriage varies greatly from couple to couple. Some couples have an "open" marriage; others have a strictly monogamous relationship. What works for one couple may not work for another. My wife and I lean significantly towards monogamy, but the one essential element is "trust." My wife and I trust each other's judgment far greater than we worry about our fidelity. We cannot control each other and we each, often, fail to do what the other expects. We view each other as a self-sufficient independent person who chooses the other to share life with.

I believe if Barry were assured that Janice and the kids would be there when he got out, he could be happier and not worry so much about her day-to-day life,

I believe if Janice could be assured of a loving faithful husband when he was released, she could show her support easier and more readily.

It is extremely difficult to build trust in the present separation. It's a goal you can share and work towards. It won't be easy. You will have to give each other, many times, the benefit of the doubt. Only the two of you can decide if the struggle is worth it.

With your future—and the kids—in the balance don't sweat the small stuff. And, Barry (you may not agree), I think going out with friends to a nightclub to be small stuff.

These words are only mine. I know little about your history together, so I could be wrong. Trust and Share.

Sentencing + 264 days. I got my library pass today. I didn't expect it for three more days. It again conflicts with yard exercise. An unexcused absence from library results in a suspension from library privileges for a month. I thought my library pass would always come on the same day of the week. Guess not.

Later: Never question providence. It rained and yard was cancelled. However, there was no rain during my trip to and from the library.

I finished "The Jungle." The last third of the book is proselytism for socialism. Not much plot, so one can scan it. Sinclair wrote the book as an epistle for socialism, but, instead, reformed the meat industry. He was surprised at the result. The legislative response was quick. The book appeared in 1906 and laws were passed the same year.

Two inmates that I know leave for home tomorrow.

Sentencing + 265 days. Commissary went OK. I bought sweat socks. Thin material.

I'm reading "All the Pretty Horses" by Cormac McCarthy. The style is a bit odd to the point that it detracts from the story. But, I'm enjoying it.

Sentencing + 266 days. As I walked today, I listened to Sibelius's "Symphony #1"—not as familiar as #5 but enjoyable.

Sentencing + 267 days. You're right—we have to start thinking about retirement. Where to put our assets. What can we live on? Will we, when I get out, be able to travel?

Sentencing + 268 days. My catalog order has not yet arrived. I did get my medicine.

I'm going to share some thoughts about beauty–specifically feminine beauty. Watching the lead actresses on some TV shows and my isolation, no doubt, has caused these thoughts to re-emerge.

Do beautiful women know they are beautiful? I suspect that most do. The question is complicated because of the lack of a universal acceptance of what is "beauty." I remember walking past beautiful women and although they wouldn't make eye contact, find a way to discover if I watched her. Others dress provocatively and then acted annoyed is you noticed them. I'm sure it was an act. It is also interesting to note the reaction of guys as a beautiful woman walks past. Some unashamedly and unabashedly stare. Others try to play it cool and make like they don't notice. The interplay of the sexes is amusing. Remember the ultimate purpose is the continuance of the species. The ritual and dance is so subtle that it is surprising that it is possible to get beyond the nuances and actually produce a kid. Why would a woman ever let a man impregnate her? What criteria does she use–an immediate animal magnetism or a long-term evaluation of prospects and stability?

Sentencing + 269 days. Slept well last night. I wore the Walkman all night. At one point PBS played a medley of Schubert themes, which included the theme from the A-minor string quartet. The familiarity awoke me. I'm on page 230 of "All the Pretty Horses."

Sentencing + 270 days. My catalog package came in. The walking shorts are a bit large, but will do fine.

I enjoyed the visit. I was amused at your attempts to get us moved to a more remote area of the visitor's room. As you discovered, even if there are only two inmates receiving visits, they and their visitors are placed next to each other while the rest of the huge room remains empty. That minimizes the work on the COs—the prime consideration.

I listened to the radio while you were driving home. Did you hear the "Brandenburg Concerto #5" followed by Copland's "Rodeo?"

Sometimes I talk and write about trivialities. Maybe I'm filling the silence, or telling you what is happening in my life and sometimes it's not much.

Sentencing + 272 days. They're painting the tiers today. No rec, no laundry. The schedule is messed up.

Sentencing + 273 days. I requested to return stuff to you in a week. See what happens. I showered and I swear that the water is much hotter in the summer. My laundry is done. Clean sheets, clean body and clean thoughts.

Sentencing + 274 days. Sorry you've been sick. If I had been there, I would've made chicken soup for you and taken *good care* of you.

Sentencing + 276 days. Not much happening. Had yard exercise and treated myself to ice cream. Spoke with Barry. The relationship with his wife is deteriorating, but he did get a good job as a clerk in the library. I envy him for that, but I'm glad something good came his way.

Sentencing + 277 days. According to my calculations, in the worst-case scenario (no more job credits), we're over halfway through.

I'm making myself a summer hat out of an old sheet. No scissors, but one cuts the material using an old razor blade. I made a bill out of cardboard and glued the sheet over and under it. It will be white and, thus, cool. It will be lightweight. I need protection against the sun while walking. I'm also designing a shower bag. Needs to be big enough to hold a towel. Creative busy work.

Sentencing + 278 days. Ben has a cold. He snored heavily last night and I didn't get much sleep. He says he feels better this morning.

Sentencing + 279 days. Got a library pass this morning, went to the library, and found it closed for maintenance. What's the saying about the left hand and the right hand? It's a cloudy day so yard should be cool.

Heard Hummel's "Concerto in B for Piano." Has nice themes.

From the food section, I'm enclosing a review of my favorite Cabernet. It's nice to know I have such good taste in wine, women and song. ☺

I finished my shower bag. Simple. Will launch it on its maiden voyage tonight.

Sentencing + 280 days. I've requested special visitation hours for out-of-state visitors. Routine, I understand.

In the mail I got a puzzle game called "Tangoes" from Jessie. It's more difficult than I would've guessed.

Sentencing + 281 days. Had a surprise visit from Brad and Walter. Enjoyed it.

I heard Tchaikovsky's "Symphony #4" last night. I much prefer his 5th. During the afternoon yard walk, I listened to Sibelius's "Symphony #2." Big expansive finish.

It was hot and muggy this afternoon and sweat dripped from my chin as I hurried around the track.

I got a note from the visitor's room telling me to see the housing lieutenant to get permission to return a package. We'll see what happens.

Sentencing + 283 days. Nice phone call this morning. I imagine you sitting at the table in your robe. The cup of coffee is to your right hand and the paper propped up.

I've written to the housing lieutenant asking permission to return a package to a visitor. I've written Ms. White, my case manager, asking how to get on the preferred job list, and I've written the parole case manager asking what happened to my appeal.

Sentencing + 284 days. Our cell is infested with little sugar ants. There is no effective way to control them except squishing them. Their number depends on the temperature—the hotter outside, the more inside. Any stray bits of food get massively attacked.

I went to the library. Checked out, "Pale Blue Dot" by Carl Sagan and "Web of Dreams" by V. C. Andrews. I'm going to write the librarian and see if I can get a job using my computer skills. Can't hurt.

Got the permission for the additional visits. Note that the Thursday visit is only approved for an hour. I enclose the permission slip. Remember to bring it with you in case of a problem.

Sentencing + 285 days. Surprise—my parole appeal was refused.

If Ben moves out of the cell to be with his friend, I have a possibility for a new cellbuddy. He's white, mid-sixties, and was a protestant Minister. His name is Paul Wilson. He's trying to reconstruct his marriage and gets a visit from his wife every two weeks. He doesn't like Jerry Springer (yeah!). His release date is in six years, but he has an appeal pending. Knowing that I have a compatible person moving in is a big relief.

Sentencing + 286 days. I haven't heard a thing about my request to return a package to you. I expect nothing will happen. Instead of telling me what to do, they just ignore my request.

Had a shower and fresh linen.

Sentencing + 287 days. I may have blown it. I can't believe I lost control like I did. An inmate is not to have any jewelry in the visitor's room. That policy is to prevent visitors from passing valuables to the inmate, which could then be used for barter. I was already upset about the screw up with the package return, so when they called me from my cell I forgot about having my wristwatch on. Even that wouldn't've been a problem if the regular CO had been at the desk in the visitor's room. The regular CO had in the past, on a couple of occasions, allowed me just to put the watch in the locker along with my coat. However, the substitute CO insisted that I return it to the cell, which meant a walk to and from the housing unit—a twenty-minute delay in initiating the visit. I asked him deferentially if I could leave it in the locker. He said, "No," and that he didn't want to be responsible for it. I told him I didn't care about the security of the watch and I trusted him. He demanded that I return it to the cell. That's when I took it off and threw it on the floor. I just lost control of myself. I thought I was imperturbable. Any display of anger or resistance to obeying an order from a CO can mean all sorts of reprisals. As soon as I threw it, I apologized by muttering something about frustration, retrieved the watch and said, of course, I'll return it to the cell. As I trekked across the prison compound and back, I fully expected them to deny me the visit. When I got in the visitor's room again, I made a lame joke by commenting about how time flies. I'm not sure it was heard or understood. At least we had our visit. There may still be repercussions. Nothing to do except wait and see.

After you left, I had a great walk in yard. Walked with a new inmate named Howard. He was in the Lincoln County Detection Center, awaiting his trial, for ten months because he couldn't make bail. He lost his company, his home and two cars. His wife rarely visits him and he tries to maintain contact with his eleven-year-old daughter. He had a public defender and received the maximum sentence—twenty years—allowed in the guidelines. I'm not sure of his crime. I didn't ask and he didn't say. He has a neurological disease and his medication, on the outside, costs $1000 a month. For four months (two at Classification) DOP hasn't given him anything. His symptoms involve uncontrolled movements and clumsy walking. He says it used to be totally controlled by medication. His emotional state is extremely low. His sentence isn't just prison time. His health may be destroyed. His business and professional life is destroyed. His family life may be destroyed. His financial well-being is destroyed. It will take a miracle for him to salvage enough to continue when he gets out. I don't know his crime, but his sentence is for life. Maybe it is justice—or a compounding of injustice. I'm lucky.

I see both Howard and Paul Wilson as kindred spirits and welcome their arrival. Maybe they can be the friends that Don Miller didn't turn out to be.

Good news! Ms. White, at my request, put me on the waiting list for the data processing workshop. This is an elementary introduction to computer technology. Since I failed to get in at the high end, I thought I'd try at the low end. I doubt that they could teach me anything new (after twenty years of involvement with computers), but while in the course, I'll get ten-days per month work credit.

The waiting list is about one or two months. If I get into the workshop in two months, I could be released in eight months! I'm not counting my chickens before they hatch—God knows I've been disappointed every time I've anticipated a good turn of events—but one searches for something to keep spirits healthy and hopeful. I hope there's no problem in getting the credit for the time spent in County.

I'm still worried about the watch incident. At lunch today, a CO pulled me out of the line and asked to see my ID. When I showed it to him, I asked if there was a problem. He replied that he was wondering where my watch was. I had left it in the cell. His remark doesn't make sense—why should he care where my watch is?—but it increased my paranoia. Mind games. I could've lost my visiting privileges for causing a disturbance in the visiting room and, with Carl coming specifically for a visit, that would've been a disaster. If nothing formal happens tomorrow concerning the event, I'll be OK.

Sentencing + 288 days. Nothing about the watch yet. I may be lucky and not suffer any consequences.

Had a nectarine for lunch. It was small, but the taste was novel and welcomed.

Paul Wilson's denomination, he says, is the "Assembly of God." He is conducting impromptu Bible study groups with the inmates in the rec hall and places all of his hope on God and Jesus. All is going according to a cosmic plan. I envy people who can escape responsibility for the past and place their future to a power beyond their own control. I'm reminded of the question that John F. Kennedy, Jr. asked of Billy Graham—*"Where does God's will end and our own freewill begin?"*

If Paul and I were to become cellbuddies, I suspect we'd have many interesting conversations. He doesn't actively proselytize, but is unrelenting in introducing religion into every conversation.

Sentencing + 289 days. Thunderstorms this morning brought a refreshing breeze down the tier. By the time I went to the dispensary to get my medication refill—which appears to be on schedule now—the sidewalks were wet, but the rain had stopped.

I learned more about the data processing workshop. It can last no longer than six months and lasts about seven hours per day. If I work fast and complete the course earlier than six months, then I'm kicked out and earn no more credits. So, my challenge will be to work slow enough that I get maximum benefit of all of the credits. Boredom might be a factor, but I'd rather be bored in front of a monitor than at the end of a broom. Two months reduction would be great!

The cell was treated for the ant infestation. See if the cure works.

Oh, Ben does tattoos. It's against the rules, of course. He wanted the power supply that I bought for my Walkman that didn't work. He can make a tattoo gun out of it, I guess. I don't want to know the details. I thought I could get an arrow-pierced heart on my left biceps inscribed with "WIFE." What do you think? Maybe on the buttocks is better? ☺

Sentencing + 290 days. The ant treatment has worked. A few stragglers remain, but the massive invasion is thwarted. Had a pleasant visit with Sam and Lucy.

Sentencing + 291 days. I had a good walk with Howard in yard last evening. His wife visits him infrequently and always unannounced. Creates a cruel tension. Got about two miles in before the rain started. The yard is going to be shut for a few days. They're doing construction work.

I wrote the Minister and said that if he ever does a pulpit swap with the local UU Church, I'd appreciate a visit. See what happens. I'm not optimistic.

Commissary tomorrow. I've been treating myself to a can of soda on Saturday and Sunday. Something to anticipate. I'm also going to buy tobacco for Jerry as well. Told him he could repay me with stamps. He's a nice guy. He's a good friend with Ben and they would like to be cellbuddies. I suspect Jerry wants some tattoos. Jerry plays chess—relatively poorly. His sentence is for fifty years, recently reduced from life by an appeal. No chance for parole for fifteen years. He's going to wait a "few years" and ask for another appeal. He has a fifteen-year-old son. Jerry is in NA and studying for his GED.

I've asked Ms. White to put me on the commissary preferred job list. She said she'd do that. It's an option independent from the data processing shop. Not sure which waiting list is longer. The commissary job isn't limited to six months, but would be physically harder. I'm still on the tier sanitation job list. I'm trying, honey.

Finished "Web of Dreams."

Sentencing + 292 days. The book, "Pale Blue Dot" by Carl Sagan might be a good choice for the book club. A deep question: If you knew (don't ask how) that there was no other intelligent life in the universe, would your religious views change?

Reading Sagan's book renewed a thought from the past. I believe the idea is labeled as "the finiteness of science." If science has a finite number of fundamental laws, e.g., conservation of energy, momentum, lepton number, quark color, electric charge, and the finiteness and invariance of the speed of light, etc., then eventually all of those laws will be discovered. When these laws are all discovered, science is then finished. It has done what it can and nothing remains except for technology to make use of the limited science. After time—perhaps millennia—technological progress will be slower and slower. The easy innovations will have been done and the difficult ones will come less frequently. The technology changes will slow to such an extent that the difference from one generation to the next will be indistinguishable, must like the lack of variation from one generation to the next of 5000 years ago. We, now, may be at the cusp of maximum technological change.

The significance for society and culture is immense. My father knew nothing about computers and could not pass insight and lessons on to me. Many children today view their parents as being dated and not worthy of respect. *"If you don't know about the Internet, why should I listen to you about behavior?"* If, however, technological changes slow then the knowledge of parents remains relevant. Family life should stabilize and parents teach useful skills—as they did in the distant past.

The technology of the future will reduce the amount of human labor required. The numbers of hours of work per week will drop enormously. Most of time will be leisure. Those on welfare today portend the norm of tomorrow. The necessities of life will be available to all without the need to "earn" them. When solar energy is harnessed, energy will be abundant and with enough energy, all problems are solvable. The future will be calm compared to the hectic today.

I've developed a habit of taking a siesta (and pondering deep thoughts as above ☺) in the afternoon—refreshing and addictive. As I was snoozing today listening to PBS, I heard Bernstein's "West Side Story" and Mendelssohn's "Symphony #5."

We had nectarines for lunch again and two other inmates gave me theirs. I view them as a treat. One can find extraordinary acts of kindness herein. These guys are people.

There is a cellbuddy move anticipated this Friday. One inmate is leaving so that causes a domino effect. Ben will move up with Jerry and Paul Wilson will move in here with me from the rec area. Of course, one cannot count their chickens before they hatch.

Rochelle State Prison, Housing Unit 1, Tier A, Cell 17, Feathers.

Sentencing + 293 days. A surprise! I was moved to the honor tier. Completely unexpected. Already, I appreciate the better access to showers. Each inmate does his own laundry. One can use the telephone anytime it's available. The biggest difference is that one has a key to their cell. Sounds weird, of course, but movement <u>outside</u> the tier is still governed as before. There are periods, lock-down, when you must be inside the cell. Otherwise, one can go back and forth between the rec area and the cell at will. This is a significant freedom. Violation of the rules means you are kicked back into the "ordinary" tiers, so there is a strong impetus to behave.

I wonder if this means that I won't share a cell with Paul Wilson? I don't know. Don Miller is over here. Maybe I'll rekindle the idea of sharing a cell with him. I'll give it time. My new cellbuddy is a lifer (murder/rape) called "Feathers"—in deference to his claim of Native American ancestry. His former cellbuddy was transferred, under the aegis of a new policy, to another prison because of a history of escape attempts.

Feathers has a TV, a fan, and a radio. He smokes and likes to stay up late. As a lifer, he's not going to change his routine for me, but I expect a comity to evolve. He's been in prison for twelve years. He's about six feet tall and has a paunch. He keeps his hair short and has lost all of his teeth. He has a set of false teeth and wears glasses. He talks tough to those who talk tough, but has good self-control.

The tier clerk told me if I gave him $4 in tobacco that I could start a tier sanitation job tomorrow. The job earns five days credit per month. He may be hustling me. I may be in line for the job in any case and he has access to that information. From my point of view, $4 is a pitiful sum to pay to get job credits so I can get out days or weeks earlier. Even if it is a scam, why risk losing an opportunity? Thus the subversion and the selling of the soul starts.

Let's calculate a worst-case scenario. If I work sanitation for ten months, I earn fifty days credit, which would mean I would be released in a bit more than ten months. If, however, I work on sanitation for three months and then start the computer shop (ten days credit per month) I would be released in eight months. The light at the end of the tunnel may be small and distant, but I see it!

Sentencing + 294 days. I just finished my first job shift. I cleaned the upper tier showers—took about ten minutes. Scrub it down with disinfectant. There are two shifts each day. Each shift lasts about fifteen minutes. As the newest member of the sanitation team, I also have the honor of cleaning the commodes in the rec area. My "off-days" are the next two. A great time to start. This job is much better than the kitchen job was.

Many good things have happened recently—honor tier, job and job lists. Most of our friends are still friends and all of our family is supportive. Life is good and will get better. We have much to look forward to and much to be thankful for.

I wrote a CO who has helped in the past about the problem returning books and old correspondence to you. See if he can offer advice.

Sentencing + 296 days. Had a good walk yesterday and showered before evening chow—a long missed privilege.

The housing unit sergeant—a tough old bastard—talked to me about the watch throwing incident. He told me that any further such event would cause an eviction from the honor tier. I suspect that if he had known of the incident before I moved in, he would've vetoed the move. Anyway, it's all behind me now.

I sauntered to the rec area last night, popped corn, sat at a table with my feet propped up on a chair, and read my book. A much more relaxing environment. In the rec area inmates play pool and table tennis. I haven't tried them and suspect I won't. Competition can lead to misunderstandings. The prison rules about table tennis seems to be that anything you can get away with is OK. Eightball is exclusively played on the pool table and there seems to be honor code to enforce fair play.

Parts of the Sagan book are too technical and arcane for the book club. I suspect that an in depth discussion about the experiments to determine the atmospheric content of Saturn's moons wouldn't be of general interest.

Don Miller told me that one's position on the computer data workshop is determined by the length of time remaining on an applicant's sentence. Presumably they want to train you immediately before your release—not years too early. An inmate, Roger, also asked me if I would like a job in the appliance repair shop—fixing TVs, radios, fans, etc. It's a ten-day a month job as well. Roger works there, but is due to be released soon and is helping find his replacement. I replied that I would be interested. The more options, the better.

It looks as if I will be able to return stuff to you on the next visit. I'll believe it when it happens. I get lonely for you.

I enclose my next poem.

The Chowhall

Across the prison yard
    the spittle speckled sidewalk
    blotched with squashed banana peels
    and milk half-pints
        leads us to the chowhall.

Our uncloven feet plod
    thrice every day, to and fro
    prodded hard by herding COs
    to keep on time
        getting to the chowhall.

Metal tray and a spoon,
    a glob, a bunch and a slice
    we carry by fours to a trough
    called a table
        arranged in the chowhall.

Hunker and cram it down.
    "Gonna eat that bread, buddy?"
    Stuff crackers into a pocket
    to eat later
        away from the chowhall.

Tomorrow would be empty
        except for the chowhall.

Sentencing + 300 days. It's hard to believe that our visit was two and a half-hours. I hope you have a good return trip home. The trip to Pinesburg and the visit with family will do you good. I hope Carl can come back with you. I'd enjoy a visit with him.

Finished "Remember Me" by Mary Higgins Clark. I enjoyed it—good escapist fiction. I've started "Affliction" by Russell Banks.

I got lots of mail. Probably a couple of day's worth that finally caught up with me after the move. I got a personal letter and material from the new Minister of *The Church of the Larger Fellowship*. I appreciate her effort.

I wasn't called to the appliance repair shop this afternoon—didn't expect it. I'll let it be known that I'd like to go on a volunteer basis until the vacancy occurs. Give the CO in charge a chance to evaluate me.

Sentencing + 301 days. Went to the repair shop for three hours in the afternoon. They hire three inmates and have a hard time finding three inmates out of the 2400 in the prison who have enough technical knowledge. Another impediment is the CO in charge, a sergeant, who has no technical knowledge of electronics. I'm told that he doesn't understand why a schematic for a particular electronic device is useful. Consequently, a repair is generally effected by part-swapping with spares. A rudimentary oscilloscope is available, but without a schematic of the malfunctioning device, it is more difficult to use. I'm amazed that the guys who work there get as much done as they do. At least, it's a job where mental effort is required.

Sentencing + 303 days. The repair job still looks probable. I will be called back on the next day they work. I suspect that I'll participate on a volunteer basis until Roger goes home in three weeks. That's how Roger got the job when his predecessor left.

Lunch was a grilled cheese sandwich, pea soup and carrot and celery sticks. It's one of my favorites, but a few chunks of ham in the pea soup would be welcomed.

I heard Saint-Saëns' "Sonata in E♭ for Clarinet and Piano." If we don't have a recording, we should get one.

Sentencing + 304 days. My release date seems so close—fewer days remain than have passed—but yet so far away. I want out! I think of servicemen who leave families behind not to be seen for months. I'm comfortable and lucky.

Yesterday, I walked, showered, did laundry, watched a NASCAR race, ate potato chips, drank a root beer and read.

I received a letter from an inmate who was transferred to minimum. He has to cross the street to go to commissary and thus is "out" for a brief period—but is required to return. He says he has to suppress thoughts of escape.

I'm spending more time outside the cell in the rec area. Because the inmates can come and go to the rec area, it's not as crowded as the rec area in the other tiers. In the other tiers, if you return to your cell (allowed only every half-hour) you must stay there. Feathers has dominion, sort of, over the cell and prefers to stay in there. He does artwork and likes to "spread-out."

I'm on page 160 of "Affliction"—a good book.

Sentencing + 305 days. Ten months we've been separated. I can't imagine the feeling I'll have when I walk out of here. It will seem as I'm awaking from a bad dream.

I wasn't called to the electronics repair shop this morning. My paranoia is flourishing, but I have to tell myself that plan "B," the computer data workshop, is still a good possibility.

Later: No call to the repair shop in the afternoon either, so I had a good walk in the yard. I walked with Don and he was receptive to continuing to see each other when we get out. He spoke of his family and his plans for retirement. We have to be so guarded in here and it's hard, sadly, to know whom to trust. Some of the guys are expert in creating a trusting and amicable relationship that can be taken advantage of. Don is due to be released in three or four months. It's *de rigueur* to be vague about release dates. Howard joined us late in our circuits.

This is a place of false hopes—parole, appeals, visits, mail, money, medication and jobs. These small illusions of hope are what enable one to go from one day to the next. There's an unspoken conspiracy among inmates to bolster the probability of these filaments of optimism. *"Of, course, you'll get parole. You deserve it," "Your girl will visit you next week, Dude, wait and see,"* etc., *ad infinitum, ad nauseam.* It's pitiful to receive such tripe (because you're tempted to believe it) and even more pitiful to render it, knowing that it's false. Yet, it is all that some have to hold onto it.

My last lap was done with Paul Wilson. His therapist and attorney are formulating a plan based on restorative justice. In Paul's plan, he, his victim (of what?) and a mediator would get together in a room. *"Why did you do this?" "I'm really sorry for what I've done,"* etc., etc. The victim then walks away and supports a sentence reduction, which the judge and prosecutor embrace and all live happily ever after. I asked Paul if there had ever been an example of restorative justice within the state. He didn't know, but trusts the Lord—a filament of hope to get to tomorrow. My hope is you. You're not a filament but rather a cable of nonpareil strength, made of love.

I enjoyed the conversation and camaraderie from the walk today. The interaction picked up my depressed spirits. My mood is odd today, but I'm OK.

Sentencing + 306 days. I worked in the repair shop today. It looks like I'm at the top of the list when a vacancy occurs—probably next month. In spite of the good news, I'm feeling a bit down. Maybe it's because I realize that it won't get any better for the next seven months or so. It's heartening that the time remaining is less than the time that has passed. I must follow Carlson's advice and control my thinking.

I look forward to your visit this weekend. It will be the last for a couple of weeks while you visit our family. You deserve and need a break—to be among those who love and cherish you, where you can relax and have fun. Your being refreshed is necessary for us both. Have a good trip. I'll send my next letter to Phyllis and Warren's.

Sentencing + 308 days. Just a short note to greet you upon your arrival in Pinesburg. Nothing new and I will probably have two visits with you before you read this.

Sentencing + 309 days. I enclose an article about two inmates who abused the home detention system. The article is extremely one-sided in the reporting. The article makes the home detention system seem completely asinine and makes no mention of the hundreds or thousands of inmates who have successfully completed the home detention and for whom it was a godsend. The newspaper, by reporting only the extreme, does a gross injustice to a good social program. No social program is perfect—we should not be surprised by failures. Together with any report of a defect, the reporter should make a comparison with successes. This goes for all programs. I read a report concerning an inmate who abused the telephone access by continuing to run a drug distribution business from prison. Nowhere did the report give space to the incredible good effect that telephones have on recidivism rates. An inmate who is able to maintain contacts with family and friends is more likely to be successfully reintegrated into society and less likely to re-offend. If an inmate, while on parole, commits a horrible crime, the whole system of parole is judged culpable without looking at the large benefits that society reaps from the system. Failures will happen. Planes will fall out of the sky. However, in the case of a plane crash, no one says that all air travel should be totally halted. Why are social programs—which inherently are less well understood—held to a higher standard than engineering projects where a greater degree of control is possible? Why do newspapers report by extremes and ignore comparisons with the norm?

Carl is on a plane as I write. It will be good to visit with him and he'll be a big help to you in driving to Pinesburg.

Something unique for lunch today—-watermelon! I enjoyed it.

Walked my 10 laps (about 3 miles). In the mail I got a copy of "Against the Gods, The Remarkable Story of Risk" by Peter Bernstein from Marsha. It's non-fiction and looks interesting. According to Junior, it has a lot of "math."

Sentencing + 310 days. A good short visit this morning. I'm looking forward to a longer one tomorrow. I hope that the squalls didn't upset your plans to visit the historical sites. While Carl's interest doesn't surprise me, his fervency does.

You looked tired. Your left eye was quite red. Is having Carl there stressful? I know that from time-to-time, I've been preoccupied during a visit. Maybe that was the case with you today. Maybe I'm detecting a false signal.

Sentencing + 311 days. Wow, a three-hour visit. You looked much better. Carl has a great sense of humor.

Sentencing + 312 days. A great three days—each with a visit. You're probably about halfway to Pinesburg at this moment. Convenient that Rochelle was on the way.

A problem I have in here is that I much prefer to be left alone. I don't want inmates initiating conversations or indulging in small talk and when they try, I resent it—and am, increasingly, showing my annoyance. Not good. I'm becoming a cranky old man who doesn't want to be bothered. A young black man—probably nineteen years old—asked me if I knew anything about mutual funds. I languished and wondered, *"Where is this going?"* I replied, *"A bit."* He wanted a recommendation. I asked if he was willing to risk losing money. He said, *"No"* and I replied that he should keep his money in the bank then, and left the table. I could've been kinder and more helpful. I just wanted to get out of the conversation. Paradoxically, there are times when I wish to talk and initiate the conversation—say, with Don—only to be rebuffed in the manner I rebuff others. It's all about TRUST. I heard an inmate exclaim, *"I had no friends in here when I came, and I'll leave with no friends."* Perhaps, that's the way it has to be.

Some inmates try to sell me stuff—hand-drawn envelopes, sandwiches from the officer's dining room, hard-boiled eggs (how old?), etc. Being a recluse reduces such solicitations and yet I wonder about the correct UU religious response. I could buy the stuff and discard it and thereby, help another who is in need. But then do I mark myself as a—mark? I'm inclined to introversion and I can be happy reading and such. Additionally most of the relationships herein are "put-down" in a brutal way. I don't want to indulge in that form of parley. Example: *"Hey, you bald-headed mother-fucking prick, got any coffee I can borrow?"* Response: *"For an ass-hole like you…etc."* The guys enjoy this!

I don't want to exaggerate this. It's just a moral/religious dilemma I'm mulling over. How much should I reach out and become vulnerable versus how much should I withdraw? Seclusion is safer, but may be more cowardly.

Sentencing + 313 days. Glad to hear your trip went well. Relax—enjoy the leisure—refresh yourself.

Some minor good news here. When Roger goes home (at which time I hope to get the repair shop job) Feathers will move in with Roger's former cellbuddy. A guy named Neil asked if he could move in with me. Neil is in the adjacent cell and I pass the newspaper to him when I finish it. He's a decent and quiet type. He has about a year left on his sentence. He isn't getting along with his cellbuddy and is looking for a quieter type. He works in the Education Department and will try to get me a job there.

Don—with only four months left—doesn't want to move again and I don't blame him. Don moving in would create a couple of problems. I'm not sure he would take the upper bunk and because he has such a short time remaining, I'd have to find a replacement when he went home. Anyway many "maybes" and "perhaps," but Feathers moving out is almost a certainty. There are friends from my old tier I'd like to move over, but that is beyond my control.

I paid the tier clerk the $4. Arghhh…

Give my love to all there with you.

Sentencing + 314 days. I may be called to the repair shop tomorrow, Roger has warned me. The probability of a teacher's aide job is increasing. I'm to write a letter—because of the intervention of a couple of teacher's aides here on A tier—requesting a position.

Sentencing + 316 days. Had a great visit with Walter and Brad. They—knowing you would be gone—made a special effort to come during your absence.

No news on the job front. I saw Barry on the walk after lunch. Talked for a bit. Not much time for more.

Troy and Sue are going to move from California to Wisconsin. They can buy an equivalent house for half as much. I teased him about "winters."

It's cooler here today. My yard walk will be nice.

I have the following possibilities—electronics repair shop, teacher's aide, clerk in the Ed. Dept., commissary worker and data processing workshop. Something has to happen. Probably two or three things at once. If nothing happens, I still have the tier sanitation job and a release date in eight and a half months.

Sentencing + 318 days. Just got off the telephone with Bud and Jessie. The seriousness of her medical problems just requires time to assess. They sound in good spirits. They're young—they deserve the best.

I'm torn between two scenarios for the future. The first ("inactive"): We garden, travel, socialize but keep our involvement in reform and social action minimal. The second ("active"): We do our hobbies, but also pursue involvement in prison reform movements, social justice and civil rights.

I'm afraid of the second. If we become visible the system could set me up—a routine traffic stop and a planted bag of white powder or a doctored sobriety test and I'm incarcerated again with no credibility ("ex-con"). I trust the system much less than before because of what I've learned about those who run the system. Power is everything and dealing with questioners is a nuisance. The reaction to scrutiny is a resistance to change—a desire for the status quo—laziness—incompetence. My life would have less meaning if the "inactive" role is chosen, but the "active" role has dangers. What would the reaction of DOP be if I were publicly critical of DOP while on probation? Yet, who else has greater experience from which to be critical of DOP except for ex-cons?

I saw Barry again and he said he was pushing my application in the Ed. Dept. Who knows what that means?

I'll send my next letter home to await you on your return from Pinesburg.

Sentencing + 319 days. I enjoyed the telephone call this morning. I got my laundry done. Coloreds and linens. The steps in the routine—walking, washing, showers, etc., measure days but they are getting dull, dull and dull.

I submitted a request for Neil to move in with me when Feathers moves out. Neil has eleven months to go, so he could be my last cellbuddy.

I'm ordered the correct power adapter for the Walkman. The Walkman is my escape. The weak link is the headphones. If they break, I lose music. Why do I worry about things that haven't happened?

I wake up expecting to be called to the repair shop or to the Ed. Dept. for an interview and dress appropriately. I'll do so this week and then return to my slovenly ways—sweat pants and undershirt, which are adequate for retrieving the newspaper and excursions to the chow hall, but not to the library, Ed. Dept., or repair shop. Bermuda shorts are allowed only in yard, gym, and within the housing unit. I find it incongruous that they are not allowed in the chow hall.

Sentencing + 320 days. I'm told and I believe that the CO in charge of the repair shop has submitted the official forms to start me in the repair shop. I have mixed feelings. You're right; I have gotten lazy. Prison does that to you. But the job will require technical and problem solving skills. I will learn something new.

Objectively speaking, it is a good development. The ten days credit per month is the primary motivation. I will also earn a dollar a day—whether I work or not, because we're on call. When inmates are transferred into Rochelle their TV and radios (if they have any) must be opened up and checked for contraband. Those of us that work in the repair shop perform that operation.

But the job reduces the time I have for doing laundry, shower and exercise. The most assured way of doing something is to have the greatest flexibility in doing it. Once I learn the routine it will be OK.

I'm much better at the crossword puzzles in the paper. I complete most within two hours.

Sentencing + 321 days. During the night, I felt I had a cold, but once I got up and moved around the symptoms disappeared

Commissary was today and had to buy for two weeks. Cost $26. The commissary schedule is a complicated algorithm. Which housing unit goes first? Is it inventory week? In what order do the tiers within the housing unit go? I rely on a published schedule, which upon scrutiny has hints of an arcane logic, but is unpredictable. I try to keep a bit extra of the essentials in case something goes awry

I saw Barry on the walk today. As I fetch the newspaper, he is often on the way to his job. He tells me all the teachers think I'm overqualified for a teacher's aide job and will be bored—more bored than lying in the cell? Anyway, I believe the electronics repair shop will work out.

Later: Had a good ten laps. Walked with Howard for several laps. His wife and eleven-year old daughter finally visited him. His sentence is for twenty years! He credited the Lord for his visit. I didn't contradict him—whatever brings comfort and hope.

Sentencing + 322 days. You should be leaving Pinesburg now. Have a safe and enjoyable trip. I just returned from a good visit with Harry. Walter had a last minute conflict and couldn't come.

Not much new. I'm accommodating to the tier sanitation job.

I renewed my medication—every ten days, like clockwork now. This month is flying by. I anticipate that the holidays will be harder for me this year, but maybe this realization will be an ameliorating factor. The realization that there is a short time remaining will make the period more difficult, but I've also become more accustomed to my environment.

I just had a good thirty-minute talk with an educated inmate named Manuel. He's a Hispanic from Nicaragua, speaks flawless English and will be deported by the INS when his ten-year sentence is over. He has done much good in here—tutor, and counselor to other Hispanics. His world-view is sophisticated and he acknowledges his guilt (of what?)—a rarity, indeed, herein. He has family both in the US and in Nicaragua and has support in both countries.

The last two nights, I've played chess for the first time since moving from B tier. There is good competition and I have a winning record against the others—but deem that may change. My nighttime cold was less severe last night, although I had a coughing spell.

Sentencing + 323 days. I was officially notified that I've been assigned a job in the electronics repair shop. So that's done. Looks like I start immediately. Doing the calculation for job credits and county time, my best guess is that I will be released in 202 days!

The data processing shop is still a possibility, but since it is of limited duration and would probably bore me to tears, I'm probably not interested.

Release—200 days. Watched football. Ate a bag of chips and drank a root beer. They let us out for yard at 7:15PM and call us in when it gets dark. Because of the shortening of the days, the exercise period becomes shorter and shorter. I only did seven laps instead of my allotment of ten. Afternoon yard doesn't suffer this fate, but when I start the job, afternoon yard will be a rarity. I will do what I can.

The greatest joy of a telephone call is the ability to converse with someone who <u>cares</u>.

One of the sets of batteries I bought for the Walkman must've been old—they didn't last long. The reception sensitivity degrades rapidly with weak batteries and the PBS station is not strong here. I'll be glad to receive the correct AC adapter.

I think about the time left—just over six months. Depending on the job, the time will go quickly or slowly, but it will go. Now that my job assignment is definite, I'll request library passes again. I suspect I'll get evening passes.

I've been informed officially that I'm no longer on tier sanitation. Do not have to clean the commodes tonight. Got new batteries in the Walkman. Will walk in yard tonight.

Release—199 days. As happens to everyone eventually, I understand, our cell got shook down this afternoon. The COs take you out of the cell, handcuff you, and go through all of your stuff looking for contraband. They found nothing in my stuff, but took extra linen from Feathers. They also tear away (sometimes) the self-made cardboard shelving. They scrutinized all written material. Feathers's papers were examined in much more detail than mine were. My massive array of stuffed manila envelopes scared them, perhaps. They took some of his stuff only to return it later. I do have extra linen, but they are mixed in with my cloths and escaped detection. Feathers files many legal "motions" and "writs," not only for himself, but also for other inmates (for a fee). Feathers is also the tier representative and I'm told that the tier representative, in the last eight months, has been shook down six times. Doesn't make sense, but that's what I'm told. Feathers has only been the representative for two months. He was shook down about a month before I arrived. Shakedowns are often successful. On B tier, they found one inmate who had been hoarding prescription medicine; another had a tattoo gun, and another who had a radio left to him by a departing inmate. The first two offenses led to cell restrictions and the last resulted in forfeiture of the radio.

No work in the repair shop this morning—maybe in the afternoon. I'm told that one works only about half of the scheduled time. Various forms of conflicts arise; for example, tomorrow morning Sergeant O'Reilly—the boss, i.e., the CO in charge—is having his car worked on and won't be in. Without him we can't work.

Release—198 days. I watched "Rebecca" on Masterpiece Theater. I enjoyed it. I was never called for work, but nevertheless, I am paid and receive my work credits. Yesterday, I did my ten laps in the afternoon, showered and played chess.

Lots of mail—three cards and two long letters.

Release—197 days. No work this morning. Been on the job for six days and haven't been called to work. I'm being taught responsibility and reliability.

If I don't work this afternoon, I'll walk my ten laps.

Later: No work. Walked. Five letters including seven photos from Carl.

Release—196 days. I worked today for about three hours. I got your letter relating the Dali Lama's attitude towards anger. I agree. I see much supporting evidence herein. Some inmates harbor a deep anger and destroy themselves because of it. I met Barry on the walk. His wife, Janice has filed for a divorce and Barry is plotting revenge. Feathers, as I imagine most lifers would be, is angry at the whole world and it makes him an ugly person.

Are there two types of anger? My father, like Warren, became frustrated and vented his anger horribly, but he felt good about himself and his place in the world. He didn't brood, fret and plot revenge. He didn't bear grudges. I believe that self-esteem dictates how we react to feelings of anger and frustration.

In a few months, we'll drive away from this place. You'll take me home. Perhaps we'll stop on the way for a meal—something different. I'll explain how the simplest things and freedoms are so precious—an infinite number of trivial things; to shower in privacy, to have the ability to laundry at ease, to write a check, to water a flower, to be with you, ad infinitum.

I reflect often on the words that you told me early in this journey. You were sitting on the couch as I told you the deplorable details. You said, *"We can get through this."* Do you remember? I'm tearing as I write. Those words come back and are always there for me to hang onto. There were a plethora of destructive words you could've said. You said what I needed to hear. You said the truth. You spoke with conviction and confidence—*"We can get through this."*

Release—195 days. Another if-I-don't-go-to-work-I'll-go-walking day.

I read in the paper about an archeological dig. That's something I could do and have fun. My problem may be there's too much for me to do upon release! The future will be good.

Later: No work. Walked. When I returned to the cell, I finished a bag of potato chips that I opened three days ago. Starting to read "Stealing Jesus."

What do you think of the legal argument that mandatory sentences violate the separation of powers, i.e., the legislature assuming a role constitutionally reserved for the judiciary? Mandatory sentences don't allow for the extraordinary exception. If allowed, the judge can accommodate on a case-by-case basis, the exigencies and render appropriate remedies. The legislature is reacting to stereotypes and pandering to re-election fervor while making bad laws. Lawmakers should lead, not follow.

Release—194 days. I wasn't called to the repair shop today, although Roger was. Maybe the sergeant didn't call me because there is no bench to work at until Roger leaves. Paranoia creep.

Did you read the newspaper article about Smith? He was indicted for a crime, fled the country and then successfully fought extradition. The prosecutor complained because, *"...the law was used to the defendant's benefit."* I'm not sure that justice was served by the turn of events, but I find it ludicrous that a prosecutor would complain about the use of law. The prosecutor uses the law routinely to circumvent justice. Since when does the prosecutor have a monopoly on defining justice? Smith's case is interesting as well because it draws attention to the disparity between American justice and justice elsewhere. Extradition was denied because of the potential harshness of the penalty. Before one experiences the legal and penal system at work, it's easy to stick one's head in the sand and trust all is OK.

Dinner last night was good. We had roast beef (from which I made a sandwich, using commissary bought mustard), corn-on-the-cob and watermelon. I listened to Vaughn Williams's "Suite for Viola and Orchestra" on PBS. Are you familiar with it? It sounds twentieth century, but it is melodic.

The walk to and from the chow hall was tranquil. The sunset variegated the sky. A symmetric vee of geese honked their way south.

Release—193 days. I gave Don Miller our home telephone number and address, and your work number. His wife's name is Lottie. Don hopes to be released within three months. Yesterday, he received a visit from his son and learned that Lottie's only brother, who had just retired, was killed in a car wreck in Alabama. I tried to console and comfort him. I feel his agony in not being able to comfort his wife during her time of need. I told Don that if Lottie wished to, she could give you a call. I think they're good people. I also understand that Don could easily see me as someone working his sympathies. What a cruel view is imbrued in us denizens herein.

A good day for TV sports—tennis, football. My favorite team is whoever plays Notre Dame. ☺ I also will walk ten laps.

I am enjoying "Stealing Jesus" more than I would've guessed. I'll finish it time to submit my report to the club.

Later: Did my laps and watched football during which I drank a grape soda and ate a partial bag of chips (NOT a whole bag!).

Release—192 days. I called my brother, David, last night. We had a good talk. Nancy had surgery and is doing much better. I hope she finds peace. Did he leave a message on the answering machine while you were in Pinesburg?

I listened to PBS last night. I awoke at the end of a violin piece that Joshua Bell had played. The announcer said that Joshua had become an actor and was in a movie called "The Red Violin."

Release—191 days. I called you early this morning because I couldn't resist the temptation. ☺ I got my laundry done—linen changed. We had gym instead of yard because of the weather. I followed the exercise with a root beer and a shower.

I've finished "Stealing Jesus" and enclose my notes for the book club.

Dear Book Club:
Re: "Stealing Jesus" by Bruce Bawer.

This book surprised me—I found it interesting. I appreciated the book more for the questions it generated than for the answers it provided.

I like the dichotomy created by the author—*The Church of Love* and *The Church of Law*. It served the purpose of the author well and avoids the political baggage of "conservative" and "liberal." I was not aware of the role that Paul, the prophet and lawyer, played in creating the chasm.

A rhetorical question—if *The Church of Law* had been accepting of homosexuality, but otherwise were as they are, would the author have bothered to write the book? Was the intolerance of homosexuality the spur for the author?

First question: Was Jesus inevitable? I mean Jesus in a generic sense of a charismatic loving giver of a code of morality. To set the context of the question, imagine a multitude of planets upon which intelligent life develops. As that life evolves socially and politically and forms a primitive civilization, they start with nothing to explain the universe and the activities therein. The intelligent life evolves from forms (e.g. protozoa) that have no morality or ethics. The early intelligent life has no science, therefore superstition and the creation of gods fills the void of explanation. Different groups create differing morale codes and rules of behavior concerning fundamentals of life. When, if ever, is it acceptable to kill another? What is the nature of spousal commitments? Confusion abounds. What is right? What is wrong? In this cauldron of superstition and confusion, is it not inevitable, that at the auspicious time, a figure like Jesus appears?

Second question. Our population has evolved with traits that enabled us to survive as a species. I speak not only of physical traits but social and cultural ones as well. One of these traits, I submit, is the ratio of leaders to followers. If everyone insisted on being a leader, then neither "hunting party" nor community structure could have emerged and the continued survival of our species would be doubtful. Likewise a community with no leaders and only followers would have perished because of the lack of direction. A few leaders and many followers are needed. To tie this thought with the book, is it not plausible that a majority of the congregation in *The Church of Love* are more apt to be "leaders", i.e., independent thinkers and less likely to follow? And similarly *The Church of Law* would attract those that are more comfortable in following. If this characterization has truth, then it follows that *The Church of Law* will always be significantly larger than *The Church of Love*.

I wish I could be there for the discussion. Good things have happened to me and I'll let my better-half fill in the details.

Release—190 days. This morning I went to the library. I had a abundance of reading material, but to combat lethargy I went and checked out a book of two novellas by D. H. Lawrence: "St. Maur" and "The Man Who Died."

I worked in the repair shop this afternoon. It went OK. Instead of being just a spectator, I actually did hands-on stuff.

Release—189 days. Eleven months down. About six to go. So close, yet so far.

I worked in the shop this morning. There are three other "technicians" who work in the repair shop: Roger, who is soon going home and whose place I will fill; Al, who knows a lot, but gets caught in rat holes satisfying his curiosity instead of actually repairing things; and Ed, a young kid, whose heart is in the right place, tries like hell, and gets an amazing amount done considering that he doesn't know what he's doing. It's a good group to work with. Al, with a good theoretical and practical basis, serves as a knowledge source and general direction giver, but accomplishes little.

We weren't needed in the shop this afternoon so I went to yard and did ten laps. I talked more with Howard. I have great empathy for that young man. I have no idea what his crime was, but he is suffering mightily. His sentence is twenty years! He is going to appeal. He had a public defender, pled guilty and got the maximum sentence. He's devastated and worries about his family and his daughter. He strikes me as quite intelligent and sensitive. Why is he—why am I—in here?

Release—188 days. I just returned from commissary. I now have an adequate supply of stamps, coffee, grapefruit juice, envelopes, paper and pens—the essentials. All else are treats—nice treats, but still treats.

News here—Al, from the repair shop, got into a fight in the chow hall and will lose his job. Another inmate apparently assaulted him for a grudge from the outside. The rumor is that the assailant is the brother of a girl that Al raped. The policy is, however, if there is a fight, both inmates are put in segregation and are disciplined. Al didn't fight back, but merely covered himself with his arms and ducked his head. There will be no investigation, no interviews and no determination of responsibility. This saves work for the COs. I hate to see anyone get into more trouble. It's already bad enough.

Al's departure will create an immediate vacancy, which I will fill. More will be expected from me sooner—I have to carry my share.

The blood test results—all OK. The cholesterol level was especially good. Blood pressure was 151/89—a bit high for comfort, but there's nothing I can do about it. They'll measure again in three months.

Release—187 days. Didn't get called to the repair shop for work yesterday or today. Did ten laps in yard. My Hispanic friend from the Commons, Jose, has been moved onto the honor tier. I enjoy talking to him from time to time. He trusts me and frequently asks me questions about English. I never denigrate or tease him. There are several other Hispanics on this tier whereas he was culturally alone on our old tier. Perhaps that expedited his transfer. Phil, the inmate who came into the commons area when Barry left, also came into the honor tier. He's made the transition quickly.

Release—186 days. I awoke this morning depressed. The days are so monotonous. I've talked myself out of it a bit. Can you send Bud a check for his birthday? I can't locate my checkbook. ☺

Release—185 days. Good morning. Did you feel my fingers stroke your cheek as you awoke? Did you notice me gazing into your eyes? Did you sense my breath in your hair? I was there.

I included in my Sunday services yesterday the CLF sermon by Rev. Michael McGee, "Necessary Losses." It was good and you'd get something out of it. I don't say that about all of them.

I am looking at the end of the tunnel and asking questions about when I get out. How receptive or tolerant will our community be? Will the church abide me returning and attending services? Will the neighbors parade and hoist protest placards? There's part of me that believes there will be no issue; that I'm exaggerating. But there's a part of me that says, of course, there will be an adverse reaction—nothing will remain the same and to believe otherwise is naïveté.

If forced to, I could enjoy life immensely without involvement in community and church. I could enjoy you, travel, a dog, gardening, reading, writing, movies, music, family—I could have a fantastic life! I would like community, but may be forced to create a new one. How about ballroom dancing—interest you? Maybe we could play duplicate bridge again. I could enjoy chess competition. There's so much new that we could enjoy that the loss of the old is lamentable, but not catastrophic.

How much do we push the church to accept us (me)? If they're not accepting of me, I want to force them to face their hypocrisy. I want them to have the debate, to discuss the issues—to grow! I am willing to be the vehicle. Is that hubris?

Probation may be abrasive, but it's an easy issue. One does what is necessary. I suspect it will be inanely controlling in the beginning, but with time, become less oppressive.

I will go to yard this afternoon. The wind is blowing wispy cirrus clouds from east to west—no threat of a thunderstorm.

Release—183 days. I had a good walk yesterday. Howard did a few laps with me. We had a meaningful discussion about religion. You can guess how it went. Christianity provides some with a convenient escape from responsibility—*"This is all part of God's plan for me."*

I worked both morning and afternoon. If an inmate has a broken TV, radio, fan, or electric razor, apparently there is no other recourse than to request us to repair it. He cannot, even if he has the funds, send it outside. If we can't fix it, then the inmate is out of luck. We also repair, as needed, the microwave ovens from the tiers of the housing units. There is a six-month backlog of repair requests. Sergeant O'Reilly is in no particular hurry to process the submissions. *"When we get to them, we'll get to them,"* is his attitude.

There are several cell moves in the offering. Roger is going home. Feathers wants to move into Roger's vacant bunk. That leaves a vacancy in my cell. I wrote the tier CO expressing preferences, which is the most I can do. I hope I get someone decent.

The last six months may be the worst. Before, I was waiting for something to happen. I now have a compatible job. I am now on the honor tier. The cell movement will happen and is beyond my control. After a couple of weeks, all will be routine. Six more months. There are no further good developments to happen. Lots of bad things. Waiting.

Release—182 days. I hope your trip wasn't affected by the storm. The TV showed extensive rain. Traffic snarls probably dotted your travel. I washed my linen this morning—didn't have to work.

When I get out and we get a sheltie puppy, we'll have to train it to get us out of bed when the coffee is made. Do we want to get two puppies and breed them? You could name the male and I could name the female. It would be as easy for you to walk two as one. ☺

I'm in a better mood today. I'm not sure why. I fight depression by thinking of good. I look at the flowers when outside. I savor my daily candy bar. The coffee I prepare with hot faucet water in the morning is a welcome to the new day. I listen to music at night and the birds outside. I try not to dwell on—to worry about—things I cannot control. Acceptance. The mail delivery is most often the highlight of the day.

Release—181 days. The telephone call last night lifted my spirits. The elevation in my mood was unexpected because I didn't realize I was feeling low. I'm not feeling insecure, but it is important to talk to you and realize that you will be there when I get out in 5.8657342 months. ☺ This environment is so barren that a reminder of what awaits me is a big impetus to keep going—to be positive and take advantage of what good is available.

Worked this morning and afternoon. I actually fixed a TV this morning. The problem was minor, but I had to diagnose it. The owner had a bit of luck. I had no particular assignment in the afternoon. Straightened up a bit. Looked into nooks and crannies to see what is in the shop. Sergeant has a staff meeting in the morning so the shop will be closed.

I'm requesting a library pass for next week. Get out of the cell, read magazines. I have $152 in my account so I'm OK for some time.

Rochelle State Prison, Housing Unit 1, Tier A, Cell 17, Elliot.

Release—180 days. Feathers has moved out and Elliot has moved in. I'm not a happy camper. Elliot is loud and loves to yell to his "friends" on the tier. Elliot wanted to move into this cell because it is quieter than the noise in his old cell, which was across from the rec area. I suspect most of the loudness follows him and is his doing. He is white, about thirty years old, has big buggy eyes, and a receding black hairline. He smokes incessantly. I recognize that I have a prejudice against him because I wanted someone else and Elliot was forced upon me. He has twelve more years on his sentence. He works in the officer's dining room and has a flourishing business in selling purloined food. I worry about being too close to questionable activities—about being set-up, having the cell shook down. Elliot brings a lot negative. His daily habits and mine are terribly incompatible. He likes to watch movies all night and sleep during the day.

Release—179 days. The first night with Elliot was not restful. He's too busy—watches TV, goes in and out of the cell, ostensibly in connection with his job. I'll probably get used to it. It's not as bad as the Commons.

What I nice day! I went to yard and did my ten laps. It was warm enough that I removed my shirt.

I worked this morning in Intake. I opened the TVs of three inmates that were transferring in. The CO looks inside for contraband and then I close them again. The newer TVs—with transparent cases—don't require my attention. I also engrave the inmates prison ID on the set. Worked for two hours.

I'm having my weekly soda and chips as I watch tennis on TV. Showered. I have answered the three letters I received yesterday.

If I am offered the data processing workshop, I'll probably take it. The job in the repair shop invites many requests from other inmates for "special" favors. *"Hey, my good man, can you fix my headphones?" "I need a bit of solder." "Can you get a knob for my TV?"* They are willing to barter a noodle or a candy bar for the favor. Most of these requests come because the waiting list for appliance repair is so long. Because the system is not working, the inmates try to circumvent it. I worry that I'll either incur the enmity of other inmates if I don't cooperate, or I'll be caught smuggling if I do. It's a Catch-22. Roger told me, before he left, that Sergeant is fully aware of the problems we face and trusts us to use our good sense. A bit of solder or a TV knob is not a problem, but something from which a weapon could be fabricated would be a major transgression. Maybe Roger was just rationalizing his own behavior. As we leave the shop, Sergeant inventories the tools, but doesn't frisk us.

I've used the third sermon in the last set of four. Could you order a new set for me?

More thoughts about anger. There is the anger felt by victims who think that revenge will assuage their loss and pain. This anger is unproductive, unhealthy, and impedes healing. Another type of anger spurs action that can make a situation better. A person can become angry at pollution and arouse the community and legislature so that the problem gets fixed. To rephrase—there is an anger that grows out of frustration that leads to, perhaps, revengeful acts that bear no productive fruit, and then there is an anger—let's call it "indignation"—that elicits a call to a positive action to correct a systemic wrong. I'm not sure there is a difference between the two in terms of physiological response. The first type of anger is something from which one needs to be healed. It is intrinsically unhealthy. Therapy helps the first, but therapy cannot cure indignation—although therapy can ease the acceptance of anything. Revenge never cures anger, but the elimination of pollution can assuage indignation.

I find myself caught in the process of: Feeling powerless—> feeling frustrated—> feeling indignation. I want to change things!

Release—177 days. What a refreshing visit. It's nice to have someone who cares. I have to accept that no one in here cares an iota about me. It's a stark realization.

In the mail today I got your package with "I Know This Much is True."

I'm anxious about your surgery—albeit minor. I've put us in a situation where we are totally dependent on you.

I have an extra Rochelle Inmate Handbook, which I'll mail to you. The cover emphasizing rehabilitation is ironic.

I have discovered more about Elliot's food store. At night, he is summoned by the COs to go to the officer's dining room to retrieve a midnight snack for them. In exchange for this personal service, he is allowed to bring back a supply of food to do with as he wishes. When he returns to the cell, he packages sandwiches, etc., for resale and that accounts for his nighttime activity. I'm sure that if some higher authority knew, it would be stopped, but who will complain? The state (loss of goods) and me (loss of sleep) are the only ones being harmed.

Release—176 days. These last few months will be pure drudgery with Elliot as a cellbuddy and a job that is frustrating. To create darkness, at night I hang sheets from the upper bunk and tent my bed to the extent possible. One has to keep the end of the bunk unobstructed so the COs can look in for the counts. To shut out extraneous noise, I wrap the headphones from the Walkman onto my head.

I should be thankful that it is only a few months. I'm settling into the job and it may be OK after I get used to it. My eyesight lacks for close up work and small details. My shaky fingers betray me at times. The lack of tools, parts and schematics is especially annoying. With just a bit more we could do so much more. The job fills time, but I had no trouble filling time in any case. But I get the work credits and will get out of here sooner. I shall stick with it, of course, and do my best. My enthusiasm increases greatly when I remember the kitchen sanitation assignment. ☺

It's fortunate that I ordered the AC adapter for my Walkman. With Elliot wandering around, I wear the earphones all night, every night, to listen to the radio.

Release—173 days. I'm greatly relieved that the surgery went well. It was nice of Walter to give you rides back and forth. I know it was advertised as minor, but when a loved one is involved and you're locked up, nothing is minor. I slept well last night. Listened to the Walkman all night.

I went to gym last evening and walked for an hour. No fresh air, but the exercise was good. I also did laundry yesterday, so, all in all, a good day. A pretty sunrise this morning. I can see it from my cell window, reminiscent of my view from Classification, an eternity ago.

I got the package in the mail. Thanks. The postcard of the sheltie puppy is darling. I placed it on my locker door. How many do we want? The photos you sent are from several events. Remember the walk we took on the river? The ride in the antique train in the mountains? The drive to the valley? At least three different events. They brought back memories of things past and promises of things future.

I'll take care of the sheltie puppy and return it to you in due time.

Release—172 days. What a beautiful day! From my interactions with other inmates, I have formed a psychological theory. None of them see themselves as a "bad" guy. There are extenuating circumstances, there are excuses, there are rationalizations, there are cognitive distortions but none say, *"I did my evil because I'm* *a bad guy. "* My theory is that at a deep level (the Freudian superego?) the primary psychological need is to think good of ourselves and we create a view of reality that satisfies that fundamental need. A trivial example—if one has no scientific or mathematical ability, but is gifted in art, then one's worldview is that art is the paramount achievement of mankind. As an aside, the distorted view of scientists by Hollywood is noteworthy. I doubt that most of the directors and producers of movies, an art form, had a great fondness for science. If one does poorly in school, then gang relationships, where one can gain self-approval by using baser instincts, have an allure. *"I'm a good guy because I protect my gang's turf and harm my gang's enemies."* If one has a view of the government and the social system as being bad—perhaps because of an abusive interaction with a renegade cop or a corrupt prosecutor—then, because the opposite of "bad" is "good," one can develop anti-social (i.e., anti-bad) behavior and feel it is the good thing to do. All of this is probably sophomoric, but it does explain the ubiquity of blameless self-images encountered herein. Some even take the road of admitting every offense and sin they have ever committed, or thought about committing, so they can feel religiously forgiven, be saved, and, thus, feel good about themselves. I maintain that the only possible opinion from the superego is *"I'm a good person,"* and the dials governing the perception of reality are adjusted until that opinion is obtained. When the dials don't turn far enough, suicide, for many, is the last effort to redeem an aura of goodness. *"Only a truly good person could see how evil they are."*

Imagine: You and I are walking in a park. We each have a dog leash attached to sheltie puppies. The small dogs know each other well and romp and play. They dart off of the path to trace a scent. A squirrel runs through the leaves and the puppies go into a spasm. The leashes get crossed and tangled. We swap places, we swap leashes, we twist and turn to undo the chaos. We call their names, but they're too young to do anything except ignore us. From time-to-time they freeze, perk their ears and then dissolve into a furry blur. Other walkers stop and pet the puppies. The shelties wag their tails in appreciation. At a creek they timidly touch a paw to the gurgling water before courageously wading in. What a new and wonderful world for them—and for us.

Release—171 days. Some in here have more than 171 <u>months</u> to go.

Release—170 days. Your visit this morning elevated my spirits. I'm glad the surgery succeeded and you're happy with the results.

I've been musing about your observation about my propensity to express sentimentality. My thoughts haven't come to closure. I do enjoy being romantic and expressing emotion. Do you remember early in our relationship I expressed the desire that you would show more affection? As I learned to know you, I recognized that you expressed affection in non-verbal ways. You showed affection by sharing companionship, participating in joint activities and interests. Your listening to my rambles and debating issues were showing affection, respect and interest in me. These are not things you do easily or lightly with people. You allow only a select few into your inner circle. I've learned to accept your rendered signs and be happy and secure. I learned how to interpret you and see the affection. There are things I'd like to hear you say, but if I ask for them they lose their significance because they're not spontaneous. Perhaps I've broached a subject better discussed while holding hands.

Release—169 days. I feel good today! I've had a couple of successes at work—from among a few jobs on my bench I actually fixed a TV and a radio. A sense of accomplishment. I'm not a doting old man incapable of anything productive. Has this place eroded my ego that I have to grasp at such trifles?

I'm looking into the eyes of the puppy. He's sad for what I've done. He's sad because my actions have separated you and me. He looks at me not with condemnation, but rather with compassion and unquestioning love. He sees the good in me. He'll lick my hand and fetch the ball when I throw it. He's alive and his life makes me more alive.

I'm fighting a crick in my neck. It was quite bad yesterday in the afternoon, but is better this morning. Medical worries are magnified herein because of the lack of concern and treatment.

Release—168 days. Have my recent letters been maudlin?

Among other things, I've been working on a TV in the shop for six days. No schematic. I'm the third person to work on it. I don't know what to do next. The owner is pissed. No one wants to work on it. It's a source of frustration and depression. During my work on it, I do meaningful stuff, but I recognize that what I do has a low probability of helping. *"Let me swap this resistor and see if that helps."* The power won't stay on. It has a protective relay that immediately turns the set off—hard to troubleshoot even with the proper equipment. Anyway, the damn TV set is my hell at the moment. I dread going to work because the TV is there waiting—a sign of my failure and incompetence, an obstacle I can't overcome. I keep reminding myself that I'm doing the best I can, but it's hard to find the positive.

At the commissary today, for only the second time, I bought a can of mixed nuts. Expensive, but a treat. Bought ten stamps. My neck is better perhaps because of a good night's sleep.

I plan on going to the gym tonight to walk and showering later. It's been warm enough that I've been sleeping on top of the bunk in my sweat pants, socks and T-shirt.

Our cable TV antenna is not working—supposedly because it's being upgraded. No one is saying when it will be back.

Release—167 days. I received the AC adapter for my Walkman. My current set of batteries died last night so the timing was good. With the new power supply the stations come in well. I'm listening to PBS at the moment.

I went to gym last night. Looks as if, with the repair shop job, exercise twice a week will be the norm.

I worked this morning and probably will this afternoon as well. My "TV from Hell" still waits for me. Another inmate working in the repair shop fixed a problem TV and that adds to my feelings of frustration and ineptness. I'm trying to be stoic and rise above it. It looks like we won't work tomorrow or the day after. The weather is predicted to be great. Maybe I can go to yard.

For holiday visitors how about: First day, Phyllis, Warren and Carl; second day, Bud, Jessie, and you; and the last day, whoever wants to come. I'll need to alter my visitor's list. I can eliminate local people who have never visited to make room for out-of-state family members.

Take care, love. You'll get this after your beach trip. The ocean breezes bear my caresses. The waves whisper my love. The gulls speak of my devotion.

Release—166 days. Thanks for carrying the phone conversation this morning. I didn't expect you to be there and was surprised when you answered. I forgot the item I wished to discuss (beginnings of Alzheimer's?). You sounded cheery and upbeat.

I had no visit from Walter, Brad or Harry last month. During a long sentence, time would gradually erode support. People have to get on with their lives.

Several trivialities are conspiring to lower my morale, but recognizing the cause enables me to endure.

I suggest we name the sheltie on the postcard, "Tuffy." If or when we get a puppy we'll have a name ready.

Played chess. Won. Maybe I'm not getting Alzheimer's.

I'm thinking of writing a book, "The Thinking Person's Guide to Prison" or maybe a better title is "A Dummies Guide to Incarceration." What do you think?

Release—165 days. I heard Jimmy Carter interviewed on PBS. He said a lesson he learned is that any personal disaster—if you have courage, patience and a willingness to learn from it—can be turned into an opportunity. The words carried wisdom for me.

I went to yard and walked my ten laps. I talked to Paul Wilson—the Minister I thought of celling with. He has an appeal coming up. His victim (of what?) will be there, but according to Paul, will support his early release.

I revisited my disappointment with the Unitarian church. When the official church asked me to volunteer to serve on the board, to run a pledge drive, or to join a committee it was always a representative of the official church or the district that called me. Through the church I made friends. During this crisis many of the friends have visited me, but <u>no one</u> representing the organization. No Minister, no board member. When they needed me, I was there. I need them—where are they?

Release—163 days. A misty morning. Bits of fog drifted by me as I walked to the chow hall. I hope the weather at the beach was bright.

Worked at the shop today. I passed the "TV from hell" to another worker. *"Another pair of eyes might have better luck."* I'm working on a radio and am confident I can fix it.

I watched "Masterpiece Theatre" last night. An escapist English comedy.

I finished reading "I Know This Much is True."

Release—162 days. I'm sorry I missed you last night. I did call Pinesburg to check for any messages to be relayed. I'll try again tonight. It may be late, however. We have to be in our cells from 10:30PM until 11:30PM. Although access to the phone is much easier, it is by no means guaranteed.

I fixed the radio I was working on. The "TV from hell" remains recalcitrant. I also did a better job—almost professional—of repairing the nose pad on my glasses.

Release—161 days. I enjoyed our call. I told Tuffy you were OK. He barked, softly, at the mention of your name. Looking forward to tomorrow's visit.

I had a nice dream recently about my sons when they were five and three. I enjoyed being a father. The boys were imbrued with innocence, joy and curiosity. I felt a heavy responsibility and pride.

I worked this afternoon. I had to swap the motor out of a fan.

To: Book Club
Re: "I Know This Much Is True" by Wally Lamb

This book was immensely enjoyable. Too bad it was so short. ☺

The obvious question is, "If they're identical twins how can only Thomas be schizophrenic?" Lamb does not address this point. I concluded that some slight—perhaps random—difference in early nurturing was magnified and manifested itself in Thomas. The author may very well have intended the reader just to accept the premise without question.

Dominick is truly stuck by life. There is no one else to care for his ill, volatile twin brother and it is impossible for Dominick to abandon him. Dominick has total empathy with Thomas's plight but, nevertheless, is embarrassed of Thomas's public behavior because of their shared identity. Dominick—as are many of us—is trapped by events in life not of our own making.

The interplay of the therapy and events in Dominick's life is poignant. The process of self-revelation and understanding is entertaining and illuminating. It would be idyllic if all therapy was as successful.

Lamb does a great job of making Dominick a real person by introducing his loves—his ex-wife and his girlfriend—and his hates—his stepfather and the boyfriend of his ex-wife—but in the end, all are human. Even Ray, the stepfather, who seemed sadistically brutal, is uncovered to be a human who was trying to do the best, as he understood it. Ray, too, is a victim of life and, through the haze of misplaced beliefs of human interaction, further victimizes. The humanization of Ray is insightful of the author.

The true brute in the story is the system. The uncaring, go-by-the-rules, system that places Thomas in a maximum-security hospital and treats him—and consequently Dominick—as <u>something</u> to be processed. *"I'm just following orders."* The future predicted for Thomas by the system is self-fulfilling.

The diary of the grandfather plays an important role in guiding Dominick through the self-discovery regime. *"If Grandfather could be so wrong about himself, what am I deluding myself about?"* was the tacit question.

I wish I could hear your comments.

Release—160 days. Lovely visit. The benefits of a visit splash onto the anticipation and the remembrance.

Commissary went OK. No hot chocolate yet. After my current supply of lemonade and Tang runs out, I'm not buying anymore. Changing seasons. I'll continue drinking grapefruit juice for breakfast.

Tuffy is doing well. I'll get him back to you soon. I told Phyllis and Warren about him. Through his eyes, I'll see you. Through his eyes, you'll see me.

Another silly British comedy, "Last of the Summer Wine" has started on PBS. It's almost too silly. British humor is either sophisticated or silly. The eccentricity of the characters maintains interest.

I asked Don his opinion of his current cellbuddy, Vic Darsey. I'm formulating a plan that entails me taking Don's bunk when Don goes home. Vic is quiet, a non-smoker, who keeps normal hours. Vic has the lower bunk, but I survived on the upper bunk when I celled with Barry. Don thought it would work out. Vic subscribes to "The Wall Street Journal" and I see him frequently in the walk. I deduce that he has his own money and won't be "borrowing" things. I'll talk to Vic—if I can get him to talk. When I greet him on the walk, he grunts—quite reticent. He seldom comes to the rec area.

I have $103 in my commissary account. There is also, for each inmate, a release account into which money, only from job earnings, is slowly accumulated until there is $50. The release account is given to the inmate upon release. My release account has $17.41. I have 46 stamps. I didn't know I had that many. End of financial report. ☺

Release—159 days. My mood is good today. I heard Sibelius's Fifth last night. I got a haircut as well. I didn't work this afternoon and was able to do ten laps in the yard. I talked to a sparrow that was on the fence. I gave him directions to our house and a message to give to you. He flew away. To get the message you have to be in the back yard. You must listen. You'll recognize the bird. A little brown sparrow chirping the message. The message is *"I love you."* He'll chirp it twice.

I haven't talked with Vic about the cell move. Another inmate told me that Don was going home this month. Why would Don tell me differently? Weird. But, if true, I may be out of this smoke filled cell and the nightly ramblings of Elliot sooner.

The nature of my existence seems to be fixed for the days remaining. The only potential development is the data processing workshop. My gut tells me that that won't happen.

I feel some of my letters are content-free. Most of my days are content-free.

Release—158 days. A rumor has arisen that there will be a significant increase in phone charges. Could you e-mail Phyllis, David, Troy, Bud, and Carl and ask if they have seen the increase? Some are saying that the minimum charge is $30 for a thirty-minute call. If true, it sounds like a good strategy by the system to curtail family support and increase recidivism. We have to keep the prisons full to provide jobs for the DOP personnel.

Has the sparrow delivered the message?

I wrote the librarian for a library pass. See if I get an answer. The repair shop job conflicts with the normal library schedule. Things are never simple.

I also determined that a quarter of one's earnings are routed to the release account until the limit of $50 is reached.

I had a good visit with Sam and Lucy.

Release—157 days. The phones were busy last night. I didn't make an extraordinary effort to get access since I had no agenda to discuss.

I spoke to Vic about moving in with him. The idea was new to him. He had someone else in mind. He said he'd get back to me. He has the reputation of being a bit eccentric—as I do, probably.

I brushed Tuffy's hair. He looks sleek and glossy. I mention your name and he gets agitated. He misses you. I miss you.

Release—156 days. My sermon this morning was "The Sin of Gambling." A good sermon, but not apparently relevant. If the aim of a sermon is to induce thought, then it succeeded.

I'm entering into a contract with Phil to do my laundry. He'll do eight loads a month for $4.00 of commissary goods. I've known him and he'll do a good job. He has no outside money. Paradoxically, laundry is more difficult on the honor tier than the other tiers. On the other tiers, there are two inmates officially designated as the laundry guys. In principle, they do all of the laundry except for those in the Commons. On the honor tier, because leaving the cell is so much easier, each inmate is expected to do their own, hence no laundry guys. I'm sure the COs know of Phil's contracts, but since it eases the functioning of the tier, they tolerate the arrangements. Inmates have been known to fight over perceived violations of protocol at the laundry. *"Hey, I was next!" "Nah, I had my clothes on the drier."* Phil gets along well with all, so he won't have a problem.

A light sprinkle prevented yard exercise, but I walked in the gym for forty minutes followed by a hot (rare) shower. The heat has been turned on and the cells are hot. We opened the window and turned on the fan. I slept under a sheet on top of the blanket.

Release—155 days. After your visit, I worked today. However, Sergeant said we wouldn't work in the next two days. I've been thinking of your question about the young mother visiting her ex-husband in prison so that he could maintain contact with the son. A hard question. He will, of course, blame her for the troubles. *"If the bitch hadn't only been interested in money, I wouldn't've had to rob the store. All she talked about was child support. Shit, I gave her what I could. She just wouldn't let me see my boy—my very own son—unless I paid her money. I hope to hell she's happy now."* Consistent with my superego theory, he'll see himself as a good father who was merely obtaining the means to interact with his child. Will he change while in prison? Lamentably, I don't believe so. There will be no therapy for him and other inmates will feed his sense of persecution. I worry about her personal safety. *"No one will keep me from my son."* He'll dwell on that night after night as he lies in bed.

I spoke with an inmate on the walk a couple of days ago. I asked him if he had much time left. He replied, *"Oh, no. Just two and a half years."* Made me appreciate my situation.

My change in my visitor's list has been processed. Should be OK for the holidays.

Don Miller will go home within the week. I have written the tier officer stating that I'd like to move in with Vic to get into a non-smoking cell. Vic never responded to my inquiry. I figured, hell, they didn't ask me when they put Elliot in with me, so I won't wait for Vic's approval.

A year ago I was sitting in the County Detention Center wondering where I'd be in a year. I'm now in Rochelle wondering where I'll be in a year. Only five months remain. Twelve down.

Release—154 days. I have a small circle of friends on the tier. Manual, Jose, Paul, and Ernie, but loneliness is still the biggest problem.

Tuffy sniffed the letter you sent. He knew it came from you. I have someone to miss you with.

I'd like to order Christmas gifts for people. The catalog ordering period is in a couple of months. If you send some catalogs and I charge things to our credit card I should be able to do so. I don't remember our credit card number, but you can send it to me encoded. 0=J, 1=E, 2=M, 3=A, 4=L, 5=V, 6=U, 7=K, 8=I, and 9=O. There is no pattern to these substitutions. My outgoing mail is unopened so this code won't be intercepted. This will be fun! I'll figure out who can open which package and wrap individual gifts. I may need some sizes if I order clothes.

Release—153 days. A busy day. I will get a medication refill, go to yard, go to library and telephone you. Phil has already done one load of laundry for me.

Release—152 days. You sounded harried on the telephone last night. Installation of new financial software on our PC is a task that, seems to me, could've waited, but you've started. You need to make your life simpler. Remember that I'll need something to do when I get home.

I had a good morning in the shop. Diagnosed and repaired a problem with a TV. Helps self-esteem. The inmate clerk in the repair shop was fired this morning. Sergeant was wrong and the incident illustrated to me his volatility and irrationality. The clerk merely questioned the procedures for getting spare parts and offered alternatives that are more efficient. The puerile CO, accustomed to total deference, interpreted the clerk's actions as a questioning of authority. *"What do you think you're doing? I run this shop, you don't. No inmate is going to tell me what to do. Get out the hell out of here. Go back to your cell. You're fired."* The CO has total discretion and the dismissal will not be reviewed. The system taught the clerk that creativity and efforts to improve matters are summarily punished. The clerk will lose the ability to accumulate work credits and suffer the boredom of no job until he can find another job. Difficult.

The milieu induces a particular form of insanity. The psyche is molded into something that can survive. Normalcy cannot survive. Nothing normal in here.

I'm not going to dinner. I have an apple and two slices of bread that I brought back from lunch. I'll make a peanut butter and jelly sandwich. I'll also make noodle soup. I seldom miss lunch or dinner. I rarely go to breakfast.

Release—151 days. There are two possibilities next week. Don goes home and perhaps I'll change cells. He is also trying to have me hired as his replacement as a teacher's aide so maybe I'll change jobs.

I had a great night at chess. Won against the best players.

Release—150 days. A cloudy lugubrious morning. Good yard exercise and shower yesterday. I talked to Carl last night. His car isn't running. I have to fight the parental urge to solve his problems. I must step back and let him solve his own problems and mature.

I heard Telemann's "A-minor Recorder Concerto." Michala Petri showed amazing virtuosity.

I read the first sermon of the new group, "Angel, Devils, and Yikes…Us" Very good.

An official letter from the Inmate's Representatives (an officially recognized and sanctioned committee) to the warden was posted on the bulletin board in the rec area. The letter protested the recent rise in telephone charges. The letter states that the rate was $1.85 for the first minute and 14¢ to 16¢ for each minute thereafter. Now, the letter claims, the rate is $4.95 for the first minute and 59¢ for each additional minute. Is the DOP so insipid as to be unaware of the importance of maintaining family ties as deterrence to recidivism? Most of the guys come from impoverished backgrounds—indeed, that's what brought many here.

Do you realize that since I started counting the number of days until release, 1/4 of them have elapsed? Soon it will be over.

It's 8:00AM and I'm in the upper level rec area, sitting next to a lambent window. I have a cup of hot coffee and a sugar roll. No one else is here. I have my mail spread out and am answering letters from Phyllis and Warren, Carl, Elgin and Kathy, and Mary. As I look out the window, fog hides the walkway. The tier is quiet. As far as Rochelle goes, it doesn't get much better.

I return Tuffy to you. The card is enclosed. Place him where you can see him. Return him after he is acclimated and let him be a messenger of our love.

Release—149 days. It was good seeing you again. It must be quite a burden on you to make the trips from home to Rochelle. Can you imagine the day when I'll be in the car when you leave?

Worked this afternoon. I have made progress on the TV on my bench, but it is still not working. The "TV from hell" is still not working, but it's not my problem. Bye for now.

Rochelle State Prison, Housing Unit 1, Tier A, Cell 9, Vic.

Release—148 days. I changed cells! I moved into Don's old spot with Vic. Don went home. I have the upper bunk, but it will be OK. From his reaction, Vic was expecting someone else.

If the Education Department wants to interview me for Don's job, they may call me. I'll miss Don, a kindred spirit. I am happy that he went home, but I am ecstatic to have his bunk. By making the request for the transfer and expressing my unhappiness in a reasoned way, I accomplished an improvement.

Release—147 days. An excellent day. Received lots of mail. Vic was impressed that I got <u>five</u> letters. It'll work out fine with Vic. He's about 35 and has spent 14 years in prison, the first 7 at PEC (the state psychiatric institution). He has 11 more to go. He got a college degree while at PEC. He inherited money from his father a few years ago and has investments. He loans me "The Wall Street Journal" and I loan him my paper. He has a job as a clerk in the administration office. He doesn't smoke and sleeps normal hours.

About sleeping patterns—I believe there are rhythms of week's duration during which one easily wakes early and is ready to go. Then comes the antipode, during which one cannot get enough sleep, wakes reluctantly and is plagued by morning lethargy. I have no idea what causes the difference.

At midnight, I was called to the dispensary. They took a blood sample for the annual DOP physical. Apparently, I will be called back in a couple of weeks to discuss the results.

I had one success and one failure at work. These combination radio/cassette/CD players are like a 3D puzzle. They are difficult to disassemble, to access the components and to reassemble. In some cases, I'm sure we do more harm than good, but there's no alternative. Inmates are not allowed to send them out for repair. Another inmate has told me that I'll be interviewed for the teacher's aide job in two weeks. However, since the story comes from an inmate, I'll believe it when it happens.

Writing letters is a nexus to the real world for me. It forces me to think beyond the razor wire ambit and to form images of what awaits me. I must not accept this environment or the inmates or the COs as representative of reality. I recognize that the letters I receive are written because of a concern for me.

If my sentence were long, I would have to come to grips with the existence herein. The need for discussions and sharing of thoughts would force me to reach out to the other inmates. I could not maintain the isolation that I now self-impose.

Release—146 days. I slept well last night without resorting to blindfold and radio headphones. Work went well today. Fixed a TV and a fan.

My day-to-day life has improved. I have a cell in which I can rest. I have a job that is engaging at times, and I don't have to struggle to do my laundry. All is relatively stress free. I'm in the best situation since incarceration. Must be time to go home. I trust you have received Tuffy by now. Mention my name. Does he perk his ears?

I see flowers and birds. I see sunrises and I rejoice in all of them. I believe it is healthy to search for beauty in the small things, to make beauty in the everyday routines, and take comfort.

Release—145 days. I fixed a Walkman at work. Itsy-bitsy parts. The pickup head had broken a support. I replaced it with a spare and all worked—lucky inmate.

I had a jovial visit with Brad, Harry and Walter. It was shortened because they never paged me at work. When I asked why, they responded, *"We didn't know where you were."* I thought that was ironic—they have me in prison and they don't know where I'm at? In reality, they were sending me a message. For those of us who have a regular job, exiting the tier and housing unit at the designated times becomes routine. Some COs are irritated if you tell them where you're going. It interrupts their reverie. They have to put their coffee cup down and write. They prefer that you just come and go. Other COs obey all the rules and will write a ticket if you don't ask permission to leave the tier. The inmate doesn't necessarily know which CO is on tier duty and can be entrapped. I made such a mistake this morning. I left the tier and went to work without checking out. This is acceptable behavior with many COs, but not this morning. When they had to page me for the visit, I was paged only on the tier—not at work. The message being sent was, *"You must check out."* I'll make sure in the future, if I err, to err on the conservative side and check out if there's any question.

I've written Herb to ask that he petition the judge to modify my sentence so that I am credited for the county time. It's only four days, but four days at the end of the sentence will seem an eternity.

There's an inmate on the tier, Shawn, who two days ago had an appeal hearing scheduled. Matters were supposed to have all been settled—*"A done deal."* His attorney, the prosecutor, the judge and the victim were in agreement for a reduction in sentencing. It was even conceivable that Shawn would walk out of the appeal courtroom as a free man. Shawn made the arduous trip to the county courthouse, stopping at Classification to spend the night trying to sleep on the floor and feasting on cold sandwiches. When he arrived at the courthouse, he was informed that the judge had had a heart attack, and the appeal was postponed indefinitely. Shawn's wife and family had driven 800 miles to be present—all for naught. Terrible things, beyond anyone's control, can happen.

I've seen beautiful sunsets recently. I remember those I saw from Classification. I blow kisses to the evanescent reds, oranges, pinks and gold. The clouds shimmer as they bounce the kiss to your lips. The kisses warm you and impart their colors to your eyes and cheeks. Before tomorrow, I dream, I sleep. I join you and share happiness and one more day is gone.

Release—144 days. I joked this morning in the shop that I didn't want to help repair the electric chair. Even Sergeant O'Reilly smiled.

Release—143 days. The sermon I read this morning was "Meaning in a Random Universe." It explored a phenomenon that causes awe and shivers in many—the coincidence of independent events creating an illusion of correlation. For example, once in Detroit, Bud, Carl and I were driving to lunch. We were discussing whether we wanted hamburgers or pizza. No one was strongly inclined one way or the other. As we were stopped at a light, I looked at the car in the adjacent lane; I saw that its vanity plate was "PIZZA 3." Surely, that was a sign from heaven, so we had pizza for lunch. I believe, as does the author of the sermon, that the congruence of such random events is inevitable because the opportunities are so numerous. We don't notice the lack to coincide—only the coincidences. Read the sermon if you get a chance.

Vic sleeps all weekend. He stays in the bed all day and only arises to eat commissary food from the locker and goes back to bed.

I feel lonely at times. Do you? I can be in a crowd of inmates and feel isolated. The best I can do for myself is to get the most from each day—read, write, exercise and dream of tomorrow.

Release—142 days. A nice visit. A reminder—send me "The House Sand and Fog." I've not heard of Andre Dubus. Have you?

Vic runs a lending library of pornographic magazines. He charges other inmates a fee (candy bar, a bag of chips) but the COs have free access.

Release—141 days. The authors I confuse are Henry James and Henry Adams. They both come from distinguished American families. They were contemporaries and have the same first name. Both men were citizens of the world. Adams is known for non-fiction, where James is known for fiction. When one of the names is mentioned, I pause for an instant to make sure I have the correct one in mind. I wonder if they ever met—I suppose they did. I've finished "The Turn of the Screw" by James. It's a quintessential gothic and gives credence to the role that the editor of the anthology assigns James, *"…first of the modern psychological novelists."*

I'm starting a non-fiction book, "Evil, Inside Human Violence and Cruelty," by Roy F. Baumeister, a professor at Case Western Reserve University.

Had step two of my DOP physical today. Blood pressure was 120/80 as measured in a hurried manner. I don't trust these medical people. They must be subjected to enormous pressure to economize. They also did an EKG.

I've made a "remote control" for my TV. I cut apart a plastic coat hanger and glued the parts together to form a long stick with which I can poke the control buttons. It works well. It enables me to change channels and volume without climbing down from my bunk. I keep the 'mote stowed underneath the mattress. It could be considered as contraband.

Vic and I have a routine. I get up first; have my grapefruit juice, medicine, coffee and pastry. I dress and then read while he gets up. He has a morning orange juice. He snacks frequently during the day and misses many meals. Vic is a collector. He has weeks, perhaps months, of issues of Wall Street Journals stuffed in nooks in the cells. He has past copies of (porno?) magazines under the bunk. Even the COs borrow magazines from him.

Release—140 days. Worked today and fixed a fan. There is an ample supply of spare parts from broken fans left by inmates as they depart. I believe our clerk was fired because he talked to the COs in charge of departing inmates about the possibility of retrieving more discards for use as spares. Sergeant doesn't want his inmates talking to other COs about the innards of the operation.

Commissary shopping was successful. I bought a supply of hot chocolate mix, which, together with milk brought back from lunch, makes a nice nightcap.

Four and a half months to go.

Release—139 days. I repaired a tape cassette today. I'm becoming the "official fixer" of such problems. Often the problem is a broken belt or a belt that has slipped from the capstan. I'm the one in the shop who knows how to use an oscilloscope and the principles of a capacitor. What I lack is a working knowledge of the technology.

Baumeister's book is enjoyable. He offers a deep perspective of the societal views of evil. He especially attacks the characterization of behaviors and attitudes as one extreme or the other.

Winter is coming. Picture us sitting in a glass-enclosed solarium. Big soft flakes of snow flitter down, gradually covering the roof. Cups of cinnamon coffee warm our hands as our sock-clad toes play with each other on the shared footstool. Birds flutter on the feeder outside. Vivaldi's "Four Seasons" wafts from the radio. Our robes invite love. The world is our solarium. The rest is an illusion.

Release—138 days. My new cell is much closer to the telephones so I can more easily monitor them for availability. I did go to the library last night. The procedure is different than I had been led to believe. One doesn't have to get a pass, but merely show up at the front of the housing unit when there is a "library call." None of this is documented, of course. No wonder I never got a response to my requests for a library pass. My request could've provided an opportunity for an explanation of the process, but official silence is never punished. Information control.

I received "The House of Fog and Sand" in the mail. I'm sure I'll finish it in time for the book club report. I have finished Baumeister's book.

No work today, for the first time in some time. Strange to have so much time. Four and a half months to go. I remember when I thought I'd spend two and a half years in here. We were convinced we could endure that period. We could've, but it would have been difficult. Thirteen months have gone by. I remember the joy at Classification when I was told that my release date, given good conduct credit, was a year and eight months. That seemed so much shorter than two and a half years. Time goes by.

I remember a year ago when Mr. John and I shared appreciation of the sunsets as we walked to chow. He and I mused that the younger guys didn't know what they were missing.

Release—137 days. Vic—our cell—was shook down last night. Like last time, we were handcuffed and taken out of the cell. The COs went through my stuff lightly, but they scoured Vic's belongings. Some materials (paper, pencils) are missing from the administration building so they shook down every inmate who works there. Vic did get a warning (hooray!) about the quantity of newspapers and magazines that he has stuffed here and there.

I had the third and final part of my DOP physical—ears, hernia, prostate, throat and heart. They did hear my heart murmur.

Release—136 days. I'll try to repair my wristwatch in the shop. The buttons no longer work so I can't correct the time. The back is held on by tiny screws, which I can undo in the shop. Last year it read one hour early for six months. Worst-case scenario is that I ruin the watch and have no watch for the next four months.

Each morning when I awake, I hear a CD stuck on a track that says, *"Four months, four months, four months."* Am I staring too intently at the light at the end of the tunnel? There are things that can go terribly wrong in spite of my efforts.

I try to get the most out of each day. I try to be smart. I interact with the other inmates minimally. I am not versed in their method of interaction and worry that I would violate some unspoken code and get into trouble. I have developed into an recluse. There are inmates whom I talk comfortably with—Barry, Jose, Phil, Howard, Manual, Paul…. We all play a role and try to get to the next day. I am infinitely blessed compared with all others. I have you and, at this moment, I'm doing what I enjoy—writing you, an act of sanity in an insane world, an act of beauty in this world of ugliness.

Release—135 days. Our visits are becoming predictable. No less enjoyable, just more predictable.

I enclose pictures—clipped from catalogs—of ideas for Christmas presents. Reactions?

Release—134 days. I successfully reset the time on my wristwatch. I removed the back and shorted out a couple of the traces. I lucked out. I won't need to worry about it again. I'll be out before the time needs to reset again.

The Education Department didn't work last night so there was no opportunity for an interview. I'm not optimistic, but merely relaying information.

Thinking about your conversations with the neighbors, it's gratifying when the nicest people stay supportive.

Imagine Tuffy on the beach chasing gulls. The puppy and the birds are about the same size and the gulls are more annoyed than frightened by the troublesome interloper. Some don't bother to fly unless they're pushed hard. Tuffy would be surprised if he actually caught a gull and seems to avoid making the last lunge. His instincts urge him to gather the gulls and herd them. But where? Into the water? But he doesn't have to make that choice because the gulls won't bunch. Damned birds. They're white, but they don't bleat. He barks in frustration. The surf roils. White caps stretch to the horizon.

Release—133 days. I'm almost finished with "The House of Fog and Sand." I want to yell at the characters.

No work today, but I did see my case manager. She gave me a time credit summary. The dates seem in order. I asked about the data processing shop—*"You could be called anytime."*

I ordered $310 worth of presents from "Signals," and $273 worth from "LL Bean." It's a fun way to do Christmas shopping.

Release—132 days. A busy day. Fixed two TVs at work. I had to swap out the picture tube on one. I did commissary shopping and got my medication refill.

Release—131 days. Finished "The House of Fog and Sand" and enclose my book report.

I did not get the teacher's aide job. I'm not disappointed. I'm becoming acclimated to the repair shop job and becoming better at it. Patience is an virtue.

Have you been following the newspaper reports of the abuses at the prison in Colenth? The authorities characterize the inmate's complaints as being "self-serving" while conveniently ignoring that their own official denials of any problems are also "self-serving." Ayn Rand would not view "self-serving" as pejorative.

To: Book Club
Re: "House of Sand and Fog" by Andre Dubus III

This book was difficult to read because it captured the reader. I, on several occasions, had to put the book down because I was too involved with the characters. I wanted to yell at them for their stupidity—shake them to their senses.

Dubus did a good job at creating the diverse voices in which the story was told. The Iranian Colonel and his wife, the Behranis, were, perhaps, stereotypes—as was Kathy, but the characterizations were believable.

The biggest problem with the book was the initial conditions. It was hard for me to believe that Colonel Behrani, given his persona (revealed later in the story) would have degraded himself by picking up garbage. Would the Colonel's anger remain quiescent in the face of Mendez's taunting? Why was the sophisticated sheriff so vulnerable that he took actions that resulted in his ruination? Why would Kathy blithely throw away official tax documents concerning her dearly held heritage?

But, given the initial conditions, the book is a powerful and insightful story into human behavior. The internal conversations of the characters were especially poignant for me because I had just read "Evil, Inside Human Violence and Cruelty," by Baumeister. Some of the constructs of Baumeister, e.g., "the myth of pure evil" were well illustrated by the mental attitudes and images that the characters formed of each other. As the reader bounced back and forth among the minds and internal thoughts of each character, the humanness of each is revealed and the evil that others detected was indeed shown to be a myth as Baumeister maintains.

It's a story of human tragedy with no winners. If there is a moral, it is that life and personal relationships are so fragile that it takes only few small misunder-standings and inattentions to destroy what is held dear.

Release—130 days. I'm reading "High Tide in Tucson" by Barbara King-solver. I find that she writes well, but her subject material is trite. Her insights aren't particularly deep and she arrogantly gives undue importance to events merely because they happened to her. I'm about a third of the way so my opinion may change.

Change of pace—what do we do if ugly incidents happen when I am released? If some believe that I haven't been punished enough and damage our cars or spray paint our door? Silent telephone calls in the middle of the night? How stoic can we be?

We had yard today. The chill prodded me to walk two extra laps just to keep warm.

Release—128 days. Enjoyed the sermon "Living with Integrity" by Kerry Mueller. She defines "Living with Integrity" as:

1. Discerning what is right and wrong.

2. Acting on what you have discerned, even at personal cost, and

3. Saying openly that you are acting on your understanding of right from wrong.

She gives examples from times of slavery and Nazism. She waffles a bit—*"Under conditions of tyranny, true integrity may not meet the full criteria...."* Wish we were together to discuss it in depth. Good sermon. Relevant.

Release—127 days. Sorry to hear about the garbage disposal. It <u>will</u> get fixed.

My Hispanic friend, Jose, was transferred this morning from a cell that he shared with a young black man into a cell with an older white guy. Jose had been unhappy in his first cell because the young man insisted on playing rap music loudly. I know of no exception to the pairings in cells of whites with whites and blacks with blacks. However, Hispanics are placed with either.

I heard a Franck Sonata in A last night. Originally for Violin and Piano, it had been transposed for Viola and Piano. The violist was Imai. I wanted to share it with you.

Release—126 days. No work this morning and none tomorrow. I need a job on the outside that has as many off-days.

I finished "High Tides in Tucson," a collection of disjointed essays and lectures that have been previously published or given. The later chapters have more depth than the early ones. A great aphorism—*"The purpose of fiction is to create empathy."* Many inmates don't read, so I wonder if Kingsolver has unearthed a nugget.

An acquaintance from B tier went home today, but he left at 10:00AM, not 8:00AM because of twice-a-month morning CO training. Those two extra hours must have been hell. What bad luck to have your release date fall on a day that the COs can't release you early.

My case manager tells me that when one is within sixty days of being release, the release date is firm and is not recalculated in case of a job loss. Four months to go.

Release—125 days. I read about similar cases as mine in the newspaper. Some result in more lenient sentences than mine—some harsher. Justice is a crapshoot.

Release—124 days. Indulge me in a fantasy. If we were to emigrate, to which country would we go? My choice—The Netherlands, somewhere close to Amsterdam. The Dutch drive on the correct side of the road and there is a cornucopia of culture. Holland is close to German wine. The Dutch are friendly people and most speak English. France, à la Hemingway, is impossible because of our inability to speak French. We could vacation in Paris.

I heard Sibelius's "Symphony #2."

Release—123 days. I had a good ten laps in yard today, except for unwelcome company. There's an inmate, middle-aged white guy, who works in the lobby of the housing unit. He's known as "Lobby Dick," a name he answers to, but doesn't particularly like. Lobby Dick has a medical problem and a mental one. He has seizures, which narrows significantly the jobs he can work. Medication reduces the number and severity of his seizures, but doesn't eliminate them. His mental problem—perhaps associated with his medical status—is that he talks incessantly and repeats himself. His stories are cogent and he doesn't talk nonsense. He may be friendless and, because I am a kind soul, has latched onto me. He searches me out on the walks to the chow hall to tell me the story that he told me two days ago. On my walk today, he found me and, in a newfound desire to become more physically fit, walked eight of the ten laps with me. I nod, mutter and grunt. There is no deterrence. I should feel that this is an opportunity to do a kindness.

Release—122 days. I heard on the radio that a recording of Joshua Bell playing the Sibelius Violin Concerto is soon to be released. The announcer had a preview copy and was laudatory—compared him with Heifetz. The announcer said that Bell had Hollywood-star good looks. The kid has gone a long way since we heard him as a child prodigy.

I called my brother Troy last night. He repeated to me his belief that I am fortunate to have you as my wife. I agreed with him and said that I was fortunate to have my entire family stand with me and give me support, him included.

Most inmates, often for reasons not understood by the inmates themselves, have lost their family. In many cases, I suspect, the inmate has victimized their family. In other cases, the family may be in such a crisis that the financial burden of maintaining contact is too much. Visits, telephone calls and postage require money, which may be better spent supporting, perhaps, the inmates' children. Some inmates are not literate. From our fortunate vantage point, we may not be able to appreciate the conditions of many inmates and families. The severance of family ties may not be an act of volition, but a necessary one.

Release—121 days. Went to work this morning. Ed, a co-worker, had been working on a radio for a couple of weeks and screwed it up worse than it was. Noise, at least, came out of it when it arrived. Ed convinced Sergeant to pass it on to me. Ed thinks that by using the oscilloscope I can fix it easily. The lack of a schematic makes an oscilloscope less useful. Damn. I feel that I could've fixed it when it came in. Of course, I'll be a hero if I can fix it. Not likely.

Release—120 days. Commissary went OK. No work today, but since it's not our day for yard, I can't take advantage of the time to exercise.

Last night I heard "Pastoral Fantasia for Viola and Orchestra" by the British composer Alwyn. The British Government, during WWII, had commissioned "uplifting music" to help the national morale and this piece was one result. My spirits were uplifted.

Release—119 days. From the library I got, "The Vintage Mencken," assembled by Alistair Cooke, to help educate me. I know of Mencken, but not about him.

Release—118 days. I worked today, but made no progress on the problem radio. When I returned to the cell after work, I missed the call for lunch somehow. I made some noodles and had a candy bar. I'll be ready for dinner.

I've started a new habit. If milk is served for lunch, I bring it back to the cell for making hot chocolate at night.

I wonder if Jesse Jackson roiling against the policy of zero-tolerance within the schools and the juvenile justice system might be an impetus to look at the entire justice system? Zero-tolerance further enhances the dichotomy of defining people into good-bad, no in-betweens. When I watch "Cops" or "America's Most Wanted" the question, *"Why did Joe (or Jane) behave this way?"* is never asked. The supposition, planted by the announcer, *"Because he/she is bad,"* is accepted by the audience and by the police. The theme song of "Cops" (*"Bad boy, bad boy. What'ja gonna do when they come for you."*) illustrates this perception. Putting an 11-year old on trial. Charging kids with felonies for putting soap in their teacher's drink. Is this where get-tough-on-crime has brought us? Zero-tolerance implies no forgiveness. Is that a lesson we wish to teach?

I think of the agony of the families of the two boys who committed the Columbine massacre. Some in the Columbine community didn't want to note the boys' deaths. Does the community not see the tragedy of the boys' lives as well as the tragedy of the shootings? Are there any that see the inmates in here as victims as well? Some were born without an adequate ability or talent, into a fragmented family, which offered little love. Such inmates are doomed from the beginning.

Release—117 days. A year ago, I arrived at Rochelle. Much has happened. Four different cells. Three different jobs. No trouble. If I look out the window, will I see some poor guy walking toward the housing unit with a box of state clothes, not sure where he is going nor what tomorrow will bring? A whole year has gone by. Suppose it was the first of many? Could I survive? Could our love survive? Thankfully, we don't have that test. In 117 days, I'll get out and I predict that I will be surprised how quickly normalcy returns.

I got a card from Amy saying you had agreed to be a casino dealer at the annual party. Are you sharpening some potential retirement skills?

I did have to work so missed yard. I'm making some progress on the radio. Still a long way from repair however.

Release—115 days. A fantastic day. The moon was almost full. The sparrow tree next to the chow hall was almost full. My sermon this morning was by Rev. Taylor of Cedar Lane Unitarian Church. The title was about love, but the sermon was really about spirituality and the ways to achieve it. To paraphrase—*"UUs shouldn't have to believe that dancing in the aisles and shouting 'hallelujah' is the only expression of spirituality."* I enjoyed it.

Release—114 days. I worked today. I believe I ended my involvement with the problem radio. After trying all I could think of, I told Sergeant that our only option was to order a new output amplifier circuit board. This, I knew, would mean that he'd have to have to use the telephone to locate a vendor and I doubt that he will do that. I was successful with my next assignment—fixed a radio. I forgot my jacket in the repair shop. I'll worry about it until I can retrieve it (when?). It should be OK. I have my heavy state coat if the weather turns bitter cold. Sergeant is vacationing the month after next, so there will be little, if any work then.

I'm impressed with the hope that Christianity brings to many inmates. Instead of dealing with the reality of spending the next 25 years herein, they believe that divine intervention will shortly free them. Is this hope good or bad? I keep quiet, although I want to draw attention to their plight and the need to deal with it. Perhaps they are. Their belief gets them through the next day—not a trivial accomplishment. They pray a lot and discuss with other adherents some scripture in the Bible. Maybe that, too, gets them through today.

Release—113 days. I awoke after a night of eclectic dreams to a foggy morning. I used hot water from the tap to make a cup of coffee. Vic had to go to work so I have some blessed time alone in the cell. I can defecate in private.

Release—112 days. I had my first pre-release informational meeting. The system knows I'm supposed to be released. I learned that 1) I don't have to be employed. I can retire. 2) I will be tested for drugs while on parole and probation. Twice a week in the beginning and then tapering off at a rate dictated by the parole officer. 3) I pay $50 a month for administration costs. 4) I pay a one-time fee of $100 for the drug testing. 5) There is nothing in the standard parole requirements about alcohol abstinence, but there are individual stipulations. 6) Permission from the parole officer is required to travel to other states. 7) When the parole officer visits your home, they are accompanied by a police officer. 8) They may speak with the neighbors.

Release—111 days. Had a great visit with Warren, Phyllis and Carl. The mood and discussion was very upbeat. I bet the day is hectic for you. I hope that being surrounded by loving and caring family is worth the hassle. I know the answer. Warren says they may be able to return on the release date. That would be welcomed.

Release—110 days. A good visit—even if it was short. It was great to see Bud and Carl. I'm aware that I push the conversation, to fill the silence. Do I appear idiotic? I want people who visit me to enjoy their visit and leave feeling that I'm well and coping well. I don't want to engender pity or worry. I want out.

I sometimes regret my "fun-poking," as when Bud asked me about financial record keeping. My lame attempt at humor probably did a disservice to all the work you do. My heritage dictates that one is able to poke fun only at those you love. It's a form of intimacy.

Release—109 days. I won every chess game last night against my nemesis, Rasheed. Good games. Time passed. Rasheed is a short muscular black man of thirty. He has a genial countenance and dancing eyes. He grins readily, which is an affectation to show his dimples. He plays chess exclusively with me, no doubt because I let my play and not my mouth speak for me. He has a temper. A few weeks ago, during the third game we played, he got upset because I didn't announce a check until after he quickly responded without realizing that he was in check. He claimed that I just wanted to see his "plan." He's a good enough player to know that only poor players don't realize they're in check. I also know that the official rules of chess don't require that check be announced. I don't have a copy of the official rules and suspect, in any case, that official versions of rules are moot herein. After his invective, I slowly rose and walked away. After a couple of days of contemplation, he asked me to play again and we have had a good series since. I do now announce checks, although he, as a mental ploy, often doesn't.

Yesterday, the visit was timed such that I missed lunch. In such circumstances the institution has to feed you. The CO asked me when I returned if I wanted a sack lunch. I had sardines and cheese from the commissary so I told the CO not to bother. I finished the feast with a candy bar.

Release—108 days. My sermon this morning was "Men, Anger, and Friendship," by Rev. Roger Fritts. Again, the sermon was successful—it caused me to think. Father-son relationships are discussed and my father, from the vantage point of a more enlightened time, was toxic in many ways. Yet consciously, I feel no anger toward him. I don't idolize him as much as I used to—I recognize his humanity. Am I in denial about my father? Denying what? I don't feel strongly about these questions and don't have a strong reaction. My opinion is that it's a non-issue.

Is there an age beyond which psychotherapy is senseless? Therapy is to enable one to live more successfully. But if there isn't much more life left...? In TV sitcoms, I don't remember any episode where "old people" were receiving psychotherapy.

I believe that parole officers—given their typical caseload—will see me as a dream case and won't hassle me once I've proven my acquiescence.

PBS had a show about home detention. It varies widely in application from state to state. They reported on some egregious failures. Again, a program benefiting hundreds is curtailed because of a few unavoidable failures.

Release—107 days. A day of no merit or demerit. I worked both morning and afternoon. I'm neutral—neither down nor up. Three and a half months to go. Could be longer. This letter is largely content free.

The real world is out there. This environment is artificial. Bits of the real world come into my space—visits, letters. Out there is important, so I write to there. I put, at times, nonsensical words down to maintain sanity and perspective.

Release—106 days. A year ago, you sent me a calendar and I started a daily log on it. Paradoxically, I look back a year and it seems a long time ago and yet the time has gone by fast. One year ago, I had orientation.

My newspaper subscription runs out in two and a half months. I need one month's extension. The mail has become slow. I'm getting letters from Phyllis dated two weeks ago. I still haven't received the letter from Herb about the time credits.

Release—105 days. At the library last night, I got a mystery by Daphne Du Maurier. I haven't read a mystery in a long time. I will finish it before I receive the next book club selection, "The Red Tent." Take your time in finishing it. We have a whole month.

No work this morning. Not sure about this afternoon. I need some exercise, but the cold weather may confine us to the gym. I hope they sort and distribute some of the mail.

Later: No work. I went to the gym, but had only forty minutes of walking instead of the usual fifty-five. It was the best I could do.

If I get a copy of the judge's order giving me the additional six days credit. I may send it to Ms. White, my case manager. You have a copy, right?

Release—104 days. I got a lot of mail yesterday—the judge's order, letters from Mary (she had her 90th birthday), Dianne (she writes long beautiful letters), and crossword puzzles.

I didn't like the dinner last night. I compensated by playing chess, popping corn and showering.

Release—103 days. The visit was too short. They always are. I did get to lunch. Bologna sandwich, black-eyed peas, pickle chips, coke and an apple. I saved my apple for later.

I was officially notified by DOP of the time credit of six days.

A bulletin concerning telephone rates and policy was posted on the bulletin board. It says that the maximum cost for a thirty-minute call within the state is $11.75 and out-of-state is $20.75. It further details the complaint procedure. Someone is making a lot of money at the expense of inmate's families.

Remember the story about Shawn—the inmate whose judge had the heart attack before an appeal hearing? Shawn did have his appeal hearing yesterday and got no reduction. All of the anxiety, two trips through classification, and sleeping on the floor for nothing.

Release—102 days. Worked today. Had to open two TVs of incoming inmates.

Barry will get me a copy of the telephone policy bulletin. I'll mail it to you.

Release—101 days. I read the latest issue of "Quest" for my sermon this morning. The act of "giving thanks" was discussed in columns.

I enclose a copy of the telephone bulletin.

I had a night filled with unremembered dreams. To go to sleep, I blindfolded myself, don the headphones from the Walkman and let my thoughts carry me anywhere.

Had ten laps in the yard.

Release—100 days. I worked this afternoon. Fixed a mechanical problem with a fan and provided the technical advice that enabled a microwave oven to be repaired.

I enjoy our planning. We have much to anticipate. It will be fun. As we navigate the roads to the future we can yell at each other, *"Turn here."*

Release—99 days. Double digits! Worked today and fixed two radios. Customers happy. I wrecked no havoc.

I'm thinking of what you can bring with you when you pick me up in 99 days—a thermos of cinnamon coffee, my wallet and a brimmed hat. We'll need to renew my driver's license. Probation office. Lunch (a hamburger). Dinner (a steak).

Commissary is tomorrow. Kipper snacks are available and I'll try some. I have eaten the second can of sardines. I also need coffee and stamps.

Release—98 days. At work, I was assigned a TV that the inmate had dropped. The picture tube and case was broken. I believe I can fix it by using parts from discarded sets.

A new policy—all new entrants on visitor's lists must have their birthday noted.

I got a note from DOP stating there was an error in the date in the six-day petition that Herb filed. He is not a detail person. Luckily, we have time to correct matters.

Release—96 days. We had heavy continuous drizzle today.

I got the broken TV fixed. It's my *magnum opus* in this job. The inmate is lucky because we had a spare for each broken part.

I had a visit with Brad, Harry and Walter. We talked about politics and the church. They were interested in my release date, retirement plans and relocation ideas. The sub-title I read was, *"Are you going to be around the church as an issue to deal with?"*

After release, as a volunteer, I don't want to spread myself too thin nor do I wish to charge windmills. I also wish to enjoy life and not be consumed with social reform battles. Candidate issues: 1) arbitrary definition of types of crimes as violent or non-violent, 2) mandatory sentencing, the boon of prosecutors and the bane of justice, 3) the vulturine phone system, 4) capital punishment, 5) the penal medical system, 6) the penal mail system, 7) the classification of people as "good" or "bad," 8) racism in the justice system, and 9) the charade of parole hearings. I could be consumed.

Release—95 days. You may get a call from Barry's father concerning the costs of telephone calls. He may wish to participate in any reformation efforts.

Sorry to hear about your problem with the credit card company. I, and presumably you, didn't realize your name wasn't on the application. They should've listened to you since you sent them a power-of-attorney and we both have cards. I've written the credit card company; although I'm not optimistic it will have an effect.

I went to the gym. I was limited to 40 minutes only of walking.

Release—94 days. This morning I read the sermon on "Rational Humanism." Characteristically cerebral.

A beautiful sunset blessed me yesterday. A sliver of a moon crowned wispy clouds. The thin silken strands were painted gold, blue, red, and all colors in between. I wanted your hand in mine.

I started reading the Mencken anthology.

Release—93 days. What I lovely time I have with you. You do ruffle your feathers at times. Thanks for pursuing the six-day order. Probably no intervention will be needed, but if a snafu developed and we hadn't done anything, we would regret our negligence.

I didn't work this morning, but did this afternoon. I won't work next week or the day after tomorrow.

No mail today. The mailroom is backed up. An inmate with a subscription to a hometown daily newspaper hasn't received an issue for three days. Nothing to be done about the laziness and inefficiency.

Release—92 days. A day of languid drizzle and high humidity. I'm still glowing from your visit.

I've started a project at work. We have several non-functioning TVs that inmates have donated. In reality they didn't want to carry them on the bus and couldn't afford to pay the shipping charges. I've found one for which, miraculously, we have the schematic. I will try to repair it. Assigned repair jobs consume about a fourth of the time I work, so I have time to devote to this project. I'm making progress. It had no picture or sound. I fixed the picture. The sound should be easy. I look forward to going to work. There is no urgency to get it working. No one cares if it works or not. I take my time and follow my curiosity. When I succeed with this one, I may start on a second.

I heard Saint-Saëns' "Concerto #5 in F for Piano" last night. I associate Saint-Saëns with quiet, moody music, but this piece was quite dramatic—bordering on eccentric.

I'm on page 80 of Mencken. Because of the nature of the anthology, it is impossible to be bored. Each entry is a few pages and the topics are wide-ranging. I look forward to re-entering it.

Mail—the dam broke, five letters and two magazines. Lack of work tomorrow will enable me to answer the letters. My mood is good. The numbers to release are getting small. Eight more refills of my medication are all that remain. I had a good night at chess. I also had a cheese and crackers snack. They could become addictive.

Release—91 days. A cloudy day, no work, an easy crossword puzzle.

The nose pad broke off my glasses again. I had to search for it, but did find it. I'll re-glue it tomorrow at work.

If I were offered the data processing shop, I'd refuse. The repair job will last until I'm within 60 days of release at which time I can't be reclassified.

We should have afternoon gym today, but I'm having a difficult time motivating myself. The gym is so inhospitable.

I'll be OK through the holidays. You worry about your own emotional well being and I'll take care of mine through this brief holiday period. I'll telephone and write. Knowing that you are with loved ones and are making the most of the situation will enable me to accept this brief hiatus. Soon this will be over.

I'm on page 140 of Mencken.

I had weird dreams last night. I don't remember much about them except they involved being in familiar surroundings—or rather surroundings with comfortable feelings. My dreams often have emotions—not images—as their primary ingredient. The brain, in response to dormant feelings, constructs an image, often nonsensical, as an accompaniment. Is the same true for you?

My letter tomorrow will be addressed to Pinesburg.

Release—90 days. Hope you had a good trip. All your holiday shopping done? ☺ I hope you can forget your cares and concerns.

I got a pass today for my medication refill and medical check, but I haven't been called yet.

I'm missing a magazine from last month. Some CO probably stowed it in his desk. The lost magazine does not irritate me, but the petty thievery that the system tolerates does. Inmates are fair game.

I repaired my glasses this morning. I had a great morning in the shop. I fixed my glasses, fixed a Walkman and fixed the discarded TV. Patience is the key.

I played a new chess opponent last night. Won four out of five. A funny guy. I've never seen anyone who gets so hyperactive over a chess game. He's quite a sight. Imagine a hectic demonstration in the end zone. The adrenaline flows.

Lots of mail—your package and three letters. Troy sent some reading material.

Later: I had the medical check. My blood pressure was 138/78. I believe the measurement was honest. As I left the quack of a doctor said, *"See you in six months."* I kept my thoughts to myself.

Release—89 days. I played chess last night against two opponents. Won seven of nine.

I worked today and was assigned a boom box. The tape player didn't work. They are difficult to work on. Cables and wires running everywhere. Three or four circuit boards interconnected. To get to the components you have to disassemble it, but to check the power and signals the parts have to be assembled. In our environment, it's a tough job.

Release—88 days. My headphones for my Walkman quit working. In the best scenario, I can take them to work tomorrow and fix them. In the worst scenario, we won't be called to work for several days.

At times, it seems that the days are getting harder—mentally and emotionally. Pre-holidays blahs? Pre-release anxiety? Natural cycle? It's the stupefying boredom. Each day has been repeated endlessly. The cycle is the same—newspaper, crossword puzzle, TV, radio. I ask myself, *"Haven't I done all of this before?"* Time is passing fast. Holidays in ten days.

Release—87 days. It was fortunate that you could stop for a visit on your way to Pinesburg. It was one of our better visits. I'll call tonight to ease my concern about your safe arrival. The weather looks like it will cooperate.

The printed sermon today was "Crime, Punishment, and Redemption," by Rev. Bumbaugh of Summit, New Jersey. It was relevant and good.

Release—86 days. Had a good series of chess games last night against Rasheed. I held my own. Neither of us was dominant.

Finished Mencken. I suspect he had an inferiority complex. He loved to denigrate academics, officials and intelligentsia. Those who have lukewarm reputations (e.g., Calvin Coolidge) receive Mencken's encomiums. His style becomes tiresome—heavy sarcasm and obscure vocabulary. I found him cynical and uncompassionate. I don't think I would have liked him.

I haven't worked since my headphones broke, so I'm still without them. I miss the music at night.

Release—85 days. It was a relief to hear your voice last night. Relax and absorb love and care from our family. No work today.

Commissary went OK. I've already started nibbling the mixed nuts. I paid Phil for doing my laundry. I've started reading "The Red Tent," and will have my report for the book club.

I plan on going to the gym this afternoon, but I may not be as assiduous in exercising these last two months. The gym is so crowded.

Three letters in the mail plus confirmation of the change to my visitor's list.

I feel old and decrepit at times. Mortality hangs heavy. I worry about the remnants of my back operation. Is there a guillotine posed on my spinal column? Will I wake some morning with no feeling or mobility on my left side? I want to live well until I die. If I were to die soon, the wastefulness of these last months would be magnified. Sorry for the morbidity. Stream of consciousness leads to whirlpools at times, sucking one down.

Light snow predicted for tonight.

Release—84 days. I went to the gym yesterday for the last time. It's too crowded. One inmate finishing a lay-up ran into me. Another, when taking off his sweatshirt, swung his elbow and hit me in the head. It wasn't intentional—just crowded. I've also been hit in the head by errantly thrown basketballs. I believe the benefit/risk ratio is wrong.

The snow did not appear.

I heard that we will work tomorrow. I can fix my headphones.

I'm watching a "travel show" on TV—New Orleans, Alaska. Wagner's swamp tour in the bayou and Prince William's Sound in Alaska look good. I'm ready to go.

Release—83 days. I had a good visit from Walter this morning. A pleasant surprise. I also worked and fixed my headphones. I'm still working on the boom box. I believe I'm making progress. Damn thing is like a 3-D puzzle. At least, so far, I haven't created more problems.

I'm on page 154 of "The Red Tent." I'm enjoying it.

I'm sorry about the LL Bean order. I suppose they automatically reject all credit card orders from inmates. You're the most affected. Your gifts were to come from them.

My letter to the credit card company was returned. A real catch-22—I can't talk to them by telephone and they won't accept my letters. The letter was stamped "Wrong Post Office Box." I suspect the real reason is a policy to refuse any letter from an inmate. I enclose the letter so that you can send it from our home address. You don't need these aggravations.

Dear Credit Card Company:
Re: My credit card.

This letter is a follow-up to the letter written by my wife three weeks ago. The facts she states are true. I am incarcerated and will be released in two months. I used my credit card to order holiday gifts for my family to be delivered to Pinesburg where my family will gather. I am in good shape financially. Because of the incarceration, I cannot communicate with you by telephone.

I appreciate your vigilance in protecting my card from fraudulent use, however in this case the use is legitimate. I request that you remove the hold on my card and honor the power-of—attorney that my wife supplied

Sincerely

Release—82 days. A good telephone call this morning. Lets me participate vicariously. I'd like to see the faces when my gifts are opened.

Release—81 days. It's early. I'm having a cup of coffee and eating a pastry. Soon—I can see in my mind's eye—the family will be gathering and opening the presents. Next year I will be there.

I skipped dinner yesterday. The entrée, again, was "fish portion." I stayed in and had a can of split pea with ham soup. The ham, as far as I could tell, was theoretical. It was not good. I also had some kippers and crackers.

We have learned a lesson about the use of a credit card from within prison. I'm sorry that your gifts were screwed up. The system allows no good deed to be done.

Release—80 days. Only eighty days to go. Since we got into double digits 20% of the time has gone. Time is passing.

For a sermon this morning, I read "Quest." It didn't inspire me. Lot's of Jewish history—Maccabees, rebuilding the Temple, meaning of Hannakah, etc. Do we UUs, in our desire for diversity and understanding of all religions, spread our butter too thin and wide?

My chess game may be getting better. The last three times I've played Rasheed I've won most of the games. We're evenly matched. It's a nice feeling to find a clever unexpected move. I feel quite creative at times. Time flies while playing.

Three weeks ago, I bought a package of cookies. I haven't finished them yet; so don't get the idea that I spend the money you send on tons of junk food. I still have my yearning for popcorn, but candy, chips, etc., are not necessities. Top priorities: 1) stamps and writing materials, 2) coffee, 3) fruit juice, and 4) popcorn.

Release—79 days. I had a nice visit from Sam and Lucy this morning. They stayed for about two hours. Thanks for arranging the holiday visits.

I worked in the shop this morning on the boom box that had been plaguing me. The CD player and the radio still work well, but I could not get the cassette player working. If I had a schematic, I would have expended more effort.

There was a dusting of snow in the leeward crevices on the walk this morning. No mail today. I suspect we'll repeat the holiday routine of several days of delay in the mail delivery.

Release—78 days. An inmate was killed last night in HU4. Someone crushed his head using a TV set while he was in his cell. He was on "B" tier—not the honor tier—so only the COs control his door. He was in my AA group, but I don't remember him. His cellbuddy was in the rec area. All housing units are on lock-down. Since a TV was involved, morbid jokes were made in the shop.

The walk to and from the chow hall was beautiful. Snow fell slowly.

Release—77 days. Lots of rumors about the slain inmate. Gay. Two assailants. The tier is still on lock-down. I worked both morning and afternoon.

Vic is becoming more congenial. Perhaps he is developing some trust. He locks up his lockers whenever he leaves. First cellbuddy to do that, but it protects me if he misses something. I generally leave mine unlocked.

I dreamt vividly of being in our family room reminiscing about incarceration. The realization that it was a dream started as a seed and grew. Reality raised its ugly head as I awoke, but I enjoyed the spiritual journey. The future will be nice.

Release—76 days. I had a visit from Walter and Harry. We gossiped about church happenings.

The latest rumor about the slain inmate is that his cellbuddy had hired two other inmates to render a beating and it got out of hand. Freshly washed T-shirts and blood-splattered shoes were discovered in the cell of the hit men. The dead inmate and the accused had requested to be separated, but the housing lieutenant had denied the request. Who knows what the truth is?

I laundered my bedding and made my bunk anew. I showered. Feeling up. I hope to get your letter today. Read your words. Touch the paper you touched.

I heard Boccherini's Minuetto last night. It was familiar. I recognize it as a theme from some TV show. I also heard Brahm's "Symphony #2." I wasn't enthralled by it.

Release—75 days. We had yard and I walked my ten laps. An unexpected benevolence at this time of the year. I have finished "The Red Tent" and will enclose my notes, when I write them.

Release—74 days. I played chess badly last night. The holidays are affecting my mood. I missed not being with the family. Will the days become more difficult as the release date draws near? I think of all the days gone by.

Have you finished "High Tide in Tucson?" Still like it?

My sermon this morning was "When Courage Fails and Faith Burns Low," by Rev. Bumbaugh. I was heartened by it. He quotes A. Powell Davies, *"When courage fails and faith burns low and men are timid grown, hold fast thy loyalty and know that truth moveth on."* As I read the sermon, I wanted to share reactions with you.

Release—73 days. I played much better chess yesterday. My success at chess affects my mood and that annoys me. It should be a pleasant pastime. The realization that I will have losses should inure me to adverse reactions.

Have a safe journey home.

Release—72 days. Your visit this morning was a gust of wind for a falling balloon. It's been over two weeks since we last saw each other.

After I get out and after the cinnamon coffee, the walk in the mall, the drive along the river, and after my favorite meal (grits and hot dogs ☺), what then? Will there be an anti-climatic reaction? Will I find the excess time of retirement to be a burden? In a year will this be a distant and forgotten memory? Will the events I anticipate become mundane, once again common?

No mail today. More for tomorrow.

Release—71 days. Glad to hear the household was in good order. Surprisingly, I worked this morning. I also refilled my medication.

I had another dramatic dream of being free and with you. It's always a disappointment when sentience reveals the truth, but—soon!

Mail delivered six letters today.

I enclose my book club notes.

To: Book Club
Re: "The Red Tent" by Anita Diamant

This novel is the story of Dinah—nothing more, and an excellent one. There is no plot, scarcely any drama. There are superb characters, but the nonpareil facet is the weaving of the time and place of Dinah's life. Diamant makes the reader believe that the people in the time of Genesis lived—and too frequently, died—as she depicts. The credibility of the milieu is no doubt due to the author's scholarship in Judaica. The relationships and appurtenances among the wives of Jacob, Dinah's mothers, are palpable. The author details the women weltering in menses, birthing, fertility, and cooking. Because of strong family ties, tragedies were incurred. Because of the breaking of family ties, hearts and lives were broken. Rest in peace, Dinah.

Release—70 days. As you know from the answering machine, I tried to call you last night. Nothing important.

I worked in the shop today, just piddling around. I'm still working on a "donated non-functional TV."

Will I bore you when I return home? I will want to do so many ordinary things and talk about trivia. I may not leave your side for hours. You'll be used to solitude into which I'll intrude. But, of course, I will be someone who can help with the housework. Will you think I'm not doing my share? We'll have to get used to the retirement budget.

Another content-free letter.

Release—69 days. I won at chess last night. Made good progress on my shop job this morning. Tonight is another eat-in-the-cell night. The chow hall is serving fish portion and scalloped tomatoes. It's my least favored meal. Luckily, it is not served often.

I will create a commissary budget for the remaining time. Stamps, juice, coffee and toiletry items are priority items. Fun to plan for the end.

Release—68 days. Good news about the court's allowance (again) of the six-day credit. I suspect I will get some internal official notification.

I'm starting to toss stuff—old catalogs and magazines. It re-enforces the view that I'M GOING HOME.

Rasheed and I are the best chess players on the tier. He (at least when he plays me), as I do, treats the game seriously, doesn't trash talk and gets the greatest enjoyment from what happens on the board itself. Another inmate, Ahmed, has been bugging me to play him. He likes to play psyche games and keeps his mouth on overdrive. Last night I played him two games and easily won both. Of course, that didn't shut him up... *"Just learning your style, Pops."* *"Hasn't played that badly in a long time,"* etc. Rasheed refuses to play Ahmed and says that he is not a good player. Chess teaches a lot about personalities and character. It amuses me that some herein try to cheat. They make an illegal knight move and then try to replace the knight in a different place. A popular ploy is to castle long, but to place the king on the knight's square—not the bishop's square. I wonder what the point is. If one has to cheat to win, does the game have value? Perhaps they see life as a game wherein if one can cheat and succeed, then the purpose of game has been met. Chess is just a metaphor for them.

Release—67 days. What a neat telephone call last night. I enjoyed the description of what you saw as you drove. I could visualize the familiar scenes. I enjoyed it more than I would've anticipated. I imagined myself seated beside you.

We had yard—a rarity this time of the year. Did my ten laps.

Release—66 days. I had a repeat dream last night, but it has evolved. You and I were walking down a dirt country road holding hands. I pulled myself next to you and said, *"I won't awake from this because it's real."* It seemed real. But then I awoke.

I enclose a letter-to-the-editor.

Until the morn of yon day...

Dear Editor:

As reported the high cost of telephone calls from inmates to their families is a matter of concern. Experts generally agree that recidivism rates diminish if the inmate, while incarcerated, can maintain contact and receive support from family, friends and community. Excessive phone charges and poor mail delivery service (also a problem) serve only to further alienate the inmate from society and, in the long run, engenders greater cost to society than a more compassionate approach.

Release—65 days. A good visit. Clearly, getting a dog is something that has appeal to each of us.

Release—64 days. I was called to the repair shop this morning. Remember the boom box that I worked on and couldn't fix? The owner wrote the warden complaining that the unit was in worse shape after the repair effort than before. I met with a Lieutenant (Sergeant O'Reilly's boss) who was investigating the issue and he seemed supportive. He said it was a minor issue.

I've been thinking about our relationship with the Unitarian Church when I am released. What do our supporters—Elgin, Kathy, Walter, Brad, Harry and Mary—want us to do? What do I want to do? There's a part of me that wants to avoid the whole issue by not attempting to attend church. Maybe church is a "necessary loss" and leaving is a necessary "transition." Reaction? What do you want me to do? You have invested time attending church while I've been incarcerated—do we cross that time off? I anticipate that the course I will take—the most rational and logical—is one step at a time and not respond to reactions before they actually happen. I have to give them a chance to formulate a just policy. I agree that any policy has a review process. Restrictions on associations and communications when not on the premises of the church are wrong.

All of this creates a mixture of emotions—anger, sadness, haughty righteousness, remorse, confusion.

Upon reflection, we have to do what we—not our supporters—think is right. If we lose them, we lose them and we can be thankful for the support they were able to give for the duration they gave it.

A major personal motivation is to correct the reaction of the church regardless of any personal benefit. If the church is so remiss in my case, I dread to think of their reaction to someone less involved and committed. The bigoted reaction to stereotypes is reprehensible.

Release—63 days. One day less. I watched a TV show last night that dealt with the issue of inmates for whom DNA evidence contradicted the finding of guilty. The inmates had been convicted before DNA testing. In spite of the DNA results, the prosecutors refused to reconsider the cases. The legal argument put forth was that once you're found guilty then the burden of proof of innocence is on the inmate. The prosecutors concoct an ulterior theory—a second accomplice who supplied the DNA is popular—although that possibility had never been presented at the original trial. Our judicial system, evolved for centuries, has some genetic deformities not easily corrected. Prosecutors, having gotten a conviction, are not motivated to pursue the truth, and, in fact, have a disincentive because any such discovery would detract from their aura of invincibility. Governors, fearful of a "Willie Horton" type of incident, when presented with petitions for clemency based on new DNA evidence, err on the side of caution. The mixture of wimpy politicians and prosecutorial intransigence slays justice.

Elgin was concerned during his last visit about my ability to fill all of my "retirement time." I worry about the opposite—finding enough time to do all I wish to do.

Release—62 days. I worked this morning and will pick up my medicine refill at noon. Two months to go!

I got two letters from you and three from Troy. He told me about recent magazine articles concerned with retirement financing.

Release—61 days. I'm depressed this morning—not sure why. Showered and wrote Troy a letter. No work today. Very cold.

Two inmates got into a fight last night. Both were kicked off the tier. Not sure of the cause—something trivial no doubt.

No mail today.

Release—60 days. Our telephone call last night caused me to think about the church more. What are our motivations for continuing to go? If we could state our motives, perhaps we could deal with the issues more rationally. My motivation may be different from yours, and that's OK. My motivation—as far as I can tell—is to make the church and the denomination more compassionate and supportive in events such as mine. I want to serve as an example to belie the reaction to stereotypes. The potential for self-deception is great, however. If I become convinced that I've failed, I can give up the fight, move on, and be satisfied that I've done what I can. If merely attending church services were my motivation, I would try to find another church or even another denomination. This issue will continue to consume.

Release—59 days. I wrote Ms. White, my case manager, to ask for a time statement. I'll see what happens—probably nothing. I hope there are no snafus.

Life is becoming eerie. When fried chicken is served, the inmates in the line get, alternately, a breast-wing or a leg-thigh. Hovering COs strictly enforce this rule. Most inmates prefer the breast-wing, but a rare few prefer the leg-thigh. The latter have no trouble exchanging. I prefer the breast-wing and have a 50-50 chance of getting one instead of a leg-thigh. The past five times that fried chicken has been served I have gotten a breast-wing. If I were a devote believer in a personal intervening God, I could view the chicken breasts as a testament to his largess. If I adopted this view, consistency would require that I view a leg-thigh as a divine censor. In some way, the breast-wing and leg-thigh issue is a metaphor for life. Much of what life gives is random and one has the choice on how to view the offering.

Release—57 days. I didn't write you a letter yesterday. The first day I've missed in my memory. We had discussed everything important during the visit.

I did submit a medical request to have my crown re-cemented. The crown fits snugly; I am leaving it in the tooth.

Our discussion about the church was fruitful. Our motivations were clarified. We may face the possibility that you attend and I don't.

I'm enduring the cold weather with the help of long johns.

Release—56 days. Last night's snow was only a dusting here. The TV shows much more snow and a traffic mess where you are.

At times, I'm surprised that I've spent fifteen months in here. How did I endure it all? How did I survive the kitchen sanitation job without hurting myself or being disciplined? How did I tolerate Elliot? I withstood it all because of you.

Next week I'll probably have to work. It's good for me, although I prefer the idleness. The idleness provides more flexibility—when to shower, read, play chess, etc. Working forces me to concentrate on something external and time goes faster.

I telephoned David and he's a grandfather again. Marsha had a baby girl and all are doing well.

Four letters in the mail.

Release—55 days. I got an official release date! I am one day off in my calculation, but I believe the official version to be correct. I didn't know how they officially round-off partial day credits. Their method is consistent and seems to ensure they release no one even a few hours early. If one is due to be released at 5:00PM, they will be held until the next morning when all releases are effected. I'll make a one-day correction in my numbering.

The night brought five inches of snow. A crisp clear winter day.

I've been considering—but not seriously—of doing consulting work when released. Employment possibilities on a regular job will be nil I suspect. Consulting is a possibility—not an attractive one.

No dental pass yet.

Release—55 (new), 54 (old) days. From studying the official time calculation, it appears that no good time credit is given for county time. One-year county time is equivalent to nine months state time.

Later: I just had a surprise visit with Harry. I shared most of our thoughts about the church with him. I find that discussion about the church causes me anguish and to mentally thrash for a long time. I re-visit the issues and try to understand the motivations and hypocrisy. Is it hypocrisy? Am I wrong to expect greater compassion and support?

I was served a chicken breast last night.

Ironic that you have tickets to the theatre on the evening of my release. I would be glad to go, or not, as you wish. I hope that some of our family will be our guests when I get out. But I'm sure the logistics could be worked out.

Release—54 days. I was awake most of the night thinking about the church. How do I control that? My ire gets agitated. My chess last evening was lousy.

I called Pinesburg last night. Warren said they would try to come on my release date.

Release—53 days. The sermon I read this morning dealt with American culture. I appreciated the insight that religion, perforce, will always be in opposition to popular culture as perfection is opposed to imperfection.

A notice was posted that as of the beginning of next month, books will be delivered to the inmates only if they come from a book dealer. I wonder why. No explanation was given. Do they worry about pages seeped with LSD? If so, a letter could be used similarly as a vehicle. Maybe they worry about a weapon being concealed in a hollow cutout. Is the motivation to reduce the workload in the mailroom? I fail to see how the work is diminished by the new policy. I also recognize that if the new policy had been in effect when I arrived at Rochelle I would have accepted it as normal. It is the arbitrariness and lack of explanation that irritates me and lends credence to the view that mere harassment is the motivation. In fact, it will have no effect on me, so why am I concerned?

Release—51 days. My crown was re-cemented. Seems OK.

When I went to bed last night, I felt as though I was coming down with a cold. However, it didn't happen. Perhaps because I followed your suggestion and had a hot cup of Tang. I'll give you the credit in any case. ☺

In a blizzard, as we're having, I wear my large, ugly, but warm state coat. I stay cozy on my walks (three this morning) across the compound, but I miss gloves and a neck scarf. The weather will delay the mail delivery, I predict.

I asked the tier CO about returning an item on my property list (my fan) to a visitor. He had no idea how to do it and offered no further help.

Release—50 days. As I predicted, there were only six pieces of mail for the whole tier yesterday.

They are implementing a new telephone registration system based on voice recognition. The process completely screws up the entire daily routine. I haven't been allowed to retrieve my newspaper yet (4:00PM).

My dream last night was insidious. I dreamt that it was the night before my release. My surroundings were consistent with reality. The mind is a wondrous instrument.

I understand that I will soon be asked to furnish a "home plan" and a "work plan" as a prelude to being released.

I'm going to try to get some Auslese at commissary tomorrow. ☺

Release—49 days. My telephone call to you this morning was successful on the third attempt. The voice recognition system aborted the first two efforts.

The commissary didn't have any Auslese. Only cheap California imitations. ☺

I'm depressed because (remember it doesn't have to be logical) there's been no mail, my chess play has been poor and I didn't get a chicken breast.

I'm also anxious about the new telephone system. Some inmates couldn't register their voice because they have no approved calling list. Isn't that sad? They have never—while being incarcerated—called anyone. How will they succeed when they get out? Does anyone care?

Have you thought about the genesis of the desire for revenge? I suspect that animals do not exhibit revenge. If a loved one of mine were a victim, would I seek revenge? If the desire for revenge was nonexistent would the nature of our penal and legal system be different? I wonder if there is a correlation between empathy and the desire for revenge? The more empathy for the victim, the greater the desire for revenge? Or is it the other way, the greater the empathy for the offender the less the desire for revenge? Does revenge, once extracted, make the seeker more serene? Does the desire for revenge appear in all cultures?

Release—47 days. Damn telephones! One of the two telephones on the tier is broken, so access to the functioning one is difficult.

I'm feeling better and my chess is improving. I'm not sure which is the cause and which is the effect.

Vic has a bad cold. My immune system must be in good shape (knock on wood). I seldom get a cold or a flu.

Another inmate was expelled from the honor tier. Not sure of the exact cause, but I do know he made a lot of noise on the tier, especially during sporting events. The COs can always find a rationale to evoke the changes they wish to make.

Release—46 days. No flu yet. The weather is blusterous. I hope you are prudent and don't feel you have to make a trip for a visit when the roads are treacherous. Be safe.

I just returned from my favorite lunch—a good vegetable soup, a dish of salad (lettuce, tomatoes, onion), coconut pudding, pickle slices, and a sliced beef product called "Steak'um." I use some commissary mustard and make an excellent sandwich from the meat and salad. I have no complaints about the food herein. Their dinner tonight, fish portion, is the worst on the revolving menu. I'll stay in the cell and make a meal.

The sermon I read yesterday was from Rev. Campbell and dealt with uncertainty. She made the point that the self-righteousness of the religious fundamentalists has a parallel with the smugness of UUs of accepting the question and discussion as being more important than the answer

I'll try to call you, but there is still only one telephone on the tier.

Release—45 days. The COs in the visiting room were really impressed that you braved the weather to visit me. I really didn't expect you, but accept your judgment that the roads are OK.

We had a bizarre event on the tier last night. Posh poured a cup of boiling water on Carlos as they watched a basketball game. I'm not sure of the motivation and no one is saying much. The COs don't know yet. Posh and Carlos are collaborating in maintaining the secret because discovery would result in each of them being ejected from the honor tier. I suspect Carlos must have provoked Posh. The hot water caused severe burns on the neck of Carlos. I doubt that the secret can be kept. I know Posh well and have spoken with him often. He is an intense Christian and always spoke a blessing before eating. My impression is that he is a mild-mannered, self-controlled intelligent man. I can't imagine him committing such an act. Carlos is Hispanic and has an attitude of defiance. He is the unofficial chief of the tier sanitation crew.

Some body lotions (e.g., baby oil) are contraband because of past episodes involving their use, after being heated to high temperatures in the microwave, as a weapon by pouring them on a victim. I saw the blisters on the neck and chest of Carlos. Carlos has received medical help by concocting some story about self-injury. Too many inmates (not me) were witnesses for the real story to remain unknown. I question whether I know anything about human nature.

My throat is ticklish. Walking to the dispensary at midnight tonight for the blood test will encourage it to flare.

Release—44 days. I did the midnight walk. My throat is quite sore. My nose is running slightly. I'm quaffing hot liquids.

No work yesterday or today.

The days are getting few, but each day doesn't know it a member of a dying breed so it mimics all the others. In a fantasyland, as one got closer to release, one would gain more freedom and privileges—the release would be gradual. There would be a supervised visit to the mall or to a fast food place. A week before your release, you'd be allowed a few hours alone in town. Totally impractical, I know. There are stories of inmates being released and immediately committing a robbery so they could return to a bed and food. Nothing awaited them on the outside. They had nothing on the outside.

Release—43 days. The weather is cold and I have a weak flu and may have passed it to you. Throat is a little sore, some muscle ache and a bit of a cough.

Nothing serious, but I'm glad I'm not working. I'll skip the chow hall tonight to minimize my external excursions.

Eddy, the dog on "Frasier" sired six puppies on the show last night. The show was filled with their antics. Cute.

I've submitted a request to return my fan to you when you visit in two weeks. I wanted the system to have ample time to complete the paper work.

The vultures are circling. *"Pops, can I have your cap when you leave?" "I could use that shirt when you leave." "Got a towel you don't need?"* I'll probably comply with the requests from "friends."

I'm still munching on my can of mixed nuts. They've lasted a whole week. I'll try to call tonight.

Release—42 days. The second telephone remained broke yesterday so I couldn't call. It is repaired today. I'll try later. No work today.

My flu is in the final stages. Muscle ache and sore throat are gone. I still have a small cough.

One letter from Troy in the mail.

In six weeks, I'll be out.

Release—41 days. The telephone call was worthwhile because I learned that nothing significant has happened. The second telephone is working.

From the library last night I got Clancey's "The Cardinal in the Kremlin" and Vidal's "Burr."

The flu has returned and I feel miserable. I have a great talent for showing discomfort and my illness has not gone unnoticed herein. I let my face contort and my steps drag. I worry that some in here may deem it more humane to put me out of my misery. ☺ To avoid another trip outside, I'm eating in the cell tonight. I'm feeling the lack of exercise.

Release—40 days. I'm feeling much better. I took my fan to the visitor's room to be given to you. This is poignant—sending stuff home in preparation of returning. My medicine wasn't renewed in time. I'll run out today.

I notice that the newspaper subscription runs out in ten days. Can one get a renewal for just one month?

Release—39 days. My flu is gone. I still haven't gotten the Procardia. I have written the nurse supervisor—as I did last year—about the problem. I spoke with another inmate who receives medication for "disc-deterioration" and he, too, has had problems with replenishment. He's a sad case—white, 38, frail. He has served three years of a 20-year sentence. He also has "trauma induced arthritis." He must be going through hell. He must have an image of the future in which, even if he gets out, he will have a crippled life caused by the lack of sufficient medical care herein. I'll be glad to escape this hell.

A disaster! ☺ My coffee order at commissary was filled with decaffeinated. I don't know how the mistake was made. I plan on giving it away and getting the "real" stuff. Why not indulge myself in these last few days?

On the radio last night, I heard Sibelius's Fifth. It's a favorite of mine. I love the passage of a long sequence of half notes. I could hum it for you. It was followed by Mozart's "Symphony #39," which I also enjoyed. The radio and the PBS station have contributed to my peace and comfort.

Release—38 days. After your morning visit, I worked in the afternoon. I lamented not being able to leave with you. I ate some jellybeans. The sugar picked me up.

Release—37 days. No medicine or response to my letter yet. I still feel well. I'll submit another request.

I worked all day and need to find time to shower. It will be a blessing to shower alone when I wish, for as long as I wish, to walk naked to the bedroom and not worry about dressing in the shower stall. The shower water is sometimes too cold, sometimes too hot. Many little things add to the hell.

Release—36 days. I finally got my medicine. Also had commissary. Got some real coffee.

Release—35 days. Sorry the telephone call last night was cut-off. We got the important things said.

I learned that Rasheed, my chess opponent, is forty-seven and has been in prison since he was eighteen! How does one come to grips with the knowledge that you're going to spend the best years of your life in a cell? No hope to marry and have kids. No trips to the mall. The latest technology passes you. A limited variety of food. Are there people so bad to the core that the only solution is to lock them up forever? Are we sure we can detect such individuals? *"You had your chance at life. Blew it big time. No second chances."* If Rasheed were to get out how could he cope with life? The road that prison builds for exiting inmates is the route to recidivism. Criminology is in the "bleed-and-apply-the-leeches" phase.

Release—34 days. No news. I resent each of these last few days. I made progress on my spare TV project. My appetite has waned. I have candy and chips that I have no desire to eat. Perhaps because of the flu. I'll force a jellybean sugar-fix upon myself and see if my mood brightens. Talk to you tonight.

Release—33 days. I was called to open the TV of an incoming inmate. I hate that duty. The COs and their inmate helpers who work on processing the incoming guys poke fun at us "electronic geniuses." If you have the slightest trouble locating a screw or let a screwdriver slip, torrents of guffaws erupt.

I called and talked with David. They're selling their house and moving closer to the city.

Release—32 days. I read the sermon "When Life Deals You a Lousy Hand."

I had a stomach ache last night. I had eaten some nuts before going to bed. Maybe I've developed an intolerance to junk food.

A change of pace—are personality and character immutable? I bet that question divides people. If one views personality and character as fixed then one is much less willing to expend resources on rehabilitation and—since crime is inevitable—much more willing to allocate for law enforcement. *They will commit the crimes regardless of what is done so let's do our best to catch them.* When I was younger, I believed that one's personality and character could be easily changed. In fact, I thirsted for someone to tell me how to improve my personality. I also believed that it was an easy matter for me to tell Joe (say*), "Joe, you'd be much more likeable if you weren't so loud and didn't dominate the conversation,"* and Joe—infinitely grateful for this wisdom—would modify his behavior to the benefit of us all. It surprised me that this approach never worked. It dawned on me later that not only do we all have different personalities, but we also respond differently to others. Some people liked Joe because of his traits—not in spite of them. Thus my belief that I knew what's best in a personality was arrogant. But the question remains: Could Joe be quieter and less intrusive? I don't know what I believe.

My heart yearns to be with you—to collude to create happiness.

Release—31 days. A nice visit. The church, the church, the church—what to do about the church? I feel they would like to make me a non-issue. I feel torn between the desire to walk away and the desire to expose the hypocrisy. Is this healthy? Is it healing? Do I react emotionally or rationally?

Release—30 days. I've said, "thirty more days" a dozen times today already.

Remember the boom box I worked on and couldn't repair and then the owner wrote the warden complaining? The inmate now says I stole the motor from it. Since it involves an allegation of theft, a captain and two lieutenants have interviewed me. I suggested that we open the box and see if the motor is still inside. The inmate *"don't want no mutherfucker messin' wit his shit."* We have a dozen or so spare similar motors lying about, so why would I want his? The system and the COs believe me, so I'm OK. I hope the inmate doesn't decide to take justice into his own hands. I spent twelve hours trying to get it working. The shop offers no guarantees. I feel sorry for the inmate. He had no choice.

I'm submitting my next medicine request. I hope it goes smoothly.

My chess game isn't good now.

On my way to get the paper this morning, the sun broke through a hole in the clouds and created an image of the light at the end of the tunnel. I got a chicken breast last night. Good omens abound. Maybe I should start a new religion, "The Church of the Holy Chicken Breast." Tomorrow is the indicated expiration date on my newspaper subscription. Hopefully you renewed it.

Ate some jellybeans—feel better. Reagan had the right idea.

Release—29 days. Twice a month the morning routine is disrupted because a majority of the COs is involved in training—learning how to kill inmates. Since only a few COs are on duty all inmate movements are minimized. I haven't retrieved my newspaper yet. I do have a cup of coffee.

I have difficulty imagining leaving here. I'm distancing myself from others—never was close.

Worked this afternoon. Got the spare TV working and have started on another. In a month, I'll be out.

Release—28 days. Are you tiring of these content-free letters? I write to chronicle the eventless days. Anything that makes one day different—no matter how petty—I can detail for you. Today, I got my medicine. I worked this morning, but haven't been called this afternoon. I worry that while I was getting my medicine, I was called for work. The COs, paradoxically, don't keep track well enough to have realized I was out when they made the call. If anything awry happens, it will be my fault because the COs are blameless and perfect.

I did get my newspaper although the expiration date is indicated as yesterday.

The voice in "Burr" describes Burr as being unsentimental and ascribes advantages to the attribute. Without sentiment one can act more rationally and be immune to the pleas of others. Is my sentimentality dictating my reaction to the church?

I'm out of jellybeans.

Release—27 days. When I called, I was surprised you were at work. I was sure the blizzard would entrap you at home. I'm glad the guys decided to skip the visit—perfectly understandable.

Shawn, the inmate whose judge had a heart attack, has 103 days to go. He started counting at 1000! Another "friend" has 143 to go. This week has gone by fast.

Release—26 days. Still getting the paper.

I'm on page 325 of "Burr"—it is dragging a bit. Vidal fully develops the humanity and personality of the founding fathers, Washington, Adams, Jefferson and Hamilton. Monroe, and Madison. I wonder how accurate his depictions are? According to the book, Jefferson was the consummate politician and his genius otherwise is overrated. Washington was dull.

Do we need to replace my name on our auto insurance policies?

I'd like to visit Barry after I'm released. He's far from home and isolated. I'm not sure what the rules are for inmates returning as visitors.

I had a good telephone call with Carl last night.

Release—25 days. Most of the sleet and snow have melted.

I read a sermon by Rev. Gallun concerning the feminist movement and the role of women today. I took his point that what is taken for granted today can be viewed as a gross injustice in the future. The inability of women to vote is such an example. The penal system of today is a prime candidate for censure tomorrow.

My chess game was better last night.

Release—24 days. I have not been able to verbalize adequately the thoughts I have concerning the respective rights of victims and society. I suspect my inability is due to a lack of clarity in my own mind. Perhaps my incomplete thoughts are bogus. I know that my sophomoric efforts at expression sound kooky.

I worked both morning and afternoon. I'm going to be purposefully slow and patient.

Release—23 days. An unseasonably nice day. I worked this morning and probably will this afternoon as well. I had my "exit" fingerprints taken. I've had my fingerprints taken twenty, or so, times. The CO told me that 8:30AM is a reasonable time for you to arrive.

In the mail, besides three letters, I got notice of a pre-release meeting to provide information about employment, education, job training, housing, shelters, etc. The meeting is not mandatory, but I'll go. It's for all inmates being released in the next four weeks—further evidence I'm getting out!

I'm in a good mood even without jellybeans—the lack thereof to be corrected tomorrow at commissary. I was delivered a chicken breast last night. Hallelujah.

Release—22 days. I'm at the point where the light at the end of the tunnel (plus jellybeans, which I now have) will keep my spirits high.

I've read another significant chunk of "Burr." Hamilton has been shot. Jefferson has made the Louisiana Purchase—Bonaparte needed $15 million.

I look at the day, 23 days from now. I need to look at today. I will enjoy a telephone call to you. I will enjoy some chess and the crossword puzzle. Today is now. Where are my jellybeans? ☺

Release—21 days. I worked both morning and afternoon. Three weeks to go. I turned in a medication refill request—should have to do that only one more time. Five letters in the mail.

Release—20 days. Brad and Harry visited this morning. We had a good time. What I read between the lines about the church was not encouraging. Hopefully I'm wrong.

Release—19 days. Although the weather was nice enough yesterday to have yard, we didn't. After a winter's idleness, the yard area has to be swept with metal detectors and that hasn't yet been done.

I got my medicine. I have thirteen days worth now.

Release—18 days. Have you thought of the relationship among "compassion," "empathy," and "sentimentality?" To me they are intertwined. "Compassion" and "empathy" are synonyms, are they not? I may be overly sentimental—do you agree? Can one be sentimental and not show it? Doesn't the definition of "sentimentality" encompass the expression of it?

Release—17 days. I'm sorry that I was in such a weird mood on the telephone. I find myself impatient and anxious to resolve the current topic of conversation and move to the next. I'm impatient with details that have no interest to me—illogical, since how do I know I'm not interested before hearing about it? I'm sure my environment is causing psychic unrest.

I feel well and am not depressed. I get so absorbed in chess when I play, that after the session (four or five games) I have to reorient myself. What time, what day is it? What have I planned for today? I completely escape into the game. At times, I hate the game because it represents imprisonment. I tell myself that when I get out, I'll never play another game.

I'm about to finish "Burr."

Release—16 days. I worked morning and afternoon. I fixed a TV.

Rasheed, my favorite and strongest chess opponent got into a fight last night and was kicked off the tier. He got into an argument with a younger black guy about whose turn it was to shower. The argument escalated. Now both are in segregation. I will not see Rasheed again. I wanted to bridge the separation that we maintain to tell him what his chess games meant to me (sentimentality?).

I had the pre-release meeting. I learned that: 1) I will be given a five-day supply of medicine, 2) my release date is official and 3) you may have to come in to sign me out. There was confusion about the latter point. I mention it only as a possibility. (How can there be confusion about what must be a rigorously defined routine?)

I have finished "Burr" and have started "The Cardinal in the Kremlin." I should have time to finish it because of the lack of chess.

Release—15 days. I had a good telephone conversation with Bud last night.

I worked this morning and fixed another TV. That makes two this week. Just when I get good at the job, I'll be leaving it.

I had to process the TV of an incoming inmate. I hate doing that—currently the worst part of my existence herein.

I'm on page 60 of "The Cardinal...." I've so far been successful at keeping the Russian characters straight—not an easy task since they have so many names.

Release—14 days. The news focused on the young boy who shot and killed the motorist. The commentators, in reporting on his background, said he never had a chance at a good life. The same is true for inmates in here. I'm not arguing that the boy should not be held responsible, but that the excuse has wider applicability. Has anyone tried to excuse a thirty-year old by saying he never had a chance? Can there be an epiphany in a life after which—regardless of the past environment—there comes a realization that one is able to control one's life and create one's own chances? All past baggage swept away? I venture there are few people who can have such an experience. Does our society view these people who cannot as "throw-away" who should be discarded in prison and forgotten about?

A different but related question: Suppose there is a person, who is deficit in some important characteristics and, in the best of circumstances, would contribute marginally to society. However their circumstances aren't ideal and they eventually are imprisoned. In an idyllic scenario, a utopian society would assemble a team of rehabilitation experts and spend the time (years?) and effort to rectify the behavior of the person. Is the result—an individual who will contribute little—worth the cost, several expert-person years? Or is it, from the crass view of society, cheaper and more efficient to keep the individual in prison? Does society owe each of its constituents the support needed so they can achieve the most? I don't know the answers and will leave here with the questions.

I processed the TVs of four incoming inmates. Poor lost souls.

Release—13 days. I've started giving things away—carbon paper, paper clips, manila envelopes.

A beautiful piece of music, a recorder concerto, awoke me last night. Scott Reiss played the alto recorder with Hesperus. I don't know the opus.

Release—12 days. I watched a show last night featuring a parrot. The bird exhibited fantastic speech. It could count to six and could identify colors. When it was tired it would say, *"I want to go back."* It had a vocabulary of approximately fifty words. A professor, researching intelligence, had trained it. The show asked the question, *"What's the difference between mankind and animals?"*

We had yard today. I walked my ten laps. I noticed the lack of exercise.

Release—11 days. I read the sermon "Pursuit of Happiness" and realized I am happy because of my friends and family.

"The Cardinal…" is a page-turner, a spy-thriller.

Release—10 days. As you could tell during the visit, I'm in a good mood. Could you make an appointment with Dr. Goldstein for me? At some time after my release.

A CO gave me a break today. An inmate, Josh and I were playing chess during the afternoon rec period. We became engrossed in the game and missed the "bar-check" call. We stayed hunched over the board as all the other inmates returned to their cells. The tier CO, Smith, came into the rec area and asked for our cell assignments. Josh and I were startled when we realized that we were the only inmates out—a clear violation. We, of course, immediately rose and headed for our cells. Smith told us to sit and finish the game. I was flabbergasted. Josh is an older black man, and neither he nor I have ever caused a problem. Smith has compassion and his attitude demands respect. I've never had significant interactions with Smith (or any other CO), but I have seen him interacting with other inmates, and he's guided by a sense of fairness. We finished our game and returned to the cell. No problem.

Josh is an interesting man. He's a large older black man, perhaps 280 lbs. and 6'2" tall. He's diabetic and walks with a limp. He has a countenance that creates nightmares. I first knew him from the kitchen sanitation job. He washed pots and pans. For hours he would stand in the hottest part of the kitchen and diligently clean the cooking utensils. I'm sure some of his slave ancestors had an easier job. Josh is gruff, but returns respect if you offer it. One chess game in a dozen with him offers a challenge. He told me kindly that I should *allow* others to win more often.

I'm sure Smith was cognizant, since a white and a black were involved, that no racial favoritism could be charged in his leniency.

Release—9 days. We did work today and I made further progress on the TV. I had a dream last night. I was driving and looking for a street named "Release."

Release—8 days. Sounds like the plans of the family are set. It is incredibly supportive for them to make the trip to greet me upon release.

I've solved all of the problems on the TV I'm working on except for an intermittent flickering. No work tomorrow. I'd like to fix this TV before release for the satisfaction.

Release—7 days. One last week. I had a final hypertension check up. 136/82. Seems under control. My total cholesterol is 163 and a ratio of 4.5. It was described as perfect. I asked for the print out of the last blood tests. They couldn't give me one. I have to go through "official" channels—irrational obstinacy.

It's a good time to go home. I've seen most of the episodes of "As Time Goes By," "Frazier," and "Home Improvement." On the other hand ☺, "Friends" and "Ally McBeal" are new. I'm adept at fixing TVs and I've discovered jellybeans.

Release—6 days. No visit yet. I've had my coffee, read the paper and solved the crossword puzzle. I'm waiting for lunch.

Later: I had a short visit with Walter. His timing was such that we only had ten minutes to talk. He came during lunch and by the time I returned to the housing unit and then back to the visiting room it was close to the end of the visiting period. Walter didn't think the church would be welcoming and would place restrictions on my attendance.

Release—5 days. Maybe we should try a different church.

Release—4 days. My last letter. My sanity is intact because of you. My humanity is steadfast. I'm optimistic about the future. I'm not depressed or bitter. In retrospect, I believe the judge was as fair and just as possible within the current flawed system.

As you read these last few words, our family will surround you. They have stood by us in spite of my faults and in spite of the pain I caused them and you. I must do what I can do to justify their love and trust. I must share in their lives to make them better. Not all would still be there.

To be able to write you and to share thoughts and feelings with an understanding loved and loving one was an ineffable beneficence. I could picture you as you read my words. I imagined your facial expressions invoked by my musings and ramblings. I will miss writing these letters. You will soon pick me up. Thank you and I love you. Hurry.

0-595-33634-5

www.ingramcontent.com/pod-product-compliance
Lightning Source LLC
Chambersburg PA
CBHW021603280526
45784CB00001BA/479